FAMILY LAW

By

MYRON G. HILL, Jr.

Adjunct Professor of Law, Antioch School of Law
Member of District of Columbia, Ohio, U.S. Court of Federal Claims,
U.S. Courts of Appeals for the Federal Circuit and
U.S. Supreme Court Bars

Fourth Edition prepared by Mr. Hill and by

STEVEN L. EMANUEL

Author, Emanuel Law Outlines Series
Member of New York Bar

THE PROFESSOR SERIES

Published by

Family Law, 4th Edition (1994)
Emanuel Publishing Corp. • 1865 Palmer Avenue • Larchmont, NY 10538

Prior editions of this work
were written in part by

HOWARD M. ROSSEN,
Director, Ohio Bar Review & BAR/BRI

and by

WILTON S. SOGG,
Adjunct Professor of Law,
Cleveland-Marshall College of Law

ISBN 1-56542-151-5

To Dominica

Abbreviations Used in Text

Areen — Judith Areen, *Cases and Materials on Family Law* (Foundation Press, 3rd Ed., 1992)

Clark — Homer H. Clark, Jr., *The Law of Domestic Relations* (West Hornbook Series, West Publ. Co., 1988)

C&G — Homer H. Clark, Jr. and Carol Glowinsky, *Cases and Problems on Domestic Relations* (West Publ. Co., 4th Ed., 1990) and 1992 Supp.

Krause — Harry D. Krause, *Family Law, Cases, Comments and Questions* West Publ. Co., 3rd Ed., 1990)

TABLE OF CONTENTS

Chapter 1
INTRODUCTION AND ANALYSIS

Chapter 2
THE INSTITUTION OF MARRIAGE

CHAPTER 3

TYPES OF MARRIAGES

CHAPTER 4

RIGHTS OF WOMEN,
MARRIAGE AND OTHER
INTIMATE RELATIONSHIPS

CHAPTER 5

ANNULMENT

CHAPTER 6

FAMILY RELATIONSHIPS

CHAPTER 7

DIVORCE: JURISDICTION AND GROUNDS

CHAPTER 8

DIVORCE: FINANCIAL ASPECTS

CHAPTER 9

CHILD CUSTODY AND SUPPORT

I. CHILD CUSTODY

CHAPTER 10
SEPARATION AGREEMENTS

CHAPTER 11

ADOPTION

CHAPTER 12

ASSISTED REPRODUCTION

CHAPTER 13

LEGITIMACY AND ILLEGITIMACY

(This page intentionally left blank)

INTRODUCTION AND ANALYSIS

I. THE MARRIAGE RELATIONSHIP

A. Generally: The principal focal point in the study of family law is the marital relationship. This includes the *formation* of the marriage, the *rights and obligations* flowing from the marital relationship, and *termination* of the marriage.

1. **Interests considered:** An aspect peculiar to family law is the concern which extends beyond the two immediate parties to the marital relationship. Because of this concern, analysis of any family law situation must also include consideration of the interests of any *children* of the marriage and of *society* at large.

   a. **Other concerns:** Family law concerns itself not only with rights and obligations between parties to a relationship, such as husband and wife, but also with rights and obligations flowing from a *status,* such as:

      i. **Married women;**

      ii. **Separated or divorced spouses;** and

      iii. **Children,** legitimate, illegitimate and adopted.

2. **Analysis:** A study of the institution of marriage requires consideration of:

   a. **Historical background;**

   b. **Nature** of the marital relationship;

   c. **Elements** of a marriage;

   d. **Contracts** preventing or promoting marriage; and

   e. **Formalities** accompanying the marital relationship. See "The Institution of Marriage," *infra*, p. 4.

3. **Types of marriage:** Consideration of the institution of marriage requires consideration of the various ways in which the status of marriage can be achieved:

   a. **Ceremonial marriage;**

   b. **Common law marriage;**

   c. **Putative marriage;** and

   d. **Proxy marriage.** See "Types of Marriages," p. 19.

4. **Modern Issues:** Because the subject matter of family law is in a constant state of flux, analysis of any fact pattern must take into account the possible impact of any of the trends of change in the law and forces

for social change, such as changing law at state, federal and constitutional levels with respect to ***women's rights, governmental regulation, birth control, abortion,*** and even ***informal "relationships."*** See "Rights of Women, Marriage and other Intimate Relationships," p. 27.

5. **Annulment:** Some marital relationships may be dissolved retroactively to the date of their formation through the process of annulment. Analysis of such a fact pattern requires consideration of:

   a. **Jurisdiction** to grant the annulment;

   b. **Grounds** for the annulment;

   c. **Defenses** to an action for annulment; and

   d. **Rights and obligations** of the parties arising from the annulment action. See "Annulment," p. 49.

6. **Family relationships:** Once the marital relationship has been established, a fact pattern must be analyzed to determine the rights and obligations arising out of family relationships. These include:

   a. Support obligations;

   b. **Support actions** between members of the family (e.g., wife vs. husband, or parent vs. child); and

   c. **Legal rights,** and obligations among family members, and special status of minors. See "Family Relationships," p. 61.

7. **Divorce:** The process by which the marital relationship is most frequently terminated is divorce. Divorce is effective from the date of the decree and thus is distinguishable from annulment. Any analysis of divorce should take this into account. Other issues include:

   a. **Jurisdiction** to grant the divorce;

   b. **Grounds** for the divorce;

   c. **Defenses** to a divorce action; and

   d. **Property rights** of the parties, and obligations to any children of the marriage. See "Divorce: Jurisdiction and Grounds," p. 84.

8. **Financial aspects of divorce:** These include:

   a. **Division of the marital property,** including community property; and

   b. **Alimony,** both temporary and permanent. See "Divorce: Financial Aspects," p. 102.

9. **Child custody:** When a marriage is terminated, provision must be made for custody and support of minor children of the marriage. See "Child Custody and Support," p. 125.

10. Separation agreements: The financial aspects of a divorce are generally provided for in a separation agreement entered into between the parties and ultimately incorporated into the court's divorce decree. See "Separation Agreements," p. 153.

B. **Adoption and Illegitimacy:** Family law deals extensively with the rights of natural children of a valid marriage. Analysis of a family law fact pattern may also bring into play two other areas with respect to the parent-child relationship: adoption and illegitimacy.

1. **Adoption:** Analysis of an adoption matter includes:

   a. Types of placement;

   b. **Consent** to the adoption;

   c. Termination of the natural parents' rights and duties;

   d. Abrogation of adoption;

   e. **Inheritance rights** arising from adoptions of both children and adults. See "Adoption," p. 158.

2. **Illegitimacy:** Analysis of a fact pattern involving illegitimacy involves consideration of the specific laws of the particular jurisdiction involved, and the identity of the natural parents and their rights and responsibilities. The rights of illegitimate persons have been expanded by a number of Supreme Court decisions. See "Legitimacy and Illegitimacy," p. 209.

3. **Artificial insemination and surrogate parenthood:** Artificial insemination and surrogate parenthood are a developing area of the law. The cases in this area consider constitutional rights to privacy and due process, as well as state public policy; see *infra*, p. 195.

THE INSTITUTION OF MARRIAGE

I. INTRODUCTION

A. **Historical background:** Although the law governing marriage in the United States has evolved to its present state through legislative action, this body of law has been influenced greatly by English matrimonial law and traditions. This influence can be seen in the *ceremony* surrounding the entrance into the marriage contract, the *guidelines determining the validity* of the marriage contract, and the use of *courts* to apply the guidelines to the marriage relation.

1. **Betrothal:** The initial step in the Anglo-Saxon marriage customs was the "betrothal," by which the family of the bride agreed to transfer custody of the bride to the groom and the groom agreed to care for, protect and make a settlement upon the bride. Following the betrothal the transfer was accomplished. The settlement involved was the forerunner of "dower."

2. **Religious aspect:** With the conquest of the Anglo-Saxons by the Normans and the increased influence of Christianity, religion assumed a prominent role in the marriage relationship. The power to regulate these relationships was placed under the jurisdiction of the Church and the ecclesiastical courts.

3. **Formalities:** Ecclesiastical courts established certain formalities of a marriage ceremony within the Church which survive today. They include:

   a. **Banns:** Marriage banns, the publication of notice of the intended marriage;

   b. **Ceremony:** Performance of the wedding ceremony by a priest in a church; and

   c. **Ring:** Given by the groom to the bride; frequently the bride also gives a ring to the groom.

4. **Disabilities:** Rules with respect to the marriage relationship developed in the English courts. The *ecclesiastical courts* prohibited the marriage of relatives of a certain degree of sanguinity and of persons below a certain age. The *common law courts* set out civil disabilities that would invalidate a marriage.

5. **Void/Voidable distinction:** A distinction developed between *void and voidable* marriages.

   a. **Civil law:** Civil disabilities, such as a prior marriage, less-than-required age, fraud, duress and insanity, rendered the marriage void.

    b. Church law: Ecclesiastical disabilities, such as marriage of persons within a certain degree of blood relationship and impotence, came from Church law and rendered the marriage voidable.

    Note: At common law there was no necessity for an annulment of a void marriage. An ecclesiastical court could annul a voidable marriage so long as both parties were living.

II. NATURE OF THE MARRIAGE RELATIONSHIP

A. Definition: Marriage is the civil status or relationship created by the legal union of a man and woman as husband and wife. It imposes certain duties and responsibilities upon each to the other and to society. These last until the death of one or the legal termination of the relationship.

    1. Relation to contracts: Marriage is contractual by nature. However, it is distinguished from other types of contracts in the following manner:

        a. Status: Marriage creates a status as well as imposing rights and duties upon the parties to the marriage contract;

        b. Restrictions: Marriage is *more restrictive* by nature than other types of contracts because of the limitations imposed upon the capacity to enter into the marriage contract;

        c. Mental capacity: Marriage generally requires a lesser degree of mental capacity than many other contractual situations.

        Example: H suffered mental impairment as a child due to illness, and was later treated over a period of years for schizophrenia. Despite those medical problems, H completes three years of high school and finds a job. When H is 28, he marries W. After three years H is hospitalized, and is placed under legal guardianship because of incompetency. His guardian brings an action to annul H's marriage on the ground that H did not have the mental capacity to enter into marriage.

        Held, there is insufficient evidence for an annulment. Absolute inability to enter into contracts—or insanity—renders a marriage void, but mere weakness of mind will not do so unless the party afflicted mentally does not possess the power to consent. A marriage is valid if the party has sufficient capacity to understand the nature of the contract and the obligations and responsibilities created thereby. The evidence shows that at the time of his marriage H had a sufficient understanding of the marriage relationship and consented to it. *Homan v. Homan,* 147 N.W.2d 630 (Neb. 1967); *Fischer v. Adams,* 38 N.W.2d 337 (Neb. 1949).

      d. **Duration:** Marriage is ***permanent*** unless it is dissolved by a court of competent jurisdiction; It cannot be revoked at the will of the parties;

      e. **Assignment:** Marriage creates rights which cannot be assigned, alienated or transferred;

      f. **Remedies:** If the marriage contract is breached, the remedies available to the parties are different from those available after breach of other types of contracts;

      g. **Constitution:** Article I, Section 10(1) denies to the states the power to enact any law which impairs the obligation of contracts. Marriage does not fall within that prohibition.

        Example: H marries W1, and they have several children. H leaves W1, promising to return or send for them. H travels to the Territory of Oregon where he settles and claims a parcel of land under a congressional act as a married man. A year later the legislature of Oregon passes an act which purports to terminate H's marriage to W1. H marries W2 and lives with her until his death. The children of H and W1 seek to compel the conveyance of the land to them, basing their claim on their relationship to W1, now deceased.

        Held, the claim is denied. Marriage is not a contract which falls within the meaning of the constitutional prohibition against the impairment of contractual obligations by legislative action. Marriage can be modified by legislative authority. The act of the legislature constituted a valid divorce, and since W1 had no valid claim to the real estate, neither did the children who claim through her. *Maynard v. Hill*, 125 U.S. 190 (1888).

2. **Basis for distinction:** The differences between marriage contracts and other types of contracts generally arise from the fact that marriage is an institution upon which the "family," an integral unit in modern society, is based. Therefore, it is considered of vital importance to the state. Due to the significance of marriage to society and the parties, the state attempts to foster and protect the marriage relationship through its courts. These unique characteristics practically make it a contract among three parties: the man, the woman and the state.

III. ELEMENTS OF A VALID MARRIAGE

  A. **Essential elements:** To enter a valid marriage the following elements must be present:

    1. **Competency:** The parties must be ***competent*** to marry, i.e., free of ***legal disabilities***. Possible legal disabilities include: ***consanguinity***; ***underage***; health problems (e.g., venereal disease); mental incapacity; and a ***preexisting marriage*** by one or both parties.

2. **Mutual present agreement:** The parties must intend in *good faith* to enter into a true and complete marriage relationship, not a sham.

3. **Opposite gender:** The parties must be of *opposite gender.*

We consider each of these requirements in turn.

B. Competency: To be competent to marry both parties must be free of any *legal disabilities* established by the state.

1. **Consanguinity:** An important type of disability is *consanguinity.* This refers to the *blood relationship* between the persons who wish to marry. All states and the District of Columbia prohibit a marriage between *parent and child*, between *brother and sister*, and between *uncle and niece*. Thirty states also prohibit marriages between *first cousins*. Areen, p. 12.

> **Example:** H marries his niece, W, in Italy after obtaining a dispensation to make the marriage valid. H and W reside in the United States until H's death. W applies for an allowance for support from H's estate. The court denies W's application because the marriage is invalid as incestuous under state law. W appeals.
>
> *Held*, the marriage is not recognized, and W cannot qualify as the surviving spouse. The general rule is that a marriage valid where performed is valid everywhere. One exception to that rule regards as invalid an incestuous marriage between persons so closely related that their marriage is contrary to strong public policy of the state of domicile even though it is valid where celebrated. "A state has the authority to declare what marriages of its citizens shall be recognized as valid, regardless of the fact that the marriages may have been entered into in foreign jurisdictions where they were valid. This state has prohibited marriages between uncle and niece for many years and made it a criminal offense. That reflects strong public policy against such marriages. *Catalano v. Catalano*, 170 A.2d 726 (Conn. 1961).

   a. **Criticism of rule:** One authority suggests that a better rule would be to make consanguineous marriages *voidable* rather than void. Such a rule would avoid the harsh result of *Catalano*. Clark, p. 88.

   b. **Persons related by half-blood:** Virtually all courts hold that the prohibited degrees of consanguinity include persons related by *half-blood*. See, e.g., *People v. Baker*, 268 P.2d 705 (Cal. 1954); *Singh v. Singh*, 213 Conn. 637, 569 A.2d 1112 (1990). Thus all states prohibit, say, a man from marrying his half-sister.

   c. **Step-relatives:** The consanguinity prohibitions also generally apply to *"affinity relationships,"* i.e., what are commonly called step-relations. For instance, where (as is always the case) a state statute prohibits siblings from marrying, the statute will usually be interpreted to prevent a person from marrying his ***step-sister***, even though there is no blood relationship between them.

    i. Effect of termination of marriage: In the absence of a statute, when a marriage ends by death, divorce or annulment, most courts ***terminate all affinity relationships*** that were produced by the marriage.

    Example: H marries W, who has a daughter, D, by a prior marriage. H and W divorce. *Held*, H may marry D, because D's status as step-daughter ended with the divorce. *Back v. Back*, 148 Iowa 223, 125 N.W. 1009 (1910).

d. Adoption: Most courts, but not all, ***allow*** marriage by persons related only by ***adoption***.

    Example: H is the natural father of S, a boy, and W is the natural mother of D, a girl. H and W marry. H adopts D, making D and S sister and brother by adoption. D and S are not otherwise related. They desire to marry, but a state statute prohibits marriage "between a brother and sister, whether the relationship is by the half or the whole blood or by adoption. ..."

    Held, D and S may marry. The prohibition here violates the Equal Protection Clause of the U.S. Constitution. The main reason for prohibiting brother-sister marriages is because of the dangers of producing genetically defective children. These dangers are not present where the relationship is solely by adoption rather than by blood. *Israel v. Allen*, 577 P.2d 762 (Col. 1978).

    i. Criticism: But the rule allowing marriage between people related by adoption has been criticized on the grounds that adopted persons are members of one nuclear family even though they are not related by blood. Clark, p. 84.

2. Age: Generally, to be competent to marry, both parties must be of a ***minimum age*** fixed by law. This age is usually ***18***, for both men and women. Where one person is under the age of consent, the marriage is usually treated as merely voidable, not void.

    Example: H, without his parents' consent, marries W1 while under the age specified by statute. H and W1 cohabit, and then voluntarily separate. There is no divorce. Subsequently, H marries W2, and H is charged with bigamy. H defends on the grounds that his marriage to W1 is void because he was under age, and therefore, he was not married to W1 when he married W2.

    Held, the defense is not valid. The marriage of one under age is not an absolute nullity, but is only annulled from the date fixed by a court in an annulment proceeding. During the time intervening the marriage is valid. Since H's first marriage was voidable only, and no decree of divorce or annulment was obtained, the marriage remained in effect, and H's subsequent marriage to W2 was biga-mous. *State v. Cone,* 57 N.W. 50 (Wis. 1893). See also *State v. Sellers,* 134 S.E. 873 (S.C. 1926).

a. **Parental consent:** Most states have statutes requiring the ***consent of a parent or guardian*** for the marriage of a minor. These statutes are ***valid***, because of the state's paternalistic power to protect and promote the welfare of minors who lack the capacity to act in their own best interests.

> **Example:** State law provides that male applicants for a marriage license between ages 16 and 18, and female applicants between 14 and 18 obtain written consent to the marriage from their parents. M and W seek to have the parental consent law declared unconstitutional as M's mother refuses to consent. They contend that the law deprives them of liberty guaranteed by the Due Process Clause of the Fourteenth Amendment.
>
> *Held,* the law is valid because it is ***rationally related*** to the state's legitimate interests. Those include the protection of minors from immature decision-making and the prevention of unstable marriages. The parental consent requirement ensures that at least one mature person will participate in the decision. The fact that some parents will not act in the best interest of their children does not render the law arbitrary. Further, the law only requires that the ***decision*** to marry be postponed. The parties may preserve the opportunity for a later marriage should they continue to desire it. *Moe v. Dinkins,* 533 F.Supp. 623 (D.C.N.Y. 1981), *aff'd* 669 F.2d 67 (2d Cir.), *cert. denied* 459 U.S. 827 (1982).

3. **Health:** To be competent to marry, the parties may be required to meet certain health standards. For instance, most states forbid the marriage of persons afflicted with venereal disease.

4. **Mental capacity:** To be competent to marry, both parties must have sufficient mental ability to understand the nature, effect and consequences of marriage ***at the time of the marriage.*** (However, a lesser standard of mental capacity is imposed upon parties to a marriage contract than is imposed upon parties to other contracts (*supra*, p. 5) — clear and convincing proof that the person lacked competence is required before a court will find the marriage void or voidable.)

> **Example:** H and W are married, but after two years W is committed to a mental institution where she is still a patient. After the commitment H learns that W had been committed to a hospital on two previous occasions and had been diagnosed as having schizo-phrenic tendencies. H seeks an annulment claiming that W was of unsound mind at the time of their marriage and was incapable of understanding the marriage contract.

Held, H's petition should be denied. The validity of a marriage is presumed; the party contending that it is invalid has the burden of proof. The parties to a marriage must have the mental capacity to understand the nature of their act. Any proof of lack of mental capacity must be definite and clear. H did not notice any abnormal behavior by W prior to or at the time of the marriage, and he did not present clear evidence that W was mentally incapable of understanding the nature of marriage or consenting to it. *Larson v. Larson*, 192 N.E.2d 594 (Ill.App. 1963). See also *Ertel v. Ertel*, 40 N.E.2d 85 (Ill.App. 1942).

5. **Bigamous marriage:** To be competent to marry, a party may not be married to another person at the time of the marriage. Existence of a prior marriage invalidates a marriage as well as subjecting the person to criminal prosecution for ***bigamy***.

C. **Mutual present agreement:** The parties to a marriage must intend in ***good faith*** to enter into the ***complete*** marriage relationship with all its obligations and responsibilities. Thus a marriage contracted for some limited purpose (e.g., immigration to the U.S.) will be found to be a sham, and invalidated.

> **Example:** W, a citizen of Haiti, and H, a citizen of the United States, marry. Their sole purpose is to allow W to immigrate to the United States. H and W have no intention of living together as husband and wife, and they have no marital relationship either before or after the ceremony. *Held*, the marriage is not valid. Marriage solely for the purpose of immigration, where there is lack of intent to assume the "status" of marriage, may be declared a nullity. *Faustin v. Lewis*, 85 N.J. 507, 427 A.2d 1105 (N.J. 1981). See also *Bark v. I.N.S.*, 511 F.2d 1200 (9th Cir. 1975).

D. **Same-sex marriage:** Statutes in all states limit marriage to persons of ***opposite sex***. In recent years homosexuals and lesbians have attempted to marry members of the ***same sex***. They have challenged the opposite-sex requirement on the grounds that this requirement violates their fundamental right to marry, or their right to equal protection, both guaranteed by the U.S. Constitution. However, nearly all courts have rejected these constitutional arguments.

> **Example:** The Ps, two homosexuals, are denied a license to marry each other. They then seek a writ of mandamus to compel issuance of the license. The court interprets the applicable statute as requiring persons who seek a marriage license to be of the opposite sex. *Held*, the right to be free from invidious sex discrimination under the Equal Protection Clause is not violated by the prohibition of marriage by homosexuals. There is no irrational or invidious discrimination. The Ps' petition for a marriage license is therefore denied. *Baker v. Nelson*, 191 N.W.2d 185 (Minn. 1971). See also

Jones v. Hallahan, 501 S.W.2d 588 (Ky. 1973) (two women denied a marriage license).

1. **State Equal Rights Amendment:** Marriage between persons of the same sex has been prohibited even where there was a *state Equal Rights Amendment* in effect. Courts have reasoned that the relationship of marriage has always been the *legal union of one man and one woman*. Relationships between persons of the same sex are simply outside the proper definition of marriage, and a ban on same-sex marriages therefore does not constitute gender discrimination. See, e.g., *Singer v. Hara,* 522 P.2d 1187 (Wash. 1974).

   a. **Possible exception in Hawaii:** But *Hawaii* now seems to be an *exception* to the rule that the same-sex ban never violates constitutional guarantees.

      i. **Facts:** The Hawaiian Constitution provides that no person shall be denied equal protection of the laws or the enjoyment of civil rights based on religion, sex, ancestry or race. This is a more expansive guarantee than contained in the Federal Constitution.

      ii. **Holding**: The Hawaiian Supreme Court has held that barring same sex couples from marrying may violate this state constitutional provision, unless the ban is justified by a *compelling state interest*. Further, any ban must be *narrowly drawn* to avoid unnecessary abridgments of state constitutional rights. The case was remanded for further proceedings in which the trial court is to determine whether there is a "compelling state interest." *Baehr v. Lewin,* 852 P.2d 44 (Haw. 1993).

2. **Transsexuals:** A marriage between a male and a *postoperative transsexual*, who surgically changed her external sexual anatomy from male to female, has been upheld. The court stated: "If such sex reassignment surgery is successful and the postoperative transsexual is, by virtue of medical treatment, thereby possessed of the full capacity to function sexually as a male or female, as the case may be, we perceive no legal barrier, cognizable social taboo, or reason grounded in public policy to prevent that person's identification at least for purposes of marriage to the sex finally indicated." *M.T. v. J.T.,* 355 A.2d 204 (N.J. 1976).

3. **Criminal law:** Homosexual relations between consenting adults is a *crime* in some states. The Supreme Court has held that the constitutional right of privacy does not protect homosexuals who commit sodomy. *Bowers v. Hardwick,* 478 U.S. 186 (1986).

IV. CONTRACTS PREVENTING OR PROMOTING MARRIAGE

A. **Types of restraint:** The validity or invalidity of contracts in restraint of marriage is dependent, in most instances, upon whether the restraints are general or partial. A ***general restraint*** which is so complete as to prevent marriage is generally deemed to be invalid. The validity of a ***partial restraint*** which does not prevent marriage completely is dependent upon whether the restraint is beneficial.

1. **Remarriage:** Contracts which would prevent remarriage or contracts regarding conveyances on the condition that no remarriage occur are usually held valid.

   Example: W brings an action for separate maintenance because of H's adultery with X. H and W enter into a stipulation of their property rights, and W amends her petition to request a divorce, which is granted. At the same time H and W agree that if either party marries prior to their youngest child's attaining age 20, such party will forfeit $10,000 to the other party. That agreement is not filed with the court. Within a year H marries X. W applies to the court for modification of the divorce decree to provide for a judgment against H for $10,000. H contends that the contract is void as against public policy and unenforceable because it amounts to a penalty.

   Held, for W. Contracts in general restraint of marriage are against public policy and void. A general restraint is construed as a restraint which binds a party from marrying anyone at any time. However, contracts in restraint of marriage, if shown to be reasonable under the circumstances and not general and unlimited, are valid. In this case, W feared the effect of X's influence on her children if H married X. Furthermore, the restraint was not unlimited, and in view of H's past conduct, it was reasonable. *Cowan v. Cowan,* 75 N.W.2d 920 (Iowa 1956).

   Note: Courts are more likely to find restraints against ***remarriage*** valid than restraints against first marriages. However, this is probably due to the fact that circumstances surrounding a restraint against remarriage are more often reasonable and may serve a meritorious purpose.

2. **Third parties:** Agreements with a third party which prevent a spouse from performing the obligations of a marriage are illegal and unenforceable.

3. **Marriage for profit:** A contract in which marriage is promoted for profit is unenforceable since it violates the policy that marriage should be entered into freely without the activities of paid third parties.

Example: Contracts in which a broker promotes marriage for profit are unenforceable. However, many cities show marriage brokers listed in telephone books. Apparently such services are utilized, and probably the fee is collected in advance.

V. CONTRACTS MADE PRIOR TO MARRIAGE

A. Antenuptial contracts generally: A contract made before marriage is called an antenuptial or prenuptial contract. The purpose of an antenuptial contract is to establish the rights of the husband and wife to property owned at the time of the marriage or to be acquired in the future.

1. Statute of frauds: The statute of frauds, which is in effect in most states, requires that a contract made in consideration of marriage or a promise to marry, other than mutual promises to marry, must be *in writing* and *signed* by the party against whom it is to be enforced. Thus, where marriage is the entire consideration or only part of the consideration for the contract, the agreement must comply with the statute of frauds.

> **Example:** H induces W to come to the United States from Europe and marry him under an oral antenuptial contract. W sues to enforce it. *Held,* enforcement is denied, because the statute of frauds requires that an antenuptial agreement be in writing. *Hutnak v. Hutnak,* 81 A.2d 278 (R.I. 1951).

> **Note:** The fact that the marriage takes place after an oral antenuptial contract is not sufficient part performance to remove the contract from the statute of frauds. This is so even where there is a change of position.

B. Validity: Antenuptial agreements are generally *valid*, provided that: (1) there is *full disclosure* of the *assets* of the parties; and (2) each spouse is *adequately supported* under the agreement.

1. Rationale for disclosure: When persons are engaged, their relationship is *fiduciary* in character. There is a duty on each partner to disclose his or her assets and income. Failure to do that renders the agreement invalid. See *Kosik v. George,* 253 Or. 15, 452 P.2d 560 (1969).

2. Reasonableness: In weighing the *fairness* and *reasonableness* of an antenuptial agreement, the courts will consider:

a. the relative *situations of the parties;*

b. their respective *ages, health and experience;*

c. their respective *properties;*

d. their *family ties* and connection;

e. the *needs* of each party; and

    f. such factors as tend to show whether the ***agreement was understandingly made.***

C. Alimony or maintenance: An antenuptial agreement may provide for the amount of ***alimony*** or ***maintenance*** payable if the marriage ends in separation or divorce.

    1. Traditional view: Traditionally, courts held that it was contrary to public policy to provide for a financial settlement in the event of a future separation or divorce. The reason was that such an agreement would be destabilizing to the marital relationship, and might promote marital breakups.

    2. Modern view: Since about 1970 courts have held that agreements which set alimony, maintenance and property rights upon divorce or separation do not violate public policy so long as they are ***fair*** and make ***adequate provision*** for each spouse in view of the needs and resources of each. *Posner v. Posner*, 233 So.2d 381 (Fla.1970); *Osborne v. Osborne*, 384 Mass. 591, 428 N.E.2d 810 (1981); Clark, pp. 6-10.

> **Example 1:** Before H and W marry they sign an agreement providing that in the event of divorce or separation W is to receive $75 per week alimony from H. Under prior state decisions this antenuptial agreement would be void. *Held*, the rule that such agreements are automatically void is abolished. Divorce is a commonplace fact of life, and there is no evidence that antenuptial agreements contemplating divorce actually encourage divorce. The clear trend of modern court decisions enforces such agreements. Changes in society render restrictions of antenuptial agreements inappropriate. The agreement on alimony is valid, provided there was full disclosure, and provided the terms are not unconscionable viewed as of the time of enforcement. *Edwardson v. Edwardson*, 798 S.W.2d 941 (Ky. 1990).

> **Example 2:** On the day before H and W marry, W signs a prenuptial agreement in which H's support payments in the event of separation or divorce are $200 per week (but in no event more than $25,000 total). At that time, W is unemployed and H earns $90,000 per year. Subsequently, H and W separate. While divorce proceedings are pending W seeks support, because the $25,000 limit is reached.
>
> *Held*, so long as there was full disclosure the prenuptial agreement is enforceable. Paternalistic presumptions to shelter women from perceived inferiority are not valid and must be discarded, especially in light of the Equal Rights Amendment adopted in this state. Therefore, the court will not inquire into the reasonableness of this agreement any more than it would for other contracts. *Simeone v. Simeone*, 581 A.2d 162 (Pa. 1990).

VI. SUITS FOR BREACH OF PROMISE TO MARRY

A. Breach of promise: About one-half of American states today permit a suit for ***breach of promise to marry***. That is, if A and B agree to be married, and B changes his/her mind, about half the states allow A to bring what is in essence a breach of contract action against B.

   1. "Heart balm actions": Such suits for breach of promise are sometimes termed "heart balm actions," because the plaintiff receives "balm" for his or her broken "heart."

   2. Either party may sue: Historically, most plaintiffs in breach-of-promise suits have been women. However, virtually all states that allow such actions at all allow suit to be brought by either the man or the woman.

   3. Measure of damages: Courts disagree about what the ***measure of damages*** should be where a breach-of-promise action is allowed. Most courts allow "direct" damages (e.g., damages for expenditures made in reliance upon the upcoming wedding, or damages for the illness brought on by the unexpected jilting). But courts are much more reluctant to allow the plaintiff to recover for the loss of ***financial advantage*** which the plaintiff would have achieved had the other party not reneged on the promise to marry.

   > **Example:** P sues for breach of promise to marry. D moves to dismiss on the ground that the action is contrary to public policy. The suit is dismissed and P appeals.
   >
   > *Held*, P may recover in a quasi-contract, quasi-tort action for foreseeable special and general damages. Thus damages for P's mental anguish, loss to reputation, and injury to health may be recovered. However, damages for P's loss of expected financial and social position will not be allowed, because a person generally does not choose a marriage partner for social or financial gain. Evidence of D's wealth or social position should not be permitted because it is immaterial. *Stanard v. Bolin*, 565 P.2d 94 (Wash. 1977).

VII. FORMALITIES OF MARRIAGE

A. Introduction: Due to the importance of the marriage relationship to the state, the formalities surrounding the marriage contract are wholly regulated by statute in each of the fifty states. The regulations may be mandatory or directory.

   1. Mandatory regulations: In some states, compliance with the statutory requirements regarding marriage is considered "mandatory." If those requirements are not met, the marriage will be invalid.

2. **Directory regulations:** By contrast, in other states, compliance with the statutory requirements regarding marriage is considered "directory." Failure to meet those requirements, in the absence of an expression that a particular requirement is a prerequisite to the validity of a marriage, does not make the marriage invalid. However, non-compliance may subject the offending parties to criminal sanctions or civil liabilities.

> **Example:** W travels with M to visit M's daughter. W had been under the influence of alcohol for the two months preceding the trip. W remembers only that she awoke the morning after she began the trip, and M told her that they had been married the previous night. The marriage was performed on the day the marriage license was issued, by a minister in the presence of only two witnesses, rather than the three required by statute. A statute of the jurisdiction requires a 72-hour waiting period between the issuance of the license and the performance of the ceremony. W petitions to annul the marriage as contrary to statute.
>
> *Held*, the marriage is valid. The statutes providing for the manner and form in which marriages are to be celebrated are merely "directory," and failure to observe them will not make the marriage null and void. Here, despite having only two witnesses to the ceremony which was performed before the 72-hour waiting period had passed, the marriage is valid. Furthermore, there was no lack of consent since the minister testified that after speaking with W and M on two occasions, he was convinced that they understood what they were doing and wanted to marry each other. *Parker v. Saileau,* 213 So.2d 190 (La. 1968).

3. **General rule:** The general rule is that *a marriage which is valid where performed is valid everywhere*. However, a state (let's call it the "forum state") may choose not to follow this rule if the marriage is contrary to a *strong public policy* of the forum state (e.g., a marriage that would be incestuous under the laws of the forum state). See, e.g., *Catalano v. Catalano, supra*, p. 7.

B. **Types of regulations:** Legislatures in all states have enacted statutes governing the formalities of marriage. Those statutes typically regulate the following:

1. **Blood tests:** Most states require that the results of *blood tests* of both parties to the marriage be presented prior to the issuance of a marriage license, to prove that neither party is afflicted with venereal disease. That requirement is usually "directory." Consequently, non-compliance does not ordinarily render the marriage invalid.

2. **Banns:** Many states, following the English practice of publishing "banns" or notice of the prospective marriage, require a *waiting period* either between the performance of the blood tests and the issu-

 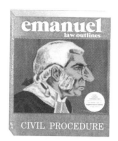 

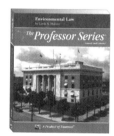 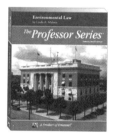 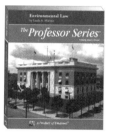

emanuel® emanuel® emanuel®

Thank you for purchasing an Emanuel title!

These bookmarks can be detached and used as you read.

If you have any comments on any of our books or flashcards, please feel free to e-mail them to **comments@ emanuel.com**.

Send in the card at right to to receive our current catalog, to get on our mailing list, or for information on becoming an **Emanuel Student Rep** at your school!

Emanuel does not sell its mailing lists to anyone.

 ## I want to learn more about Emanuel!

- ❏ **Send me your current catalog**
- ❏ **Add me to your regular mailing list**
- ❏ **Add me to your e-mail list**
- ❏ **I'd like information about becoming an Emanuel Student Rep at my school**

Name _____ E-mail address (e.g., johndoe@school.edu)

Address _____ City ____ State ___ ZIP Code

Law school attended _____ Graduation Year

Telephone Number

Visit us on the Internet at http://www.emanuel.com

emanuel®

First Year Products   E   L   S   P

Civil Procedure
Civil Procedure 2
Constitutional Law
Contracts
Criminal Law
Criminal Procedure
Future Interests
Property
Torts

Upper Year Products

Agency & Partnership
Bankruptcy
Constitutional Law
Corporations
Criminal Procedure
Environmental Law
Evidence
Family Law
Federal Income Taxation
Future Interests
Intellectual Property
International Law
Labor Law
Neg. Inst. & Pmt. Systems
Products Liability
Prof. Responsibility
Sales (UCC Art. 2)
Secured Transactions
Wills & Trusts

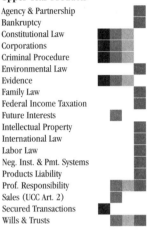

E - Emanuel Law Outlines
L - Law In A Flash flashcards & software
S - Siegel's Essay & M/C Q&A's
P - The Professor Series

Strategies & Tactics Series
Strategies & Tactics for First Year Law
Strategies & Tactics for the MBE
Strategies & Tactics for the MPRE
The Finz Multistate Method

Steve Emanuel's 1st Year Q&A's

---

emanuel®

First Year Products   E   L   S   P

Civil Procedure
Civil Procedure 2
Constitutional Law
Contracts
Criminal Law
Criminal Procedure
Future Interests
Property
Torts

Upper Year Products

Agency & Partnership
Bankruptcy
Constitutional Law
Corporations
Criminal Procedure
Environmental Law
Evidence
Family Law
Federal Income Taxation
Future Interests
Intellectual Property
International Law
Labor Law
Neg. Inst. & Pmt. Systems
Products Liability
Prof. Responsibility
Sales (UCC Art. 2)
Secured Transactions
Wills & Trusts

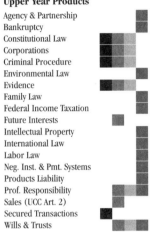

E - Emanuel Law Outlines
L - Law In A Flash flashcards & software
S - Siegel's Essay & M/C Q&A's
P - The Professor Series

Strategies & Tactics Series
Strategies & Tactics for First Year Law
Strategies & Tactics for the MBE
Strategies & Tactics for the MPRE
The Finz Multistate Method

Steve Emanuel's 1st Year Q&A's

---

emanuel®

First Year Products   E   L   S   P

Civil Procedure
Civil Procedure 2
Constitutional Law
Contracts
Criminal Law
Criminal Procedure
Future Interests
Property
Torts

Upper Year Products

Agency & Partnership
Bankruptcy
Constitutional Law
Corporations
Criminal Procedure
Environmental Law
Evidence
Family Law
Federal Income Taxation
Future Interests
Intellectual Property
International Law
Labor Law
Neg. Inst. & Pmt. Systems
Products Liability
Prof. Responsibility
Sales (UCC Art. 2)
Secured Transactions
Wills & Trusts

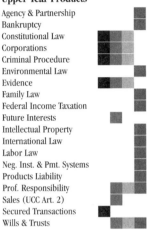

E - Emanuel Law Outlines
L - Law In A Flash flashcards & software
S - Siegel's Essay & M/C Q&A's
P - The Professor Series

Strategies & Tactics Series
Strategies & Tactics for First Year Law
Strategies & Tactics for the MBE
Strategies & Tactics for the MPRE
The Finz Multistate Method

Steve Emanuel's 1st Year Q&A's

---

name

address

city

state   zip

To: Emanuel Publishing Corp.
1865 Palmer Avenue, Suite 202
Larchmont, NY 10538

ATTN: BRC

ance of the marriage license, or between the issuance of the marriage license and the performance of the marriage ceremony. Such statute is usually "directory," so non-compliance does not ordinarily make the marriage invalid.

3. **Licensing:** All states require the issuance of a *marriage license* prior to the performance of the marriage ceremony. The precise license provisions governing issuance vary from state to state. These rules are "directory" in some states and "mandatory" in other states.

> **Example:** H and W marry in a religious ceremony. They fail to obtain a marriage license as state law requires. H and W live together for a number of years. Is the marriage void?
>
> *Held*, no. When there is no express language in the statute declaring a marriage void for failure to observe a statutory requirement, the marriage is not void. Here, no such statutory language regarding marriage licenses exists. Furthermore, the public policy favoring valid marriages is very strong. Therefore, the unlicensed ceremony will be deemed valid. *Carabetta v. Carabetta*, 438 A.2d 109 (Ct. 1980).

4. **Solemnization:** Most states require *formal celebration or solemnization* of a marriage, although the precise form that the ceremony should take is generally not prescribed by statute.

a. **Strict compliance not required:** While some sort of solemnization is everywhere required for a valid ceremonial marriage, most states do *not* treat the marriage as *void* merely because some requirements concerning the details of the ceremony are not complied with. That is, statutes regarding solemnization, like those regarding blood tests, waiting periods, etc., are usually "directory." *Hames v. Hames*, 316 A.2d 379 (Conn. 1972).

5. **Officiation:** Most states have enacted legislation with respect to the *persons who may officiate* at a marriage ceremony. This type of legislation generally concerns the qualifications and licensing of persons, and is considered "directory." The performance of a marriage ceremony by a person who does not meet the statutory requirements does *not* render the marriage invalid.

> **Example:** H and W are married by a family court judge who is acting outside the geographical limits within which he is authorized to perform marriages. H and W apply for a license, participate in the ceremony, and thereafter live together as husband and wife. H now seeks to have the marriage annulled on the ground that the judge did not perform a valid marriage.
>
> *Held*, the marriage is valid. The statute pertains only to the form and manner in which marriages are to be celebrated, and is merely "directory" in nature. Failure to meet its provisions does not render

a marriage void. Furthermore, courts are reluctant to invalidate a marriage unless the law and circumstances indicate clearly that it should be annulled. In this case, it would be contrary to public policy to allow one of the parties to deny the validity of the marriage when a difference has arisen between them and there is no mandatory reason to grant an annulment. *Helfond v. Helfond,* 280 N.Y.S.2d 990 (1967).

6. **Registration:** Most states have enacted legislation governing the *recording* of marriages. These statutes are "directory" and consequently, non-compliance does not render an otherwise proper marriage invalid.

TYPES OF MARRIAGES

I. INTRODUCTION

A. Generally: The status of marriage can be achieved in a variety of ways. The principal two are:

  1. **Ceremonial marriage:** *Ceremonial* marriages, which are provided for under the laws of all states (see *supra*, p. 15);

  2. **Common-law marriage:** *Common-law* marriages, which are recognized in fourteen states.

B. Other issues: This Chapter also explores the definitions and implications of other types of marriages, specifically:

  1. *putative marriages*;

  2. *successive marriages*; and

  3. *proxy marriages*.

II. COMMON LAW MARRIAGES

A. Definition: A common law marriage is an agreement between a man and a woman to enter into the marital relationship *without a civil or ecclesiastical ceremony*. Where common law marriages are recognized, this is either by statute or because the courts reason that marriage is a civil contract and no specific ceremony is required.

> **Note:** If the parties to a valid common law marriage separate, they must obtain a *divorce* before either may contract a later marriage.

  1. **Background:** Historically, a common law contract of marriage made *per verba de praesenti* (by words of the present [tense]) was a valid marriage. It is an express contract of marriage. *Voorhees v. Voorhees,* 19 A. 172 (N.J. 1890).

  > **Example:** Each party says: "I agree to take you as my husband (or wife) and live with you as husband and wife." These words, spoken by both parties, are sufficient to establish a common law marriage.

  a. **Promise distinguished:** If the *future tense* is used, there will only be a promise to marry.

  > **Example:** "I will take you for my husband" would create an engagement. No marriage would occur at that time.

  2. **Requirements:** Under present law, courts look to the *actions* of the parties rather than to specific words used. The elements of a valid common law marriage include:

a. **Consent:** There must be a ***present agreement*** (*i.e.,* a mutual understanding) to enter ***at that time*** into a marriage relationship. No ceremony and no particular words are required. The agreement may be ***inferred*** from conduct.

b. **Representation:** The parties must hold themselves out to the public to be husband and wife.

c. **Cohabitation:** The parties must ***live together*** as husband and wife.

Example 1: M and W told a few persons they were married although they never had a ceremonial marriage. M and W had sexual relations, but did not live together and observed great secrecy with respect to their relationship. M and W do not have a valid common law marriage because: (1) They did not enter into a present agreement to marry; (2) They did not hold themselves out to all persons to be husband and wife; and (3) They did not cohabit. *Ex parte Threet*, 333 S.W.2d 361 (Tex. 1960).

Example 2: M and W live together as husband and wife, and represent to others that they are married. They plan to undergo a ceremonial marriage because of mutual concerns over their legal status, but M dies before the formal ceremony.

Held, there is a valid common law marriage. This occurred as soon as all the elements were established. Mere plans to have a formal ceremony do not show a lack of present agreement, but are only a fact to be evaluated with other evidence of the entire relationship. *Skipworth v. Skipworth,* 360 So.2d 975 (Ala. 1978).

B. **Recognition of common law marriages:** Common law marriages are recognized in ***fourteen states*** and the District of Columbia.

1. **Prohibition:** In most of the remaining jurisdictions, ***statutes*** have been enacted which require all marriages to conform to certain prescribed regulations as to the ceremony, license and other aspects of the marriage. Such statutes, therefore, bar common law marriages since these marriages lack licensing and the requisite ceremonies. Other jurisdictions have found common law marriages to be invalid through ***case law.***

2. **Habit and repute:** ***"Habit and repute"*** appears to be the most important factor in determining the existence of a valid common law marriage. That is, a common law marriage will be found to exist if the parties ***behaved*** between themselves in a way that suggests that they thought of themselves as husband and wife, and had a ***reputation*** in the community, or among family members, as being married.

3. **Proof required:** A hard and fast rule concerning evidentiary proof sufficient to find the existence of a common law marriage cannot be

stated due to the reluctance of many courts to validate common law marriages. Some courts require **clear and convincing evidence** to reduce the danger of fraudulent claims.

> **Example:** M and W live together and hold themselves out as husband and wife for 25 years. Upon M's death W makes claims as his widow. The court did not find a valid common law marriage since there was no proof that M and W had entered into an express agreement to be husband and wife. *In re Erickson's Estate,* 64 N.W.2d 316 (S.D. 1954).

4. **Conflict of law:** Frequently a couple will spend part of their years together in a state that does not recognize common law marriage, and another part in a state that *does* recognize such marriages. When this happens, the general rule is that so long as: (1) the parties were at some part **domiciled** in a state that did recognize common law marriage, and (2) the couple explicitly or implicitly agreed during their stay in the common-law state to regard themselves as married (and to hold themselves out to the world as married), this is enough for even the state that does not recognize common law marriages to view the parties as married. See, e.g., *Travers v. Reinhardt,* 205 U.S. 423 (1906).

   a. **Marriage contracted while traveling:** Some states have gone even further, and have held that even a brief **visit** to a common-law state can be enough for a marriage to be contracted there (even though the parties were never domiciled in that state), as long as the couple explicitly or implicitly agreed to treat themselves as husband and wife in the state they were visiting, and to hold themselves out as husband and wife there. Courts are especially likely to reach this conclusion where what is at stake is some sort of ***government benefit***, such as Social Security survivor's benefits.

   > **Example:** H and W live in New York, which does not recognize common law marriage. They agree to live together "just as though [they] were married." There is never a formal ceremonial marriage, but they consider themselves "husband and wife." H gives W a wedding band, W begins using H's last name, and they hold themselves out as being married. Although H and W are always domiciled in New York, they visit Pennsylvania a total of 16 days at various times during their "marriage." After 21 years H dies and W seeks Social Security benefits as a surviving spouse. W claims there is a common law marriage under Pennsylvania law.
   >
   > *Held,* for W. There was a valid common law marriage, based on W's proof of cohabitation and reputation. H and W lived together during their visits to Pennsylvania, and held themselves out as husband and wife to family members in that state. New York recognizes common law marriages if validly established in another state.

Thus the marriage is valid in New York. *Renshaw v. Heckler,* 787 F.2d 50 (2d Cir. 1986).

5. **Effect of impediment:** When an *impediment* to a valid common law marriage is *removed* while the parties are living together as husband and wife in a jurisdiction in which common law marriages are recognized, a valid common law marriage will result as of the time the impediment is removed.

> **Example:** M and W live together as husband and wife in a jurisdiction which recognizes common law marriages, but they never have a formal marriage ceremony. W was married to H prior to living with M, and did not obtain a divorce from H before cohabiting with M. H, however, did divorce W six years before M's death, at which time she was legally free to remarry. At M's death, W claims certain death benefits as M's surviving common law wife.
>
> *Held,* W is entitled to the benefits as M's surviving spouse. M and W agreed to marry before an impediment (W's marriage) was removed, and they lived together as husband and wife after the impediment was removed. This gives rise to a valid common law marriage which was established at the time H obtained the divorce from W. *Matthews v. Britton,* 303 F.2d 408 (D.C.App. 1962).

III. PUTATIVE MARRIAGES

A. **Definition:** A putative marriage is a marriage contracted in good faith and in ignorance of some existing impediment facing at least one of the contracting parties. *U.S. Fidelity & Guaranty Co. v. Henderson,* 53 S.W.2d 811 (Tex.Cir.Ct.App. 1932); *Succession of Marinoni,* 164 So. 797 (La. 1935).

1. **Origin:** The concept of putative marriage comes from the Napoleonic Code and is recognized only in a few states with a civil law tradition, such as Texas, Louisiana and California. In addition, Wisconsin has a statute similar to the putative marriage doctrine. *Smith v. Smith,* 190 N.W.2d 174 (Wis. 1971).

   a. **Purpose:** Putative marriage is the device utilized to reach results analogous to those reached in the jurisdictions which recognize common law marriages.

   b. **Common law marriage distinguished:** Putative marriage is more restrictive than common law marriage since in putative marriages the good faith commitment of at least one participant is required; in a common law marriage both parties may be and usually are fully aware that ceremonial requirements have not been met.

2. **Essential requirement:** In an action based on the existence of a putative marriage, the party asserting a claim must prove lack of knowl-

edge of the impediment to a valid marriage. *Smith v. Smith,* 1 Tex. 621 (1846).

3. **Legal effect:** If a putative marriage is found to exist, then the spouse who entered into the marriage in good faith can claim interest in community property, inherit from the other spouse, and sue for the wrongful death of the other spouse. The decision in *Davis v. Davis,* 521 S.W.2d 603 (Tex. 1975), illustrates the application of these principles.

   a. **Facts:** H marries W1 and the following year, departs for an overseas assignment leaving W1 in Texas. H marries W2 in Singapore. H tells W2 that he has been divorced, but in fact, H was never divorced from W1. Two years later H dies, and one month later both W1 and W2 give birth. Suit is brought to determine the proper division of H's property.

   b. **W1 and W2:** W1 inherits as H's lawful wife and W2 inherits as H's putative wife. Where there are successive marriages, there is a presumption that the second marriage is valid. The evidence that H and W1 were never divorced rebuts that presumption. However, W2 married H in good faith and all formal marriage requirements were met. This establishes that W2 is H's putative wife, and she is entitled to the same right to H's property as if she were a lawful wife.

   c. **Children:** Only W2's child inherits. There was no possibility of access between H and W1 during the time her child was conceived. Thus W1's child could not have been H's child and may not inherit from H. The child of W2 was H's child and may inherit as any child. Clark, pp. 53-56.

IV. SUCCESSIVE MARRIAGES

A. **Generally:** Under case law and statutory law a person may have only one spouse at a time. In circumstances where there are successive marriages, the later marriage will be held null and void, if one party to that marriage has a spouse of a previous marriage still living and is undivorced. This rule is applicable even when the first marriage is a common law marriage and the second marriage meets all legal requirements with respect to a marriage license and ceremony. A common law marriage is valid where permitted by law and must be dissolved before remarriage. *Beaudin v. Suarez,* 113 N.W.2d 818 (Mich. 1962).

1. **Criminal penalties:** The underlying principle governing successive marriages is the concept of "monogamy," marriage to but one person at a time. Violation of the requirement of monogamy will subject a person to criminal prosecution. A person "married" to two spouses will be charged with the crime of bigamy, and a person "married" to more than two spouses will be charged with the crime of polygamy.

Note: Bigamy and polygamy are punishable even though committed in response to religious beliefs and practices.

Example: While married to W1, H marries W2. H is indicted under a federal statute for the crime of bigamy. H's defense is that such marriages are in conformance with the practices of his Mormon religion and protected by the First Amendment as part of his religious belief.

Held, H was convicted. Laws are made to govern actions. Although laws may not interfere with religious worship, beliefs and opinions, they may interfere with **practices.** To allow H's defense would make religious belief superior to law and "permit every citizen to become a law unto himself." Polygamy and bigamy have been considered offenses against society among nations of Northern and Western Europe and America. The statute is a valid exercise of legislative power. *Reynolds v. United States,* 98 U.S. 145 (1878).

a. **Rationale:** It has been suggested that the rationale in *Reynolds* distinguishing between religious beliefs and practices is an unsatisfactory distinction, and that the true basis of the decision is simply that certain marriage customs are at such odds with the widely accepted morals of society that they cannot be tolerated.

2. **Recognition:** A polygamous marriage will not be recognized in the United States even for matrimonial remedies, such as divorce, even if the marriage is contracted in a country permitting such a marriage. It will, however, be recognized for the purposes of the legitimization of children born of such a marriage or the barring of a successive marriage. *In re Dalip Singh Bir's Estate,* 188 P.2d 499 (Cal.App. 1948); *Application of Sood,* 142 N.Y.S.2d 591 (1955).

3. **Presumption of validity:** In the case of successive marriages, there is a **presumption** that **the latest of the marriages is valid.** This presumption arises since the law presumes matrimony, morality and legitimacy, rather than concubinage, immorality and illegitimacy.

a. **Rebutting presumption:** Because of the presumption that the most recent marriage is valid, the **burden of proof** is on the spouse of the previous marriage who is attacking the latest marriage, to prove, **by conclusive evidence,** the validity and the continuity of the previous marriage.

Example: When H and W1 were divorced, the decree provided that neither party could remarry for six months. H married W2 three months later. W2 seeks a divorce after cohabiting with H for 16 years. H contends that the marriage is void because it violated his divorce decree from W1.

Held, H and W2 are lawfully married. The presumption that a second marriage is valid may be rebutted only by "the most cogent and satisfactory evidence." H showed that W1 was alive at the time of the divorce decree, but offered no other evidence. The presumption that W1 continued to live is not as strong as the presumption of the validity of H's second marriage. *In re Marriage of Sumners*, 645 S.W.2d 205 (Mo. 1983).

   i. Estoppel: In *Sumners* the court noted that H produced a misleading situation when he married W2 in violation of the divorce decree. H may not now set up the invalidity of his second marriage when it is advantageous to him. W2 relied on the validity of H's divorce and acted in good faith.

   Note: It is the majority view that the presumption of the validity of the latest marriage will extend to a valid common law marriage as well as a valid ceremonial marriage. *Anderson-Tully Co. v. Wilson*, 74 So.2d 735 (Miss. 1954).

B. "Enoch Arden" laws: The term "Enoch Arden" is derived from the name of a sailor, memorialized in Tennyson's poem, who returned home after a ten-year absence due to shipwreck only to find that his wife remarried, believing him to be dead. The law at that time provided no relief to her for the bigamous second marriage.

   1. Statutory relief: Many states have statutes exculpating from criminal prosecution a person who marries for a second time after the spouse of the first marriage has been missing for a certain period of time. Those statutes absolve a person from the criminal charges of bigamy but do not validate the second marriage. Other states have enacted far-reaching statutes to provide more complete relief to the spouse who desires to remarry.

      a. Dissolution of marriage: Some statutes permit a court to issue a decree of dissolution of a marriage where a spouse has disappeared for a certain length of time and is not known to be alive. Such statutes free a deserted spouse to remarry, if a dissolution is obtained.

      b. Declaration of death: Some statutes permit a court to declare the absent spouse of an applicant for a marriage license dead after notice of publication.

V. PROXY MARRIAGES

   A. Definition and purpose: A proxy marriage is a marriage contracted or celebrated by one or more *agents* rather than by both parties themselves. Proxy marriages are not prevalent. They are found mainly in times of war to enable a person in the armed services to marry and legitimize children.

      1. Effect of statutes: The validity of a proxy marriage is dependent upon the regulatory statutes governing marriage procedures in a particular jurisdiction.

    a. State law prohibits: If state statutes require the actual presence of both parties to obtain a marriage license and/or at the marriage ceremony, a proxy marriage will be held invalid.

    b. State law silent: If the statutes are silent with respect to the presence of both parties to obtain a marriage license and at the marriage ceremony, they may be construed as allowing proxy marriages. *Barrons v. United States*, 191 F.2d 92 (9th Cir. 1951).

    c. Federal law: Where a marriage affects the ***immigration rights of the parties, it may not be recognized regardless of state law.*** 8 U.S.C. §1101(a)(35).

2. Recognition: If a proxy marriage is performed in a jurisdiction in which proxy marriages are valid, other jurisdictions, including the domicile of the parties, will recognize it as valid under the Full Faith and Credit Clause of the Constitution. *Hardin v. Davis*, 30 Ohio Op. 524 (1945).

RIGHTS OF WOMEN, MARRIAGE AND OTHER INTIMATE RELATIONSHIPS

Introductory note: A study of Family Law includes a number of contemporary issues involving the rights of women, sexual activities of individuals, informal "relationships," and laws which attempt to regulate these activities. Accordingly, this chapter deals with:

1. Governmental restrictions on marriage;
2. Women's Rights;
3. Birth control;
4. Abortion; and
5. Rights of unmarried couples living together.

I. DEVELOPMENT OF RIGHTS OF WOMEN

A. **Historical development:** At common law when a woman married, she exchanged a number of rights for the protection of her husband. These included the right to make contracts, to hold property, and to sue or be sued.

1. **Personal property:** At common law a married woman's personal property became a possession of her husband and upon his death was transferred to his personal representative, except for her clothing and jewelry which were returned to her.

2. **Real property:** At common law a married woman's real property interests were affected as follows:

   a. **Inheritance:** Her estates of inheritance belonged to her husband during the marriage, and he received the rents and profits therefrom. If a child was born of the marriage, the husband received the rents and profits for life.

   b. **Life estates:** Her life estates became her husband's and he was entitled to the use of rents and profits from them.

   c. **Leaseholds:** Her leaseholds became the property of her husband.

3. **Women's rights:** At common law a married woman's loss of property rights was balanced by the following:

   a. **Dower:** She became entitled to dower or a one-third interest in her husband's land.

   b. **Support:** She was entitled to support from her husband.

    c. **Debts:** Her husband was responsible for her antenuptial debts.

    d. **Torts:** Her husband was responsible for her torts, whether committed before or after her marriage.

4. **Development:** In England by the 17th and 18th Centuries, the courts started to modify the common law rules concerning women's rights and liabilities. By contrast, courts in the United States demonstrated a reluctance to follow their counterparts in England, so by 1850 the legislatures of various jurisdictions had passed statutes modifying the common law position. These statutes were called *"Married Women's Property Acts."*

5. **Present law:** Today, legal disabilities affecting women have been removed. The American woman has achieved more freedom than in any other period of western history. Controversial areas which have been altered, and which afford greater freedom to women, are the right to obtain birth control information and abortions. See Chart I, *infra*, p. 29.

B. **Constitutional provisions:** Discrimination and *de facto* segregation against women in employment is prohibited by the Constitution, and by federal and many state laws. Discrimination based upon sex is prohibited to the federal government by the *Due Process Clause* of the Fifth Amendment, and to the states by the *Equal Protection Clause* of the Fourteenth Amendment. Private employers, employment agencies and labor unions are covered by Title VII of the Civil Rights Act of 1964, as amended by the Equal Employment Opportunity Act of 1972.

1. **Discrimination prohibited:** Laws and practices which discriminate against women have been struck down as women assume a more equal role in society.

    Example: A school board establishes a mandatory rule requiring pregnant public school teachers to take maternity leave four months prior to the expected birth. The teachers challenge the rule as violative of their constitutional rights.

    Held, the rule is unconstitutional. It is arbitrary and violates the Due Process Clause since it has no valid relationship to a state interest. Another rule, which prohibited teachers from returning to work until after the child was at least three months old, was also struck down for the same reason. The Court stated that the school board's administrative convenience alone could not justify the rules. *Cleveland Bd. of Education v. LaFleur*, 414 U.S. 632 (1974).

    Example: H executes a mortgage on a house owned jointly with W, his wife, to pay his legal expenses. State law gives H exclusive control over the disposition of jointly owned property. Subsequently, H and W separate and there is an action to foreclose the mortgage.

CHART I. RIGHTS OF MARRIED WOMEN
COMMON LAW AND MODERN COMPARED

<u>At Common Law</u>	<u>Under Modern Statutory and Case Law</u>
1. Could not contract with husband or others.	1. Can contract with husband (except where contracts go to the essence of the marital relationship) as well as others.
2. Could not sue or be sued without joining husband.	2. Can sue and be sued without joining husband.
3. Could not make a will.	3. Can make a will.
4. Could not vote.	4. Can vote.
5. Could not serve on juries.	5. Can serve on juries.
6. Could not hold public office.	6. Can hold public office.
7. Could contract as husband's agent.	7. Can contract as husband's agent.
8. Could pledge husband's credit for necessaries.	8. Can pledge husband's credit for necessaries.
9. Personal property became a possession of the husband.	9. Personal property remains the property of the owner.
10. Rights with respect to her real property were severely limited.	10. Rights with respect to her real property are not limited.

Held, the statute violates the Equal Protection Clause. The law discriminates on the basis of sex, and there is no showing that it serves an important government objective. *Kirchberg v. Feenstra*, 450 U.S. 455 (1981).

II. GOVERNMENTAL REGULATION OF MARRIAGE

A. Constitutional protection: The right to marry has been recognized as protected by the United States Constitution.

1. **Miscegenation (segregation) statutes:** The essence of the right to marry is freedom to join in marriage with the person of one's choice. This right to marry is a right not of racial groups, but of individuals. Thus, a statute prohibiting interracial marriages impairs this fundamental right and is unconstitutional. See ***Loving v. Virginia,*** 338 U.S. 1 (1967), where the Supreme Court **struck down** a Virginia miscegenation statute and held that "restricting the freedom to marry solely because of racial classifications violates the central meaning of the Equal Protection Clause." The Court also found that such statutes deprived the plaintiffs of "liberty" without due process of law.

2. **Unreasonable restrictions:** A state may not place unreasonable restrictions on the right to marry.

Example: A state statute provides that residents who are required by any court order or judgment to support children not in their custody, cannot marry without court approval. Court permission could not be granted unless the marriage applicant could prove that the children covered by the support order were not then, and were not likely thereafter to become, public charges. P was in arrears in support payments to his illegitimate child who had been a public charge since birth. For that reason P could not comply with the statute, and he was denied a marriage license. P challenges the statute.

Held, the statute is unconstitutional. The right to marry is of fundamental importance for all persons. It is part of the ***fundamental right of privacy*** implicit in the Due Process Clause of the Fourteenth Amendment. When a statutory classification interferes significantly with the exercise of a fundamental right, it cannot be upheld unless it is supported by sufficiently important state interests and is closely tailored to effectuate *only* those interests. The state contended that the statute furnished the opportunity to counsel the applicant and to protect the welfare of out-of-state custody children. However, the statute did not require counseling, and the state could enforce support obligations by wage attachments, civil contempt proceedings, and criminal penalties. Furthermore, preventing an applicant from marrying does not achieve the objectives of the state. Thus, the means selected unnecessarily impinged on the ***fundamental right to marry.*** Finally, it created a classification of persons who must prove financial means to support their children before marrying, thus violating the Equal Protection Clause. *Zablocki v. Redhail*, 434 U.S. 374 (1978).

3. **Valid regulations:** Not every statute which regulates the prerequisites for marriage will be subjected to rigorous scrutiny as the Court did in *Zablocki.* The Court said that reasonable regulations that do not significantly interfere with decisions to enter into the marital relationship may legitimately be imposed.

   a. **Religion:** Free exercise of religion is guaranteed by the First Amendment. However, the state may regulate conduct prompted by religious beliefs when the individual's interest is outweighed by a compelling state interest.

   Example: H seeks a divorce from W. W argues that her Hindu religion does not recognize divorce, and if W returns to India as a divorced woman, her family and friends will treat her as though she were dead. W reasons that this will deny her right of free exercise of religion.

   Held, granting a divorce to H does not deprive W of her religious freedom. W may take any view of the relationship after the divorce decree as her religion requires, but the civil contract may be dissolved under the law. Further, H does not share W's religious beliefs concerning divorce. To compel H to remain married because of W's religious beliefs would be to prefer W's beliefs over H's beliefs. Such a preference is prohibited by the Establishment Clause of the First Amendment. *Sharma v. Sharma,* 667 P.2d 395 (Kan.App. 1983). See also *Reynolds v. United States, supra*, p. 24.

4. **Divorce:** The statutory scheme for divorce must allow access to the courts by all persons without unreasonable restrictions under the Due Process Clause.

   Example: A statute requires payment of court fees and costs when a petition for divorce is filed. P cannot pay such fees because of indigence, and the court clerk does not accept P's petition. P challenges the statute.

   Held, the statute is struck down. The court noted the basic importance of marriage to society and the necessity of judicial approval to dissolve a marriage. A state must afford to all individuals a meaningful opportunity to be heard under the Due Process Clause. To withhold that right because of inability to pay is the equivalent of denying them an opportunity to be heard and to dissolve marriages. *Boddie v. Connecticut*, 401 U.S. 371 (1971).

5. **Name of married woman:** At present, a married woman seems **not** to have a constitutional right to **retain her maiden name**. See *Forbush v. Wallace*, 341 F.Supp. 217 (M.D.Ala. 1971), *aff'd* per curiam 405 U.S. 970 (1972). (Although the Supreme Court affirmed in *Forbush*, the Court wrote no opinion in that case. The Court has not tackled this question since *Forbush*.)

   a. **Possible right in future:** But there is a good chance that if the Supreme Court considers whether a married woman has a constitutional right to retain her name, the Court will conclude that she does, on equal protection grounds. See Clark, p. 305.

   b. **State law allows:** In any event, most states that have considered the issue in recent years have held that as a matter of **state law**, the woman **does** have the right to keep her maiden name (or use essentially any other name she chooses). Clark, pp. 304-05.

      i. **Case law:** Sometimes, courts have done this as a matter either of common law, or interpretation of ambiguous statutes. See, e.g., *Moskowitz v. Moskowitz*, 385 A.2d 120 (N.H. 1978) (Where statute gives trial court discretion in deciding whether to allow a divorced woman to resume use of her maiden name, the fact that there are minor children is not by itself grounds to automatically deny the woman the right to make this change).

      ii. **Statutes:** Many states have amended their statutes to explicitly give the woman the right to resume use of her maiden name after divorce; see, e.g., Cal. Civ. Code §4362; Mich. Comp. Laws §552.391.

B. **Domestic violence:** States are recognizing and dealing with **domestic violence** between husbands and wives.

   1. **Rape:** Most states now **reject** the common law rule that **a husband cannot rape his wife**.

      Example: D is indicted for rape and sodomy of his wife while they are living together. D files a motion to dismiss, contending that there is an implied marital exclusion in the statute that makes it legally impossible for a husband to rape his wife. *Held*, D's contention is rejected. The common law theory that by contracting marriage a wife irrevocably consents to intercourse is no longer valid. The marriage relationship does not imply consent to criminal conduct. *Warren v. State*, 336 S.E.2d 221 (Ga. 1985).

   2. **Protection:** To protect a spouse from abuse, many states will enjoin harmful conduct. For example, a court may issue a **"protective order"** as part of a divorce decree, under which the man is ordered not to harass (or, in some instance, even contact) his former wife. See, e.g., *Siggelkow v. State*, 731 P.2d 57 (Alaska 1987).

a. **Available before divorce proceedings:** Nearly all states now also authorize judges to issue protective orders during an *ongoing* marriage, if there is reason to fear that the husband may behave violently towards the wife. Many states have set up simplified procedures, whereby the woman can request a protective order without hiring a lawyer.

b. **Arrest as preferred response:** Traditionally, police officers have usually responded differently to domestic violence than to other sorts of violence. For instance, where a woman has accused her husband of beating her, the police have in the past been far less likely to *arrest* the husband than if he had been charged with, say, beating up another man in a bar. But this, too, is changing rapidly. Many if not most police departments now make arrest the *preferred method* of dealing with domestic violence. Areen, pp. 282-83.

C. **Evidentiary privilege:** Two *privileges* in the law of *evidence* apply specially to spouses.

1. **Nature of the two privileges:** Although courts and lawyers sometimes loosely talk of "the spousal privilege," there are in fact two distinct privileges that protect the marital relationship: (1) the privilege against *adverse spousal testimony*; and (2) the privilege protecting *confidential communications*.

   a. **Need to distinguish:** It is important to distinguish between these two. The adverse testimony privilege (sometimes called the "spousal immunity") gives a spouse *complete* protection from *adverse testimony* by the other spouse. The *confidential communications* privilege protects only against the disclosure of confidential *communications* made by one spouse to the other during the marriage.

      i. **Acts:** One important consequence is that the adverse testimony privilege prevents the non-party spouse from testifying even as to *acts* committed by his/her spouse; by contrast, the confidential communications privilege generally does not bar such testimony, since the privilege applies only to communications.

         Example: W watches H shoot X to death in a public park. The adverse testimony privilege will prevent the prosecution from calling on W to describe what she has seen. The confidential communications privilege will not (since there is no "communication").

   b. **End of marriage:** Another important distinction is that the adverse testimony privilege applies only if the parties are *still married at the time of the trial*. The confidential communications privilege, by contrast, applies so long as the parties were married at the time of communication, even if the marriage has subsequently ended.

3. **Variety of statutes:** Jurisdictions vary as to whether both or just one of the privileges apply:

   a. **Federal rule:** In federal courts, *both* privileges are recognized.

   b. **State rules:** In state courts, only a slight majority of states recognize the adverse testimony privilege, but virtually all states recognize the confidential communication privilege (including those that recognize the adverse testimony privilege).

4. **Who holds:** Courts and statutes are not in agreement about *who holds* these privileges:

   a. **Adverse testimony privilege:** As to the adverse testimony privilege:

      i. **Federal practice:** In federal cases, the privilege belongs to the *testifying spouse*, not the party spouse. That is, the defendant in a federal criminal trial may not block his or her spouse's testimony; only the witness-spouse may assert or waive the right. The Supreme Court so concluded in *Trammel v. U.S.*, 445 U.S. 40 (1980).

         Example: W, D's wife, is arrested for narcotics smuggling. In return for not being prosecuted, she agrees to cooperate with the government in its case against D. She then testifies at trial about the role she and D played in a heroin distribution conspiracy. D objects on the grounds of the adverse testimony privilege. *Held*, D loses. Only the witness-spouse may assert the adverse testimony privilege. *Trammel v. U.S., supra.*

         Note: Observe that the federal rule, that the adverse testimony privilege belongs only to the witness-spouse, means that where two spouses commit crimes together, one may *obtain a better deal* for him/herself by *agreeing to testify* against the other (something that would not happen if the privilege could be asserted by the defendant-spouse).

      ii. **States:** The 30 or so states that recognize the adverse testimony privilege vary about whom the privilege belongs to. About half let the party prevent his/her spouse from giving the adverse testimony, whereas the others follow the federal approach of vesting the privilege in the witness-spouse.

   b. **Confidential communications:** As to the confidential communications privilege:

      i. **Federal:** There is no clear rule in federal cases about who holds the privilege. Most federal courts grant the privilege only to the spouse who *made* the communication, whether that spouse is the witness or the non-witness party.

    ii. States: Most states today probably follow the traditional common-law rule, that *either spouse* may assert the confidential communications privilege.

5. Exceptions to confidential communications privilege: The states have made various *exceptions* to the communications privilege. For instance, the privilege does not apply for crimes *committed by one spouse against the other* or against the children of either. Similarly, the privilege does not apply in suits by *one spouse against the other*, such as in a *divorce* suit. For more details on the spousal privileges, see *Emanuel on Evidence*.

III. BIRTH CONTROL

A. The *Griswold* case: The constitution protects the right of married couples to *practice contraception*. In *Griswold v. Connecticut,* 381 U.S. 479 (1965), the Supreme Court held that the right to use birth control falls within a constitutionally-protected *"zone of privacy."*

    1. Facts of *Griswold*: The statute at issue in *Griswold* was a Connecticut law which forbade the use of contraceptives and made their use a criminal offense; the statute also forbade the aiding or counselling of others in their use. The defendants were the director of the local Planned Parenthood Association, and its medical director. They were convicted of counselling *married persons* in the use of contraceptives. No users, married or single, were charged in the case.

    2. Majority strikes statute: The Court, by a 7-2 vote, *struck down* the statute. The majority opinion, authored by Justice Douglas, declined to make explicit use of the substantive due process doctrine. Instead, the opinion found that several of the Bill of Rights guarantees protect privacy interests and create a *"penumbra"* or "zone" of privacy. The Court then concluded that the right of married persons to use contraceptives fell within this penumbra.

        a. Why statute was invalid: Douglas' majority opinion did not specify exactly how the Connecticut ban on contraceptives violated this penumbra of privacy. But a good part of the rationale seemed to have to do with the privacy implications of *proof* in prosecutions. Thus the Court asked: "Would we allow the police to search the sacred precincts of marital bedrooms for telltale signs of the use of contraceptives?" Douglas concluded: "The very idea is repulsive to the notions of privacy surrounding the marriage relationship."

3. **Concurrences:** There were three separate concurring opinions in *Griswold*. All agreed that the Connecticut statute violated the Fourteenth Amendment's interest in "liberty."

4. **Post-*Griswold* contraceptive law:** Developments since *Griswold* make it clear that *Griswold* ultimately means much more than preventing married persons from using birth control—it means that *no person, single or married,* may be prohibited from using contraceptives, or otherwise be subjected to undue interference with decisions on procreation. As the Court said in a post-*Griswold* case, "the teaching of *Griswold* is that the Constitution protects individual decisions in matters of child bearing from unjustified intrusion by the state." *Carey v. Population Services Int'l., infra.*

   a. ***Eisenstadt v. Baird:*** Much of the expansion of the meaning of *Griswold* came in *Eisenstadt v. Baird,* 405 U.S. 438 (1972), where the Court invalidated a statute which, by permitting contraceptives to be distributed only by registered physicians and pharmacists, and only to married persons, *discriminated against the unmarried.*

      i. **Rationale:** In striking down the statute, the majority invoked equal protection as well as substantive due process grounds. The Court observed: "Whatever the rights of the individual to access to contraceptives may be, the rights must be the same for the unmarried and the married alike.... If the right of privacy means anything, it is the right of the *individual*, married or single, to be free from unwarranted government intrusion into matters so fundamentally affecting a person as the decision whether to bear or beget a child." (Emphasis in original.)

   b. **Private place no longer required:** What might be called the right of *"reproductive autonomy,"* protected by both *Griswold* and *Eisenstadt,* now exists *even in non-private situations.* In the post-*Eisenstadt* case of *Carey v. Population Services Int'l, infra,* the Court noted that the constitutionally-protected privacy interest in procreation and child rearing "is not just concerned with a particular place, but with a protected intimate relationship. Such protected privacy extends to the doctor's office, the hospital, the hotel room or as otherwise required to safeguard the right to intimacy involved."

   c. **Ban on sale to minors:** The states may not completely ban nonprescription sales of contraceptives to minors. In *Carey v. Population Services Int'l,* 431 U.S. 678 (1977), seven Justices agreed that such a ban violated the right of privacy, but they were split 4-3 as to the appropriate rationale.

i. **Plurality:** A four-Justice plurality voted to strike the regulation because it did not serve "any significant state interest [that] is not present in the case of an adult," and was therefore indistinguishable from *Danforth* (*infra,* p. 43). (This "significant state interest" test was apparently less rigorous than the "strict scrutiny/compelling state interest" test applied by the Court in nearly all cases involving the privacy rights of adults.) The state's principal argument, that sexual activity by minors would be deterred by the ban on non-prescription contraceptive sales, was found by the plurality to be an unconvincing and bare assertion.

ii. **Three concurring votes:** Three Justices concurred that the adults-only restriction should be stricken, but found much more limited scope for doing so. They would permit substantial regulation of the sexual activities of minors, but felt that a ban on contraceptives was an irrational means of deterring sexual activity. It was not only an ineffective deterrent, but also increased the risk of pregnancy and venereal disease. They appeared to advocate only a "mere rationality" standard for review of the adults-only restriction.

iii. **Regulation of sexual activities by minors:** If one adds the three concurrences to the two dissents in *Carey*, one can conclude that a majority of the Court apparently believes that states have ***substantial authority to restrict sexual activity on the part of minors, so long as they exercise that authority rationally.***

d. **Non-marital relationships:** Although *Eisenstadt, supra,* broadened at least privacy in the use of contraceptives to non-married couples, the Supreme Court has ***not recognized a general right of privacy in sexual or procreational matters*** so as to protect homosexuality, adultery, fornication or other conduct which may be forbidden by the state. See *e.g., Bowers v. Hardwick,* 478 U.S.186 (1986) (state may ban homosexual sodomy without violating substantive due process).

IV. ABORTION

A. **Abortion:** The right of privacy which the Court found to exist in *Griswold* has been extended to the ***abortion*** context. The case recognizing that the right of privacy limits a legislature's freedom to proscribe or regulate abortion was the landmark case of ***Roe v. Wade,*** 410 U.S. 113 (1973). That case has since been interpreted in a long line of decisions and, most recently, cut back in important ways in *Planned Parenthood v. Casey,* 112 S.Ct. 2791 (1992).

B. *Roe v. Wade*: In *Roe*, the Court held that a woman's right to privacy is a ***"fundamental" right*** under the Fourteenth Amendment. Therefore, the legislature has only a limited right to regulate — and may not completely proscribe — abortions. The actual result of the case was to invalidate, on privacy grounds, Texas' nearly-complete ban on abortions.

1. **Precise holding in *Roe*:** The actual holding of *Roe* was remarkably specific, almost legislative. In an opinion by Justice Blackmun, the Court divided pregnancy into three ***trimesters***, and prescribed a different rule for each:

    a. **First trimester:** During the first trimester, a state ***may not ban, or even closely regulate, abortions***. The decision to have an abortion, and the manner in which it is to be carried out, are to be left to the pregnant woman and her physician.

        i. **Rationale:** The Court's rationale for this approach was that at present, the mortality rate for mothers having abortions during the first trimester is lower than the rate for full-term pregnancies. Therefore, the state has no valid (or at least no compelling) interest in protecting the mother's health by banning or closely regulating abortions during this period. (But the state may require that abortions be performed only by licensed physicians.)

    b. **Second trimester:** During the second trimester, the state may protect its interest in the ***mother's health***, by regulating the abortion procedure in ways that are "reasonably related" to her health. Such regulation might include, for instance, a requirement that the operation take place in a hospital rather than a clinic. (The Court implied that during this second trimester, the risk of maternal death through abortion was higher than that in full-term pregnancies.)

        i. **No protection of fetus:** But the state may protect only the mother's health, ***not the fetus' life***, during this period. Therefore, a flat ban on second trimester abortions is not permitted. Nor may the state regulate in ways that protect the fetus rather than the mother's health.

    c. **Third trimester:** At the beginning of the third trimester, the Court stated, the fetus typically becomes "***viable***." That is, it has a "capability of meaningful life outside the mother's womb." Therefore, after viability the state has a "***compelling***" interest in protecting the fetus. It may therefore regulate, or ***even proscribe***, abortion. However, abortion ***must be permitted*** where it is necessary to preserve the ***life or the health*** of the mother.

2. **Rationale of *Roe*:** The *Roe* decision was premised upon the right of privacy. The Court pointed to *Griswold*, as well as to other privacy-

derived holdings. This right of privacy, which the Court found to be part of the "liberty" guaranteed by the Fourteenth Amendment, was "broad enough to encompass a woman's decision whether or not to terminate her pregnancy."

  a. **Standard of review:** In fact, the Court held, a woman's interest in deciding this issue herself was a *"fundamental"* one, which could only be outweighed if: (1) there was a *"compelling state interest"* in barring or restricting abortion; and (2) the state statute was *"narrowly drawn"* so that it fulfilled only that legitimate state interest. Texas' complete ban on abortions did not satisfy either requirement.

     i. **Fetus not person:** The Court explicitly rejected the argument that the state had a compelling interest, even before viability, in *protecting the fetus as a "person"* as that term is used in the Fourteenth Amendment. The Court reached this conclusion largely on historical grounds.

C. **The modification of *Roe* by *Casey*:** *Roe* has been *partially overruled*. This occurred in the Court's most important post-*Roe* abortion decision, ***Planned Parenthood of Southeastern Pennsylvania v. Casey***, 112 S.Ct. 2791 (1992). In *Casey*, a majority of the Court declined to overrule *Roe v. Wade* explicitly. However, important aspects of *Roe* — including abortion's status as a *"fundamental right,"* the state's almost complete inability to *regulate first-trimester abortions*, and in fact the whole *trimester framework* of *Roe* — were all *overturned*. As a result of *Casey*, the states *may restrict abortion* so long as they do not place *"undue burdens"* on the woman's right to choose.

  1. **Pennsylvania statute:** At issue in *Casey* was a Pennsylvania statute which placed a number of significant restrictions on abortion, such as a requirement that the woman *wait for 24 hours* after receiving from a doctor certain information about abortion, and a requirement that a married woman *notify her husband* of her intent to abort. Several of these restrictions were clearly unconstitutional judged by the standards of the Court's post-*Roe* decisions.

  2. **Three blocs:** There were three distinct voting blocs in *Casey*. First, two traditionally "liberal" Justices — Stevens and Blackmun (the author of *Roe*) — voted to reaffirm *Roe* completely. Second, a four-Justice "conservative" bloc — Chief Justice Rehnquist, and Justices White, Scalia and Thomas — voted to overturn *Roe* completely. The "swing" votes were supplied by a middle-of-the-road bloc consisting of Justices O'Connor, Souter and Kennedy, who voted to reaffirm the "central principle" of *Roe v. Wade*, but to allow state regulation that did not "unduly burden" the woman's freedom to choose. Thus the Court decided by 5-4 to maintain *Roe v. Wade* as precedent, but by 7-2 to allow states to regulate more strictly than *Roe* and its progeny had allowed.

3. **The joint opinion:** The three "centrist" Justices — O'Connor, Souter and Kennedy — formed a *plurality* opinion, which spoke for the Court on all points. This opinion must be closely read, since it is now effectively the law of the land. Interestingly, the plurality opinion was written by all three Justices *jointly*, rather than by a single Justice with others joining in the opinion. We will refer to this plurality opinion as the "joint opinion."

    a. ***Roe reaffirmed:*** The joint opinion began by stating broadly that it was *reaffirming* the ***"essential holding"*** of *Roe v. Wade."* The opinion saw this "essential holding" as having three parts: (1) a recognition of "the right of the woman to choose to have an abortion before viability and to obtain it without undue interference from the state"; (2) a confirmation of the State's power to restrict abortions after fetal viability, if the law contains exceptions for pregnancies endangering the woman's life or health; and (3) a recognition of the state's "legitimate interests from the outset of the pregnancy in protecting the health of the woman and the life of the fetus. ..."

    b. ***Stare decisis***: However, the joint opinion also suggested that its authors might ***not*** have endorsed the principles of *Roe v. Wade* if the issue were appearing before the Court for the first time. The opinion referred to "the reservations any of us may have in reaffirming the central holding of *Roe*." But, the joint opinion held, what tipped the scales in favor of reaffirming *Roe* was the force of ***stare decisis***, the doctrine that says that courts should not lightly overturn precedent.

    c. **The "undue burden" standard:** But what the joint opinion gave, it partly took away. Two aspects of *Roe* and the cases interpreting it should be ***abandoned***, the three Justices held: the ***"trimester framework"*** of *Roe*, and (at least implicitly) the principle that any pre-viability abortion regulation must survive ***strict scrutiny***.

        i. **The "undue burden" standard:** In place of the trimester approach, the joint opinion articulated a new ***"undue burden"*** standard: "Only where state regulation imposes an undue burden on a woman's ability to make [the decision whether to abort] does the power of the State reach into the heart of liberty protected by the Due Process Clause." A state regulation will constitute an "undue burden" if the regulation "has the purpose or effect of placing a ***substantial obstacle*** in the path of a woman seeking an abortion of a nonviable fetus." Under this standard, if state regulations merely "create a ***structural mechanism***" by which the state may "express profound respect for the life of the unborn," and do not place a substantial obstacle in the woman's path, the regulations will be upheld. Similarly, the state may regulate to further the ***health or safety of*** *the woman*, as long as the regulation does not unduly burden the right to abortion. After viability, the state may proscribe all abortions not needed to protect the health or life of the mother (a holding that does not represent any change from *Roe* or later cases).

d. **Application to Pennsylvania statute:** The plurality then applied its new "undue burden" analysis to the Pennsylvania statute. All but one of the Pennsylvania restrictions were *upheld* as not being unduly burdensome:

   i. **Informed consent:** The Pennsylvania statute contained an elaborate *"informed consent"* requirement, which the joint opinion *upheld*. First, at least *24 hours* before performing an abortion, a physician must inform the woman of the nature of the procedure, the health risks of both abortion and childbirth, and the "probable gestational age of the unborn child." (The waiting period was subject to an exception for "medical emergencies," defined as situations where an immediate abortion is required to avert serious risk of death or major bodily impairment to the woman.) Second, either a physician or a qualified non-physician must inform the woman of the availability of state-printed materials describing the fetus and providing information about non-abortion alternatives (e.g., adoption, child support, etc.) The joint opinion found that these informed consent requirements *did not "unduly burden"* the woman's right to choose to abort.

   ii. **Spousal notification:** But the joint opinion *struck down* the Pennsylvania statute's *"spousal notification"* provision. Under that provision, a married woman could not receive an abortion without signing a statement that she had notified her spouse that she was about to undergo the procedure. The joint opinion found that this spousal notification requirement was a *substantial obstacle* to abortion for some women: for instance, many fear that they will be *psychologically abused* by the husband, or that he will abuse their *children* (neither situation was covered by an exception in the notification requirement).

   iii. **Parental consent:** The joint opinion *upheld* the statute's *parental consent* provision, by which except in medical emergencies, an unemancipated young woman under 18 may not obtain an abortion unless she and one of her parents provides informed consent. The statute allowed for a "judicial bypass," by which a court could authorize performance of the abortion without parental consent, if the judge determined that the young woman had given informed consent and that an abortion would be in her best interest. The three Justices had little trouble upholding this provision, because it matched other "parental consent with possibility of judicial bypass" provisions that the court had previously upheld (see the cases summarized *infra*, p. 183).

4. **The Stevens and Blackmun opinions:** Justices Stevens and Blackmun each wrote a separate opinion, concurring in part and dissenting in part. Each agreed that *Roe v. Wade* should be maintained as precedent, but each disagreed with the plurality as to how tightly the states may regulate abortion, and each believed that some of the Pennsylvania regulations upheld by the plurality were unconstitutional.

5. **Dissents:** There were four *dissenters* in *Casey*. Chief Justice Rehnquist wrote one dissent, in which Justices White, Scalia and Thomas joined. Justice Scalia wrote another dissent, in which Rehnquist, White and Thomas joined.

   a. **Rehnquist dissent:** Paradoxically, Rehnquist's dissent read in some ways more like a declaration of victory than a protest against defeat. He argued that the joint opinion "retains the outer shell of *Roe v. Wade* ... but beats a wholesale retreat from the substance of that case." By contrast, he said, he and the other dissenters "believe that *Roe* was wrongly decided, and that it can and should be overruled...." The dissenters would have upheld *all* the challenged provisions of the Pennsylvania statute.

6. **Significance of case:** So what is the significance of *Casey*?

   a. **Abortion as protected interest:** The case certainly seems to ensure — as long as the present composition of the Court does not change — that a woman's right to decide whether to terminate her pregnancy will be an interest that receives special constitutional protection. For example, it seems completely clear that a state may not simply *forbid* all abortions, or even all abortions occurring in, say, the second trimester. Similarly, it seems clear that a state may not forbid all pre-viability abortions except those necessary to save the life or health of the mother. Any such regulation would certainly be considered by five Justices to be an "undue burden" on abortion.

   b. **Regulations easier to sustain:** On the other hand, state provisions that in some way *regulate* the abortion process are much more likely to be sustained than they were prior to *Casey*. The pre-abortion counseling requirements of the Pennsylvania statute, the 24-hour notice provision, and the requirement that a minor's parent give "informed" consent, are all provisions which either were, or would almost certainly have been, struck down under Supreme Court case law that existed prior to *Casey*. Assuming that the state is really attempting to "regulate" abortion rather than proscribe it, only the most severe kinds of regulations — the spousal notification requirement struck down in *Casey* is one of the few actually-existing state restrictions that comes to mind — will constitute such an obstacle that it will be found to be an "undue burden" by the standard announced and applied in the joint opinion.

D. Post-*Roe* developments: Post-*Roe* abortion cases have centered around several areas, the most important of which are: (1) requirements that persons other than the pregnant woman *consent* to the operation before it may be performed; and (2) the availability of *public funding* for abortions. In reading the following discussion of these cases, consider that all of them were decided before *Planned Parenthood v. Casey*, and might be decided differently today in view of *Casey*'s "undue burden" approach, which makes state regulations on abortion much more likely to be upheld.

E. Consent: A number of states have enacted statutes, usually after the *Roe v. Wade* decision, which impose requirements that third persons *consent* to a woman's decision to get an abortion, or which require *notice* to such third persons.

1. **No absolute veto allowed (*Danforth*):** The most important case about consent is *Planned Parenthood v. Danforth*, 428 U.S. 52 (1976). In *Danforth*, the Supreme Court barred the states from giving a pregnant woman's *spouse* or parents, in most instances, an *absolute right to veto* the woman's decision to obtain an abortion.

   a. **Statute invalidated:** The statute struck down in *Danforth* barred abortions unless the operation was consented to by the woman's spouse or (if she was unmarried and under 18) by her parents.

   b. **Husband's consent:** The Court flatly *rejected* the requirement of consent by the husband. Both parents have rights at stake, but since the woman is more directly affected by the pregnancy, the Court concluded, she should have the deciding vote. Also, since the state itself cannot proscribe abortions during the early stages of pregnancy, it cannot delegate this power to the husband by allowing him to veto the procedure.

   c. **Effect of *Casey*:** The principal holding in *Danforth* — that the states may not give a pregnant woman's spouse an absolute veto right over the woman's abortion decision — is clearly still good law. In *Planned Parenthood v. Casey, supra,* p. 39, the Court struck down a requirement that the woman's spouse be *notified* of the woman's intent to get an abortion. Even this lesser requirement of notice (as distinguished from consent, at issue in *Danforth*) was found to be an "undue burden" upon abortion, and this restriction was, indeed, the only restriction that the Court struck down in *Casey*. So it is absolutely clear that *the state may not require spousal consent.*

2. **Parental consent:** But the state *may* require that an *unemancipated* woman under the age of 18 obtain *parental* consent. The state may also require that this parental consent be "informed," even if this requires an in-person visit by the parent to the facility, and even if it involves a 24-hour waiting period. *Casey, supra.*

   a. **Court hearing:** However, if the state does require parental consent, it must give the girl an opportunity to *persuade a judge* that an abortion is in her best interests. This is called a *"judicial bypass."*

   b. **Emancipation or maturity:** The state must also allow an individualized judicial hearing at which the girl may persuade the court that she is in fact sufficiently *mature* or *emancipated* that she is able to make this decision for herself. If she proves this, the abortion must be allowed even if the judge believes that the abortion is not in the girl's best interest.

F. **Public funding:** States may refuse to give *public funding* (e.g., Medicaid) for abortions, even though they give such funding for other types of operations. *Maher v. Roe*, 432 U.S. 464 (1977). Also, states may *prohibit public hospitals* (or publicly-employed staff) from performing abortions. *Webster v. Reproductive Health Svcs.*, 492 U.S. 490 (1989).

G. **Abortion counseling:** The government may, as a condition of funding family-planning clinics, insist that the doctor or other professional *not recommend* abortion, and *not refer* clinic patients to an abortion provider. *Rust v. Sullivan*, 111 S.Ct. 1759 (1991).

H. **Types of abortion:** The state probably has substantial freedom to place regulations on the types of abortions that may be performed. For instance, the state may probably not require that all second trimester abortions be performed in a hospital (even though a pre-*Casey* decision, *Akron v. Akron Center for Reproductive Health*, 464 U.S. 416 (1983), says that the states may not do this.)

V. INFORMAL LIVING ARRANGEMENTS

A. **Cohabitation:** With the erosion of the concept of the permanency of marriage, the institution of marriage presently is being questioned and, in some segments of society, even rejected. As a result, a growing number of people live together outside any marriage relationship, formal or informal. These living arrangements obviously have had, and will in the future have, an effect on the mores and attitudes of society towards marriage.

   1. **Traditional rule:** Courts have refused in the past to enforce contracts between nonmarital partners if they involved an illicit relationship. Any such agreement was viewed as a contract for prostitution, and therefore, illegal or contrary to public policy.

2. **Modern rule:** The great majority of courts which have considered this issue have recognized the prevalence of nonmarital relationships in modern society, and the social acceptance of them. Accordingly, one court held that certain theories may be applied to couples living together so that one person may recover from the other if the immoral or illegal aspects of the relationship can be separated from the lawful aspects.

   a. **Express contract:** If nonmarital partners make a contract it should be enforced except to the extent that the contract is explicitly founded on the consideration of meretricious sexual services.

   b. **Implied contract:** Courts may imply a contract, agreement of partnership, or joint venture between the parties based upon their conduct.

   c. *Quantum meruit:* Courts may employ the doctrine of *quantum meruit,* or other equitable remedies such as constructive or resulting trusts, when warranted by the facts of the case, to permit recovery.

3. *Marvin v. Marvin I:* The trend toward "conferring the benefits of marriage upon persons who clearly were not married, and who had no intention of being married" began with the leading case of *Marvin v. Marvin,* 557 P.2d 106 (Cal. 1977).

   a. **Background:** This case attracted national publicity when it was tried, not only because of the issues involved, but also because the defendant was the famous movie star Lee Marvin. His female companion, who had legally changed her name to Marvin, sought one-half of the $3.6 million that Lee Marvin earned while they were living together.

   b. **Facts:** M and W live together for seven years without being married. After they separate W brings suit for one-half of the property acquired by M while they were living together, and for support. W contends that she had made an oral contract with M to share equally all property either would acquire while they were living together. W also alleges that they agreed to hold themselves out as husband and wife, and that W would render "services as a companion, homemaker, housekeeper and cook" to M. Finally, F alleges that she gave up her career as a singer, and that M agreed to provide for all F's financial support and needs for the rest of her life. M moves to dismiss principally on the ground that the alleged contract was so closely related to the supposed "immoral" character of the relationship between them that enforcement of the contract would violate public policy.

   c. **Holding:** M's motion is denied, and the case is remanded for trial.

d. **Rationale:** The fact that M and W live together without marriage, and engage in a sexual relationship, does not in itself invalidate agreements between them relating to earnings, property or expenses. A "contract between nonmarital partners is unenforceable only to the extent that it explicitly rests upon the immoral and illicit consideration of meretricious sexual services." Thus, a court will not enforce a contract if it is explicitly and inseparably based upon sexual services. However, where other services are part of the contract, and they are supported by independent consideration, that part of the contract will be enforced if it is severable from that part of the contract involving sexual services. The court reasoned that "judicial barriers that may stand in the way of a policy based upon the fulfillment of the reasonable expectations of the parties to a nonmarital relationship should be removed." Therefore, an express contract will be enforced unless it rests on an unlawful meretricious consideration.

e. **Other remedies:** The court also stated that in the absence of an express agreement there are other remedies to protect the lawful expectations of the parties: (a) The conduct of the parties may evidence an implied contract, joint venture or other *tacit understanding;* (b) Courts may apply the principles of constructive trust or resulting trust where appropriate; and (c) *Quantum meruit* recovery for the reasonable value of household services rendered, less the reasonable value of support received, if one person can show that the services were rendered with the expectation of monetary reward.

   i. **Constructive trust:** When a court determines that one party holds property that rightfully belongs to another, a constructive trust may be created. This forces the person with title to convey the property to the one who should have title. It is usually a remedy for fraud, duress, mistake or undue influence.

   ii. **Resulting trust:** This is a doctrine of construction based on presumed or implied intent. It attempts to do with property what it is presumed the transferor would have wanted if he had anticipated the situation.

   iii. **Comment:** One authority noted that neither of the doctrines above appears to apply to the *Marvin* type situation very well. However, the mention of these doctrines by the court indicates that some equitable duty is being imposed. "The meaning of the Marvin case thus seems to be that living together out of wedlock, at least for a substantial period, gives rise to claims on the part of both parties to share in each other's property on some unspecified equitable basis. The measure of the claim may be the value of services rendered, or it may be just what strikes the trial court as fair under all the circumstances." Clark, pp. 617-18.

    f. **Other issues:** M raised other grounds in support of his motion to dismiss. (a) M contended that the contract violated public policy because it impaired the community property rights of his wife. (M began living with F before divorcing his wife.) That argument was rejected because a contract involving the improper transfer of community property is not void *ab initio,* but merely voidable at the option of the aggrieved spouse. M's wife had the opportunity to protect her rights in her divorce action, and that decree fixed her interest in M's property. (b) M also contended that the oral contract could not be enforced because state law required that "All contracts for marriage settlements must be in writing." However, the statute refers to antenuptial contracts in which the parties agree to release or modify property rights which would otherwise arise from the marriage. Since the contract involved here was not made in contemplation of marriage, the statute did not apply.

4. ***Marvin v. Marvin II:*** On remand the trial court found that M and W never agreed to combine their efforts and earnings or share any property which they accumulated. There was never any agreement, express or implied, between them. W benefited economically from the cohabitation, and W suffered no damage as a result of the termination of the relationship. Furthermore, M was not unjustly enriched as a result of the relationship.

    a. **Holding:** The court awarded W $104,000 for rehabilitation because W could not return to her former career and she needed to learn new employable skills. Another basis for the award was that W had no means of support when M terminated the relationship, and that W, in equity, had a right to assistance until W could become self-supporting. 5 F.L.R. 3085 (1979).

5. ***Marvin v. Marvin III:*** On appeal, the court held that W may not recover. The award is not warranted to protect the expectations of *both* parties and M was not unjustly enriched. Merely showing that W needed the money does not establish an obligation in law or in Equity to the award. The facts showed that W benefited from the relationship; she suffered no damage therefrom. *Marvin v. Marvin,* 176 Cal.Rptr. 555 (1981).

6. **Aftermath of *Marvin:*** This case began a trend, and the majority of courts considering this issue have recognized the individual claims of unmarried cohabitants to property accumulated jointly. Those courts use an equitable or contractual basis for implementing the reasonable expectations of the parties unless sexual services constituted an ***explicit consideration.***

Example: P and D agree to live together and hold themselves out as married. P gives up her job, assumes D's surname and works in D's business. P gives birth to two children and contributes childcare and homemaking services. Several years later P starts a business with D's sister-in-law. Then the relationship deteriorates and P leaves. P sues D, alleging that they have a contract to share equally the property accumulated during their relationship.

Held, state law does not preclude an unmarried cohabitant from asserting contract and property claims against the other party to the cohabitation. Public policy does not preclude such a claim so long as the claim *exists independently* of the sexual relationship and is supported by separate consideration. P may recover on an express or implied contract if she can prove the agreement. P also has a claim based on *unjust enrichment* if D has retained an unreasonable amount of the property acquired through the efforts of both. *Watts v. Watts*, 405 N.W.2d 303 (Wis. 1987).

    a. **Comparison to antenuptial contract:** An antenuptial contract must be in writing to be enforceable. A *Marvin* type contract may be enforced even though it is oral.

7. **Minority view:** But not all courts have agreed with the *Marvin* approach. For instance, in *Hewitt v. Hewitt*, 394 N.E.2d 1204 (Ill. 1979), the court denied relief to a woman who established a common law marriage (not recognized in the state) and a promise by her "husband" to share his earnings and property with her. The court used the following rationale in rejecting her claim.

    a. *Marvin* **based on faulty assumptions:** Other courts have said that the rendition of housekeeping and homemaking services may be regarded as the consideration for a separate contract between the parties which is severable from the illegal agreement founded on sexual relations. However, it is naive to assume that such contracts are independent from the sexual activity and would have been entered into or continued without sexual activity.

    b. **Legislature should set policy:** There are more important considerations than the rights of the immediate parties. Specifically, the impact of recognition of nonmarital cohabitation upon society and the institution of marriage must be considered. It is the legislature which should set public policy in this area after investigation and fact-finding, especially when present policy is to preserve the integrity of marriage. Furthermore, a court should not create a new type of common law marriage when the state legislature has outlawed common law marriages.

ANNULMENT

I. HISTORICAL BACKGROUND

A. Introduction: Annulment is the legal process by which a marriage is invalidated retroactively to the date of the inception of the marriage.

1. **English ecclesiastical courts:** In England until 1857 only ecclesiastical courts had jurisdiction to annul marriages. The procedure, called *"divorce a vinculo matrimonii,"* was the **only** method of dissolving a marriage. It was based on conditions existing at the time of the marriage which would render the marriage invalid.

2. **Development in America:** Annulment in the United States, unlike other aspects of matrimonial law, does not have strong roots reaching back to English law. It is basically a creation of state legislatures.

   a. **Origin:** In the northeastern section of the American Colonies, annulment was authorized by statute and granted by courts and legislatures. In the southern colonies and New York, however, English traditions prevailed, and since there were no ecclesiastical courts as in England, annulment pleadings were not heard.

      i. **Court decisions:** After 1776 diverse rulings with respect to annulments began. Some courts stated that only statutory law could confer authority to grant annulments; other courts held that only equity courts could annul marriages. The grounds were *fraud, duress or insanity. Burtis v. Burtis,* 1 Hopk. Ch. 557 (N.Y. 1825); *Brown v. Westbrook,* 27 Ga. 102 (1859).

   b. **General laws:** In the nineteenth and twentieth centuries an increasing number of states passed legislation authorizing and governing annulment proceedings.

   c. **Contemporary laws:** Today most states have statutes which set forth the grounds for annulment. In states which have not enacted such a statute, a court may, nevertheless, annul a marriage based upon its equitable powers. In all situations the ground for annulment must have *existed at the beginning of the marriage.*

   Example: Mental incapacity at the time of the marriage is a ground for annulment if the afflicted party was incapable of consent. If the mental incapacity occurs after the marriage ceremony, no annulment may be granted, but a divorce may be possible.

II. ANNULMENT DISTINGUISHED FROM DIVORCE

A. Generally: A marriage which is annulled, is void from the beginning because of some defect existing *at the time of the marriage* ceremony.

By contrast, a divorce terminates a marriage that was valid. See Chart II, *infra* p. 51.

> **Example:** W sues H for divorce due to H's cruelty towards her. H counterclaims for an annulment because W refuses to stop taking birth control pills and have children. W and H agreed at the time of their marriage to have children, but to postpone having them for a while. W agreed to take birth control pills, but refused to stop taking them due to H's cruel behavior.
>
> *Held*, W is granted a divorce. A representation to have children goes to the essentials of a marriage. However, in order to grant an annulment for the falsity of a representation to have children, the party defrauded must show that the other party did not intend to have children at the time of the marriage. The evidence shows only that W changed her mind. *Heup v. Heup,* 172 N.W.2d 334 (Wis. 1969).

1. **Void—Voidable Distinction:** For purposes of annulment, there are two types of invalid marriages:

    a. **Void marriage:** This marriage is invalid for any purpose at any time;

    b. **Voidable marriage:** This marriage is valid for all civil purposes until and unless attacked by one of the parties.

    Note: Where a marriage is only voidable, it is effective until a decree of annulment is obtained. However, the effect of the decree is retroactive to the time of the marriage ceremony. Nevertheless, children born of an annulled marriage are deemed legitimate under present laws.

2. **Use of annulments:** As a method for terminating the marriage relation, annulment is not utilized as frequently as divorce because the grounds for annulment are very limited, and they are not present in most discordant marriages.

III. JURISDICTION IN ANNULMENT ACTIONS

A. **Domicile:** Jurisdiction in an annulment action is based on the domicile of one or both parties, since the state of domicile has the primary governmental interest in the marital relationship of its residents.

> **Example 1:** If both parties are domiciled in State X, then X's courts have jurisdiction to grant an annulment.

> **Example 2:** If one party is domiciled in State X, then X's courts have jurisdiction to grant an annulment. *Perlstein v. Perlstein,* 204 A.2d 909 (Conn. 1964).

CHART II. DIFFERENCES BETWEEN DIVORCE AND ANNULMENT

<u>DIVORCE</u>

1. Predicated on a valid marriage.

2. Terminates marriage as of the date of such decree.

3. Grounds arise *after* the marriage.

4. Alimony is generally granted in a divorce action.

<u>ANNULMENT</u>

1. Predicated on an invalid marriage.

2. Terminates a void or voidable marriage retroactively to the date of its supposed inception.

3. Grounds exist *prior* to the marriage.

4. Unless state statutes provide otherwise, alimony is not granted after issuance of the annulment decree. However, the statutory trend is to allow alimony.

Example 3: If neither party is domiciled in State X, even though both parties are in X's court, the court has no jurisdiction to grant an annulment. X's interest in the matter is minimal.

Note: This general principle is not followed in all states. A California court held that the interests of the state where the marriage occurred, and the interests of the state of domicile of either party, do not preclude a court in another state from granting an annulment if it has *personal jurisdiction* over *both* parties. The crucial question is whether there is sufficient contact with the state to justify the exercise of jurisdiction by a court. When this rule is applied, the doctrine of *forum non conveniens* (inconvenient forum) can be applied to prevent hardship on the defendant. *Whealton v. Whealton,* 432 P.2d 979 (Cal. 1967).

1. **Law applied:** The court of the state having jurisdiction to annul a marriage will, under its conflict of laws rule, refer to and apply the law of the state which determined the validity of the marriage.

   Example 1: By the law of State A, a common law marriage created by mere consent and the act of living together as man and wife, is invalid. State B recognizes common law marriages as valid. H and W enter into a common law marriage in State A and cohabit as man and wife. W leaves H and establishes her domicile in State B. W sues for a decree of annulment in B.

   Held, the annulment is granted. W has her domicile in B, so that state has a valid interest in W's marriage and may assert jurisdiction. B's court will apply the law of the place where the marriage took place, where the ground for annulment is the validity of the ceremony or lack of it. The common law marriage was void in A. Since W and H did not live together in B, the court will declare the marriage void *ab initio.*

   Example 2: In State A first cousins may marry, but in State B such a marriage is void. H and W are first cousins domiciled in B. To evade the laws of B, H and W are married in A. Later H establishes his domicile in State C, and sues for a decree of annulment in C.

   Held, the decree is granted applying the law of B. The fact that H is now domiciled in C gives that court jurisdiction to grant the decree. The law which determines the validity of the marriage is the state of their domicile, which was B. In B there is a strong public policy against the incestuous marriage of first cousins, which H and W could not evade by leaving the state and marrying in another.

2. **Restatement view:** The Rest. 2d, Conflict of Laws, §283(1) states that the "validity of a marriage is to be determined by the local law of the state which, with respect to the particular issue, has the most signifi-

cant relationship to the spouses and the marriage." The following factors are significant:

a. **Needs** of the interstate and international systems;

b. **Policies of the forum;**

c. **Policies of other interested states** and the relative interests of those states in the determination of the issue presented;

d. **Justified expectations** of the parties which deserve protection;

e. **Basic policies** underlying the particular field of law;

f. **Predictability and uniformity of result;** and

g. **Ease in the determination** and application of the law to be applied. Rest. 2d, Conflict of Laws, §6.

> **Note:** "A marriage which satisfies the requirements of the state where the marriage was contracted will be recognized as valid everywhere unless it violates the strong public policy of another state which has the most significant relationship to the spouses and the marriage." Rest. 2d, Conflict of Laws, §283(2).

IV. GROUNDS FOR ANNULMENT

A. **Specific grounds:** Generally, states will grant an annulment for *fraud*, *duress*, *impotency*, and *mental incapacity*.

1. **Fraud:** Under the *"doctrine of essentials,"* a *fraud* which goes to the *essentials of the marriage* is ground for an annulment. In deciding whether the fraud went to the "essentials," many courts ask *whether the defrauded party would have entered into the marriage without the fraud* (essentially a "subjective" standard). Other courts use a more objective test based upon the state's policies toward marriage.

   a. **Pregnant by another man:** Misrepresentations regarding *pregnancies* may sometimes be grounds for an annulment. For instance, if the woman is *in fact* pregnant, and she *conceals* this fact from the man, an annulment will be granted (provided that the man is *not the father* of the child).

   Example: H marries W after knowing her six weeks. W represents that she is chaste when in fact she is pregnant by another man. Upon learning of W's condition H files for an annulment.

   Held, the annulment is granted. The misrepresentation went to the essentials of the marriage. W was already bearing another man's child and could not execute the marriage contract with H which entails sexual relations and child bearing. *Reynolds v. Reynolds*, 85 Mass. 605 (1862).

    i. Misrepresentation of paternity: Where the wife does not conceal the fact that she is pregnant, but falsely tells the husband that she is pregnant *by him* when she is in fact pregnant by another man, most courts similarly grant the annulment. Clark, p. 115.

    ii. Woman not pregnant: But where the wife tells the husband she is pregnant by him, when she is in fact *not pregnant at all*, most courts **deny** the annulment. See, e.g., *Levy v. Levy*, 34 N.E.2d 650 (Mass. 1941). Contra: *Masters v. Masters*, 108 N.W.2d 674 (Wis. 1961).

b. Children: Misrepresentation of a willingness to engage in sexual relations and to *have children* is a ground.

c. Character: Some courts permit an annulment based upon a material misrepresentation of *character*, status or past life, if the marriage would not have been entered into had the true facts been known.

Example 1: W marries H, who conceals the fact that he had been an officer in the German Army during World War II and was fanatically anti-Semitic. After their marriage, H requires W to stop socializing with all Jewish friends. W sues for an annulment.

    Held, the annulment is granted. The misrepresentation upon which an annulment action is based need not go to what is commonly called the essentials of the marriage relation, *i.e.*, the duties and rights concerning cohabitation and consortium. Fraud is sufficient ground for annulment if it is material. H's concealed sentiments made the marriage intolerable, and W would not have married H had she been aware of H's concealed sentiments. *Kober v. Kober*, 211 N.E.2d 817 (N.Y. 1965).

Example 2: H falsely represents to W that H is an Orthodox Jew. W is Orthodox, and (as H knows) would not have married H if she had known that H was not Orthodox. Upon discovering that H is not Orthodox, W sues for an annulment.

    Held, annulment granted. Fraud is grounds for annulment only when the fraud is "of an extreme nature, going to one of the essentials of marriage...." To W, the religious beliefs and convictions of her husband were essential to her marriage, because she could not carry out her duties of wife and mother without the support of a husband holding the same beliefs. *Bilowit v. Dolitsky*, 304 A.2d 774 (N.J.Super. 1973).

Note: Observe that the court in *Bilowit* applied a **subjective** standard for fraud: the court treated the issue as being whether, viewed from the perspective of a party seeking annulment (not the perspective of a "reasonable person") the fraud went to the essentials of the marriage.

  i. Social standing or income: Courts are less likely to allow an annulment where the defendant's misrepresentation related to his or her *social position* or *income*. See, e.g., *Woronzoff-Daschkoff v. Woronzoff-Daschkoff*, 104 N.E.2d 877 (N.Y. 1952) (annulment denied where H falsely stated to W, a wealthy woman, that H had a job and was socially prominent).

d. Drug dependency: The concealment of *drug addiction* has been held to be a fraud going to the essentials of the marriage. Thus, an annulment was granted where W learned of H's heroin addiction five weeks after the marriage and immediately left H. *Costello v. Porzelt*, 282 A.2d 432 (N.J. 1971).

e. Illness: Misrepresentation or concealment of infirmities at the time of the marriage will sometimes be a ground for annulment. Conditions of health for which an annulment will be granted include venereal disease, mental illness and sterility.

f. Love: A misrepresentation as the *love and affection* for one's spouse at the time of marriage, by itself, is not grounds for annulment. However, lack of love and affection may be relevant as evidence to show another misrepresentation which is grounds for annulment.

  i. Obtain property: It may show an intent to defraud the spouse of property and then desert. *Robert v. Robert,* 150 N.Y.S.2d 366 (1914).

  ii. Immigrate: It may show the intent to marry for the sole purpose of obtaining an immigration visa. *Ernst v. Ernst,* 32 N.Y.S.2d 795 (1943).

  iii. Adultery: It may show an intent to continue an illicit relationship with another person. *United States v. Rubenstein,* 151 F.2d 915 (2d Cir.), *cert. denied* 326 U.S. 766 (1945).

2. **Duress:** Duress may be grounds for annulment, depending on the particular pressure brought against the spouse. The threat or use of force constitute duress and are grounds for annulment. The threat of legal action for seduction, fornication or bastardy would not normally be grounds for annulment.

   Example: H is domiciled in England, but is employed by the British government in Malta. As H is preparing to leave Malta he is arrested and charged with corrupting W, a minor. H had dated W a few times, but they did not have sexual intercourse. A solicitor is appointed to represent H. He tells H that it is not uncommon for British personnel to seduce Maltese women and then return to

England before they can be prosecuted. That fact is resented by the Maltese people and it is certain that H will be convicted. Therefore, H could expect to be sentenced to prison unless he marries W. H asks his British supervisor who confirms the advice of the solicitor. To avoid what appears to be a certain prison sentence H marries W. Subsequently, H returns to England and seeks an annulment of the marriage.

Held, the marriage is void. "In the absence of consent there can be no valid marriage; and fear may vitiate consent." H was placed in fear by the unfounded charge against him. That fear was strengthened by the advice of H's appointed solicitor and H's work supervisor. H believed that he had to choose between marriage and prison. H's reasonable fears arose from circumstances for which he was not responsible, and are sufficient to constitute duress. *Buckland v. Buckland,* 2 All E.R. 300 (1965).

a. **Test:** The duress must be present at the time of the marriage. The test for duress is *subjective* rather than objective. That is, was the person seeking the annulment prevented from freely assenting to the marriage, rather than was the fear reasonable in light of all the circumstances.

Note: Today most courts hold that a marriage entered into under duress is voidable and not void *ab initio*. Thus, the rights and duties of the marriage bind both parties until the marriage is formally annulled.

3. **Impotency:** This is grounds upon which a marriage will be declared voidable.

Example: H and W are married. W seeks an annulment on the ground that H is impotent due to psychological, rather than physical reasons.

Held, an annulment should be granted. Although the applicable statute appears to be limited to impotency caused by physical reasons, the intention of the legislature must have been to include physical incapacity caused by psychological reasons. The fact that H's impotence is caused by psychological rather than physical reasons is irrelevant when the question of W's right to an annulment for physical incapacity is at issue. *Rickards v. Rickards,* 166 A.2d 425 (Del. 1960).

4. **Mental incapacity:** A marriage will be declared invalid on the ground of mental incapacity, if the afflicted party was incapable of consent at the time of marriage.

Example: C, a child from H's first marriage, seeks to have H's second marriage annulled on the ground that H was insane at the time of the marriage and incapable of consent. H was elderly when he married. His appearance and health had declined. He had become slovenly, confused mentally, and partially paralyzed due to a stroke. His wife attended H after his stroke and H improved. H then married her.

Held, the circumstances do not warrant an annulment. A marriage contract will not be annulled on the ground of mental incapacity unless there existed *at the time of the marriage* such a lack of understanding as to render a party incapable of consenting to the contract. C did not present such evidence. *Fischer v. Adams,* 38 N.W.2d 337 (Neb. 1949). See also *Ertel v. Ertel*, 40 N.E.2d 85 (Ill. 1942).

V. DEFENSES TO AN ANNULMENT ACTION

A. **Defenses:** Among the defenses to an annulment action are the following:

1. **Ratification:** If a married couple continue to live together after one spouse learns of valid grounds for annulment, that may be considered ratification and used as a defense.

2. **Clean hands:** The equitable defense of clean hands may be asserted in some jurisdictions. In those jurisdictions inequitable conduct or bad faith by the plaintiff may be a valid defense to the suit for annulment.

   Example: M, mother of W who is 17 and below the statutory age of consent, files for divorce on behalf of W. W and H had two children, and a temporary support order is issued. Upon reaching 18, W amends the complaint and files for an annulment on the ground of nonage. H defends on the grounds of election of remedies, estoppel, clean hands and ratification of the marriage.

   Held, H's defenses are not valid. To ratify a marriage, a party must perform some unequivocal, voluntary act confirming the marriage upon reaching the age of consent, such as cohabitation. Acceptance of temporary support is neither an act of confirmation nor an election of remedies. Clean hands is not conclusive in annulment proceedings, and since the legitimacy of the children of a voidable marriage is not affected, the defenses of estoppel, election of remedies and clean hands are overruled. *Powell v. Powell*, 86 A.2d 331 (N.H. 1952).

3. **Antenuptial knowledge:** This defense may be asserted in some states when the person seeking the annulment knew of the marital defect before the marriage.

4. *Res judicata:* All courts agree on the principle that where two parties have *fully litigated* a particular claim, and a *final judgment* has resulted, that claim may not later be relitigated by the loser.

5. **Collateral estoppel:** Under the doctrine of collateral estoppel, all courts are in agreement that if a particular *finding of fact* has been made in the course of a lawsuit between two parties, that issue of fact may not later be retried by the loser, under the doctrine of collateral estoppel, even though the cause of action is different in the second suit.

   a. **Distinction:** The term *"res judicata"* is sometimes used loosely to refer to both the rule preventing relitigation of claims and that preventing relitigation of findings of fact. There are two primary differences between the terms.

      i. **Application:** *Res judicata* applies only where the *cause of action* in the second action is the same as the one adjudicated in the first action. Collateral estoppel applies so long as any *issue of fact* is the same, even though the causes of action are different.

      ii. **Effect:** *Res judicata* prevents a second suit altogether. Collateral estoppel does not prevent suit, but merely compels the court to make the same finding of fact on the identical factual issue that the first court made.

   Example: H sues W for a separation which is granted based upon abandonment. In the litigation W admits the validity of the marriage. Subsequently, W brings an action against H to annul the marriage because H was validly married when he married W. *Held,* W's suit is dismissed. The court decree in H's suit for a separation determined that the marriage between H and W was valid, even though that question was not actually litigated. To annul the marriage would undermine the factual basis of the prior judgment. Thus the defense of *res judicata* may be asserted by H. *Statter v. Statter,* 143 N.E.2d 10 (N.Y. 1957).

6. **Statute of limitations:** Many states have a statute of limitations for each specific ground upon which an annulment may be sought. Other states apply the general statute of limitations or permit the equitable defense of laches.

B. **Effect of death:** If one of the spouses dies before an action for annulment is brought, or during the action, the following consequences should be noted.

1. **Death before action:** Whether or not an annulment action can be brought *after* the death of a spouse depends upon whether the marriage was "void" or "voidable." If the marriage was *void,* an annulment action can be brought and the marriage attacked collaterally. If the marriage was *voidable,* an annulment action cannot be brought.

   Example: W and H marry. W dies leaving H and collateral relatives A, B and C as heirs. Wishing the inheritance they would receive if H were not W's husband, A, B and C file suit to have the marriage of H and W annulled on the ground that W was gravely ill at the time of the marriage. Such a condition renders a marriage voidable in that state.

Held, the petition is dismissed. Where a marriage is merely voidable, rather than void, it cannot be attacked by a third party after the death of one of the parties to the marriage. *Patey v. Peaslee,* 111 A.2d 194 (N.H. 1955).

2. **Death during action:** If a party to a *void* marriage dies during the annulment action before the decision is issued, the action may continue. If a party to a *voidable* marriage dies during the action, the action abates. *Dibble v. Meyer,* 278 P.2d 901 (Or. 1955).

VI. PROPERTY AND ALIMONY IN ANNULMENT ACTIONS

A. **Authority of courts:** In addition to ruling a marriage to be invalid, a court may also settle the property rights of the parties and award alimony in an annulment action.

1. **General principles:** Temporary alimony may only be awarded in annulment actions in certain situations:

   a. **D contends marriage valid:** *Temporary alimony* during the pendency of the suit may be awarded by the court to the defendant spouse if that spouse does not admit the invalidity of the marriage.

   b. **D admits marriage invalid:** Temporary alimony will *not* be awarded to a defendant spouse who admits the invalidity of the marriage, since there is no support owing a person who is not a spouse.

   c. **P contends marriage invalid:** Temporary alimony during the pendency of the suit will *not* be awarded to a plaintiff spouse who is attacking the validity of the marriage, since this would be an inconsistent position.

2. **Statutes:** *Permanent alimony* at the end of an annulment action will generally not be granted in the absence of statutory authorization. Many states, however, have passed legislation expanding the use of alimony by awarding alimony in annulment actions.

   a. **Treat as divorce:** Some states have attempted to provide for alimony by including grounds for annulment in their divorce statutes.

   b. **Court discretion:** Some states have specifically provided that alimony may be granted in the court's discretion.

   c. **Innocent spouse:** Other states have provided that alimony may only be awarded to an innocent spouse in an annulment action.

3. **Court decisions:** To avoid the situation in which one spouse would be left penniless due to lack of legislation authorizing alimony in annulment actions, some courts may order one spouse to pay the other spouse *fair compensation* for services rendered during their invalid marriage.

> **Example:** W2 enters a common law marriage with H, not knowing that H is validly married to W1. W2 and H live together for six years, during which time they accumulate real estate, household furnishings and equipment. W2 files for a divorce from H, which is denied due to the fact that H is married to W1. However, the court annuls the marriage to W2. W2 files a complaint asking for the value of her services as a housekeeper and reimbursement for amounts she contributed towards their property.
>
> *Held*, W2 may recover the proportion of property accumulated during the relationship that is just and equitable. Equity has jurisdiction to adjudicate the property rights between persons whose marriage has been declared void. In this case W2 entered into a supposedly valid marital relationship in good faith, and the marriage would be valid except for the incapacity of H. W2 is an innocent party who made material contributions to the marriage. *Walker v. Walker,* 47 N.W.2d 633 (Mich. 1951); *Sclamberg v. Sclamberg,* 41 N.E.2d 801 (Ind. 1942).

FAMILY RELATIONSHIPS

I. INTRODUCTION

A. **Basis of laws:** Analysis of family law problems frequently focuses on two aspects of the individuals involved: their *status,* and their *relationship* to one another.

1. **Duties:** The obligation of *support* that one spouse has for the other arises out of the marital relationship. The obligation of parents to support their children arises out of the parent-child relationship.

   a. **Torts:** The husband-wife relationship and the parent-child relationship may alter what would otherwise be causes of action as between unrelated individuals.

      Example: H is driving an automobile with his wife and child as passengers. There is an accident due to H's negligence and his wife and child are injured. Under the common law rule H would be immune from suit by his wife and child. This rule has been changed by modern statutes and court decisions to allow suit against H.

   b. **Agency:** The relationship of husband and wife, without more, does not create an agency. If the parties intend that one shall act for the other in a transaction, a principal-agent relationship arises. *Express Publishing Co. v. Levenson,* 282 S.W.2d 357 (Tex. 1956).

2. **Disabilities of minors:** A person under the age of majority, usually 18, is termed a minor or infant, and is subject to certain *legal disabilities.* The reasons for these disabilities are to *protect* the minor from the consequences of his own lack of judgment, and to *prevent* the minor from acting in situations where he does not have enough maturity.

   a. **Specific rules:** Disabilities affect the rights of minors in many ways. Some of the more important relate to:

      i. **Capacity to enter into contracts;**

      ii. **Liability for torts;**

      iii. **Property ownership;**

      iv. **Will execution**; and

      v. **Criminal liability.**

II. SUPPORT OBLIGATIONS IN A FAMILY

A. **Statutory background:** There are statutes which impose familial support obligations.

1. **Duty of husband:** Historically statutes obligated a husband to support his wife, but there was no reciprocal duty placed on the wife. These statutes, patterned after the common law, have been held to violate the Equal Protection Clause because of their gender-based classification.

2. **Family Expense Acts:** These modern statutes render the expenses of the family chargeable against the property of *both* the husband and the wife. The wife must support the husband if he is unable to support himself.

B. **Support of spouse:** What constitutes support is dependent upon the statutes of each jurisdiction. Some states impose liability only for necessaries, while others impose liability for all expenses.

> **Example 1:** H and W were married for 16 years when W left H with no explanation. Later W requests H to leave the apartment in which they had lived, since W regarded it as belonging to her. H complies, and he has no further contact with W until she files for support. W claims that H should support her since she is still his wife. W is currently receiving pubic assistance. H contends that he is not liable for W's support because W abandoned him.
>
> *Held*, H is responsible for W's support. W's abandonment of H is not sufficient reason to relieve H of his duty of support if W is or may become a public charge. The applicable support statute provides that the spouse of a recipient of public assistance is responsible for support. There is no exculpatory language concerning desertion in the law, and a court cannot alter obligations of a legally responsible spouse. *Campas v. Campas,* 304 N.Y.S.2d 876 (1969).

> **Example 2:** H and W are married and live together on a farm. H is extremely frugal and does not give W any money for household necessities. H makes all purchases he believes necessary. The house has no inside toilet and the kitchen has no sink. H never takes W to social events. H gives W only small amounts of money, although he has over $100,000 in the bank. W sues H for suitable maintenance. At trial W is not able to show grounds for separation or divorce under state law.
>
> *Held*, W may not recover. Living standards are a matter of concern to the household and not for the courts to determine so long as H provides W with necessaries, and there are no grounds for separation or divorce under state law. H maintains their house, although not well, and W continues to live there. There is no proof of extreme cruelty, and H is legally supporting his wife. *McGuire v. McGuire,* 59 N.W.2d 336 (Neb. 1953).

> **Note:** The basis for the court's decision, that W was not entitled to a decree compelling H to support her according to H's wealth and

circumstances, was public policy. Courts are not equipped to settle the countless number of family budget disputes which could be brought into court if the decision were otherwise. Furthermore, there is no assurance that courts could settle family budget disputes justly or better than the parties themselves.

1. **Mutual obligation:** Most statutes which impose support obligations on the wife do not release the husband of his support obligation. Unless an intention of a gift from the wife to the husband is shown, a wife is entitled to reimbursement from her husband for her payment of his obligations of support. Clark, p. 258.

   a. **Contrary view:** The rule is not valid in Iowa where neither spouse may receive reimbursement for support from the other in the absence of a specific agreement. *Truax v. Ellett,* 15 N.W.2d 361 (Iowa 1944).

2. **Enforcement by third party:** Traditionally, persons who furnished goods or services to one spouse were able to enforce their claim against the other spouse under the doctrine of necessaries or agency.

   a. **"Necessaries" doctrine:** Under the *"necessaries"* doctrine, a husband is responsible for necessary goods and services furnished to his spouse by a third party. The doctrine comes from the common law rule that a wife could not have a separate estate — a husband was entitled to his wife's domestic services and consortium and was in return liable for her support. The necessaries doctrine was based on principles of restitution and quasi-contract.

      i. **Constitutional issue:** The common-law necessaries doctrine does not impose an obligation on the wife for her husband's necessaries. The gender-based classification created by this doctrine probably violates the Equal Protection Clause. The doctrine is based on the now-outdated assumption that women are more financially dependent than men. Therefore, at least one court has abolished the doctrine and refused to hold a husband liable for his wife's medical expenses. *Schilling v. Bedford County Memorial Hospital,* 303 S.E.2d 905 (Va. 1983).

      ii. **Doctrine modified:** To prevent the sex-based discrimination inherent in the necessaries doctrine, some courts have broadened the rule to make the wife responsible for necessaries of her husband. See, e.g., *Cooke v. Adams,* 183 So.2d 925 (Miss. 1966).

   b. **Agency:** H can also be liable for debts of his wife on principles of agency for goods purchased by his wife or child when he has *authorized* or *apparently authorized* the purchase. The mere relationship of husband and wife, without more, does not create an agency. There is no need to demonstrate that the goods are necessities if an agency exists.

Example: W buys articles from X Department Store for her own use, and charges them by signing her own name. W does not pay the bill, and X sues H for the amount due.

Held, H is not liable. Neither a husband nor a wife has the power to act as agent for the other merely because of their relationship as husband and wife. To hold H liable, X must show that H was an undisclosed principal or that the articles purchased were necessities which H had the duty to provide. The goods involved are not necessities, and there is no evidence of agency. *Saks & Co. v. Bennett,* 79 A.2d 479 (N.J. 1951).

3. **Contemporary statutes:** There is considerable variation among states with respect to support statutes, but they are gender-neutral, *i.e.,* the duty of support is placed *jointly* on the husband and wife. They are designed to ensure support whether a spouse (or former spouse) is living within the state or in another state.

   a. **Family expense statutes:** These statutes generally provide that family expenses and the cost of educating children are chargeable against both the husband and wife. They are in force in about twenty states.

      Example: W wants to appeal her conviction of a crime committed before her marriage to H. W contends that she is indigent, so she is entitled to an appeal at the public expense. The state shows that H has ample assets to finance an appeal. The court held that H must pay for the appeal because it is within the family expense statute. *State v. Clark,* 563 P.2d 1253 (Wash. 1977).

   b. **URESA:** The Uniform Reciprocal Enforcement of Support Act (URESA) is a civil statute which allows reciprocity between states in order to provide support for members of a family. This Act, or a similar act, is in effect in all states, so there is full reciprocity; an action started in one state can be continued in another state. URESA is discussed more extensively *infra*, p. 147.

C. **Support of parents:** Many states have laws which require **children** — if they are financially able to do so — to **support their parents**. These laws are part of the state's **welfare** system. Thus when a parent receives public welfare, the state looks to their children for reimbursement of all or part of the money paid. Such laws have a rational basis and are constitutional, courts have held.

   Example: P's mother receives aid to the aged under a state law which requires P to contribute according to a fixed schedule. P brings a class action contending that the law violates the Equal Protection Clause because it places the burden of supporting the elderly on too narrow a class. *Held*, P loses. The purpose of elderly-support laws is to protect the public from the burden of supporting people who have children able to support them. There is no suspect classification based on wealth, because the law applies to *all* children to the extent of their ability. The state selects the children to bear the burden not on the basis of wealth, but on the basis of parentage, a rational basis for imposing the burden. *Swoap v. Superior Court of Sacramento County*, 516 P.2d 840 (Cal. 1973).

D. Child support: The principles relating to the support of a wife are generally applicable to support of children. That is, each parent must support his or her children by supplying at least "necessities."

1. **Amount required:** There are no hard-and-fast rules as to ***how much*** financial support a parent must give his or her child, or as to precisely what items must be supplied. In general, of course, courts only require a parent to supply that financial support which the parent is ***reasonably capable*** of supplying. (In a few cases, courts have ordered support based on what the parent ***could earn*** if he or she chose the highest-paying work for which he or she is qualified, rather than based on what the parent is actually earning. See Clark, p. 259.)

2. **College costs:** Courts are split as to whether the parents have the obligation to pay for a child's ***college education***. Probably a majority of recent cases hold that parents are ***obligated*** to pay these costs, if they can afford to do so. See, e.g., *Childers v. Childers*, 575 P.2d 201 (Wash. 1978); Clark, p. 260.

   Note: In this section we are considering the duty of child support in the context of an ***intact*** family unit. Most child support issues, of course, are litigated in the context of divorce. Therefore, child support is considered in more detail in our treatment of divorce, *infra*, p. 141.

3. **Duty to support disobedient child:** Where the marriage is still intact, the most frequently-litigated issue regarding child support is whether the parents have a duty to support a ***disobedient*** child. Usually, the issue arises when the child ***leaves home*** and pursues a ***lifestyle*** that the parent disapproves of. Courts are split as to whether the parent may cut off support in this situation, with perhaps a slight majority allowing a cut-off.

   Example: C is the minor daughter of F. F permits C to attend college out of state and provides ample support for her. C moves out of the college dormitory contrary to F's instructions. C lives with a female classmate, experiments with drugs, and does poorly in college. When F discovers this, he directs C to return home and attend school there. C refuses, and F stops supporting her.

   Held, C has forfeited her right to support. Parents are charged with the discipline and support of their children. If a child merely disobeys her parent or becomes delinquent, the duty of support generally continues. However, a parent may impose reasonable regulations for his child in return for support. If C voluntarily abandons F's home to avoid parental discipline, C forfeits her claim to support. F did not cast C out into the world forcing her to fend for herself, or make arbitrary demands on her. If C elects not to comply with F's reasonable demands, she may not enlist the aid of the court in frustrating parental authority, and may not require F to underwrite her chosen lifestyle. *Roe v. Doe,* 272 N.E.2d 567 (N.Y. 1971).

a. **State supplies welfare:** Even where the state has had to give *welfare payments* to the child because of the parent's non-support, some courts have allowed the parent to defend on the grounds that the child followed a lifestyle that was so against the parent's wishes that the *parent* should be viewed as having been abandoned and no support due.

Example: C leaves her father's home against his wishes to live with her paramour and have a child. C receives public assistance. The Commissioner of Social Services brings an action against C's father to compel payments toward C's support. The father argues that C emancipated herself by voluntarily leaving home, and thus relieved him of any obligation to support her.

Held, there is no duty to support. Although parents are generally obligated to support their children under state law until they are 21, courts have discretionary powers in these cases. This is not a case of an abandoned child, but of an abandoned parent. The father did not abuse C or place unreasonable demands on her. He did not encourage C to leave home so the public would assume his obligation of support. He supported her at home and urged her to continue school. He is not required to underwrite C's chosen lifestyle. *Parker v. Stage*, 371 N.E.2d 513 (N.Y.1977).

4. **Emancipation:** Courts generally hold that an *emancipated* child has no right to parental support. Certainly a child who is over the age of 21 and living independently would not be found to be entitled to parental support in the vast majority of states. But the concept of "emancipation" is blurry, and does not correspond precisely to the minor/major distinction — even though in most states a child is no longer a minor after reaching 18, courts usually find that a child between 18 and 21 is not yet "emancipated" for purposes of the parental support obligation. (Also, as noted, some courts order the parents to pay for college; those courts that do so seem to impose the obligation even if the child is over 21.)

5. **Necessaries:** If parents fail to support their children, a *third person* who provides *necessaries* is entitled to the reasonable value thereof. This rule is not based on agency, but on the parent's duty to provide

necessaries, from which the law implies a promise to pay. *Greenspan v. Slate*, 97 A.2d 390 (N.J. 1953).

    a. Recovery of welfare payments: The most important practical consequence of this rule that a third party who provides necessaries may get reimbursement from the parent, is that when government makes *welfare payments* to or on behalf of the child, the welfare agency may recover these sums from the parent. Thus under the federal Aid to Families with Dependent Children (AFDC) program, state welfare agencies may (and, in fact, must) pursue collection efforts against an absent parent.

E. Conflict between parents and state: The state has an interest in the education, health and safety of children, and may impose *reasonable regulations* on parents in furthering that interest.

    1. Compulsory education: Conflicts sometimes arise between the state's interest in *educating* the young, and parents' interest in *religious freedom*. Where interference with religious freedom occurs, it is not sufficient for a state to show that there are no less restrictive alternatives for achieving its goals fully. If granting an exemption will *almost* fully achieve these goals, the state will generally be required to grant it even at a small sacrifice to its objectives. This is illustrated by *Wisconsin v. Yoder*, 406 U.S. 205 (1972), where the Court invalidated Wisconsin's refusal to exempt 14 and 15 year old Amish students from the requirement of attending school until age 16.

        a. Rationale: The parents of the Amish students satisfied the Court that it was an essential element of the Amish religion that members be informally taught to earn their living through farming and other rural activities. Compulsory secondary school education would be an impermissible exposure of their children to "worldly" influences which conflicted with their religious beliefs. Applying strict scrutiny, the Court concluded that an exemption must be granted unless the state could show an interest "of the highest order," which could not be served by means other than denial of an exemption.

        b. Harm not sufficiently great: The state's interest was to have its citizens reasonably well-educated, so that they could participate intelligently in political affairs and become economically self-sufficient. The Court implicitly conceded that Amish children who failed to attend high school would not receive the same level of intellectual learning; in other words, the state's objective would not be as fully realized if an exemption were given. But the Court considered it critical that nearly all Amish children continued to live in the Amish community throughout their lives, and that the informal vocational training they received seemed to prepare them well for that life. The Court also noted that this sect has existed for three hundred years, and it has been a successful and self-reliant part of society.

c. **Significance:** The Court in *Yoder* found that the state's interest must be read ***broadly and flexibly,*** not narrowly and rigidly, in determining whether that interest could still be fulfilled if an exemption were given.

d. **Dissent:** Justice Douglas, the sole dissenter in *Yoder,* argued that the majority was wrong to decide the case without determining whether each of the ***children*** involved desired to attend high school over the objections of his/her parents. Douglas contended that the child's desires should be preeminent.

2. **Medical treatment:** Parents sometimes refuse to consent to ***medical treatment*** for their child. Frequently the refusal is based on **religious** grounds. Where the treatment creates slight risk and lack of medical treatment would endanger the child's health, courts often order the treatment over the parents' objection. But where medical treatment involves substantial risk, courts are very reluctant to order treatment. Usually, the ***wishes of the child*** are considered.

> **Example:** C, age 16, is suffering from paralytic scoliosis (94% curvature of the spine). Because of this condition C is unable to stand, and if there is no corrective surgery, C can become a bed patient. C's doctors recommend a spinal fusion, but that is a dangerous operation. C's mother is a Jehovah's Witness, and her religious beliefs prohibit her from consenting to blood transfusions which would be necessary for the operation. While the operation, if successful, would be beneficial, C's life is not in immediate danger.
>
> *Held,* further proceedings are necessary. A state may not interfere with religious beliefs and opinions, but it may interfere with religious practices where the state's interest is of sufficient magnitude. As between a parent and the state, the state does not have an interest outweighing a parent's religious beliefs when the child's life is not immediately imperiled. However, the inquiry does not end at that point. The preference of C, who is intelligent and of sufficient maturity, should be considered. *In re Green,* 292 A.2d 387 (Pa. 1972).
>
> **Note:** At the subsequent hearing in *Green* to determine C's desires, C stated that he did not want the operation. His decision was not based on religious beliefs alone, but also because he had been hospitalized for a long period, and there was no assurance that the operation would be successful. The trial and appellate courts then agreed that C need not undergo the operation.

a. **Reluctance to consider quality of life:** Suppose the child will die without the proposed medical procedure, but with the procedure will have a ***poor quality of life***. Courts are usually reluctant to hold that death is the better alternative, and tend to order the treatment in this situation.

Example: C is born without a left eye, with a rudimentary left ear with no ear canal, without any ability to ingest nourishment, and with at least some brain damage. Doctors recommend surgery on C's esophagus, to allow normal feeding and respiration. However, C's father demands that medical be treatment stopped. The hospital seeks a court order authorizing treatment.

Held, C must be given medical treatment. At the moment of birth there exists a human being entitled to the fullest protection of the law. That includes the right to life. The issue is not the quality of life to be preserved, but the medical feasibility of the proposed treatment compared to the almost certain risk of death if treatment is withheld. Since surgery is necessary and feasible, C's parents have no right to withhold such treatment. The court will authorize a guardian ad litem to consent to the surgery. *Maine Medical Center v. Houle*, Doc. No. 74-145 (Super. Ct. of Cumberland, Maine, 1974).

b. **Federal law on treatment of infants:** The law on who decides whether a handicapped infant should receive treatment is now governed partly by federal regulations. Under 45 C.F.R. §1340.15, hospitals receiving federal funds (essentially all hospitals) are strongly "encouraged" to set up Infant Care Review Committees to supervise the care given to handicapped newborns; in the event of a disagreement between the hospital and the parent about whether care should be given, the Committee is to refer the matter to a court. There seems to be a strong federal policy that medically-beneficial treatment not be denied to an infant merely on the grounds of the infant's disabilities. However, there is no federal statute or regulation expressly requiring that such treatment be given to disabled children over the parents' objections. See *Bowen v. American Hospital Assoc.*, 476 U.S. 610 (1986), in which the Supreme Court struck down regulations that would have had this effect.

e. **The right to allow a child to die:** So far, we've considered whether a parent may, on religious or other grounds refuse to allow medically useful treatment to a child. Now, we consider the converse problem: When a child (or other member of a family) is in a ***coma*** or is otherwise terminally ill, may the parents refuse to allow ***unwanted medical procedures*** that may keep the patient alive, but will almost certainly ***not*** return the patient to a useful life or even to consciousness?

  i. **Patient's own right:** Before we get to the issue of a parent's right to decline treatment on behalf of the child, let's first consider briefly the patient's *own* right to decline treatment. While there are no recent Supreme Court cases on point, a competent adult almost certainly has a Fourteenth Amendment liberty interest — probably a fundamental one — in not being forced to undergo unwanted medical procedures. For instance, a terminally ill cancer patient who is competent probably has a right to compel a public hospital to stop feeding him or medicating him, so that he will die.

ii. **Incompetent patient:** But where the patient is *not presently competent* to make or state his decision about whether he wants life-saving techniques used, the situation gets much murkier. Under the leading case of *Cruzan v. Missouri Dept. of Health*, 110 S.Ct. 2841 (1990), the state may require that life-saving measures be used unless there is *"clear and convincing evidence"* that the patient would not have wanted these techniques.

Example: P is an irreversible coma. She is kept alive by means of a feeding and hydration tube implanted in her stomach. P's parents ask the hospital to end the artificial nutrition and hydration procedures, but the hospital refuses to do this without a court order. P's parents claim that P has a due process right not to be kept alive by unwanted procedures, and that they have a right to carry out her wishes.

Held (by the U.S. Supreme Court), the state may insist that P be fed and hydrated artificially, even over the objections of her parents and her court-appointed guardian. P may have a Fourteenth Amendment liberty interest in declining such treatment, but the state may constitutionally insist that that right can be exercised only by "clear and convincing evidence" that P indeed would not have wanted such procedures used on her. Here, the requisite clear and convincing evidence was lacking, so the state could insist that P be kept alive against her family's wishes. *Cruzan v. Missouri Dept. of Health, supra.*

iii. **Living wills and health-care proxies:** Probably states must honor a *"living will"* and *"health-care proxy."* In a living will, the signer gives direct instructions. In a health-care proxy, the signer appoints someone else (e.g., a spouse) to make health care decisions. However, presumably a valid living will or health-care proxy can only be executed by an adult, or, perhaps, a mature teenager.

iv. **Child:** When the patient who is incompetent to express her present wishes is a *child*, the issues are even murkier. There are no Supreme Court cases on point. There is a good chance that a court would hold that the unconscious child-patient nonetheless has a constitutional right not to be kept alive where this would be of no conceivable benefit to the child, and that the state must give to the parent the right to exercise this constitutional right on behalf of the child. Under this approach, if P in the *Cruzan* case had been a young child (too young to have possibly given clear and convincing evidence of her wishes about artificial life-sustaining measures), her parents would have had a constitutional right to make the decision to terminate the measures.

d. Mental institutions: The parents or guardian of a child have a duty to provide ***psychiatric care*** for their child, just as they must provide other medical treatments. When the care involves commitment to a ***mental institution***, however, the parents' right and duty to make medical decision can come in conflict with the child's ***due process*** right to be ***free of unwanted imprisonment and treatment***. In general, the Supreme Court has held, these two principles are to be ***balanced*** by presuming that the parents have the maturity and experience to act in the child's best interests, but by also having a "neutral fact finder" (e.g., the admitting physician) review the case and decline to admit the child to the institution if admission is not medically warranted. Due process does not require that the child be given a ***judicial hearing*** before being admitted. *Parham v. J.R.* 442 U.S. 584 (1979).

Example: State law provides for the voluntary admission of children to a state mental hospital. Initially the person is admitted temporarily at the request of a parent for observation and diagnosis. If the child is "suitable for treatment" he is admitted. The child may be discharged at the request of the parent or by the hospital superintendent if the child has improved sufficiently so that hospitalization is no longer desirable. A class action challenges the procedure for admission and confinement in state hospitals, contending that a judicial hearing is required to assure the minor child of his due process rights.

Held, the procedures do not violate the due process rights of patients. The traditional presumption that parents act in the best interest of their child should apply. However, the child's rights are such that parents cannot have unreviewable discretion. Therefore, a "neutral factfinder," such as the admitting physician, must review the child's background using all available sources and interview the child. This decisionmaker must have authority to refuse admission to anyone who fails to meet the medical standards of the hospital. An adversarial judicial hearing may cause disharmony in the family unit and discourage families from seeking necessary care, so it is not required. Finally, the child's continuing need for commitment must be reviewed periodically. *Parham v. J.R.*, *supra*.

e. **Criminal liability of parents:** If a parent refuses to obtain necessary medical care for a child and the child dies as a result, at least some courts have allowed the parent to be *prosecuted* for manslaughter. This has been true even where the parent acted in good faith pursuant to religious beliefs.

> **Example:** D is a member of the Church of Christ, Scientist. D's child, C, becomes ill. D treats C with prayer rather than medical care, consistent with the tenets of D's religion. C dies and D is charged with involuntary manslaughter. D moves to dismiss, contending that her conduct was constitutionally protected.
>
> *Held*, the prosecution of D does not violate federal constitutional law. The First Amendment protects the "free exercise" of religion, but religiously motivated conduct is subject to regulation for the protection of society. The state's interest must be balanced against the severity of the religious imposition. The state has a compelling interest in the lives of children. This governmental interest justified the restriction here on the practice of D's religion. *Walker v. Superior Court*, 763 P.2d 852 (Cal.1988).

3. **Political asylum:** Just as the rights of parent and child may conflict with each other when medical treatment is at stake, so these interests may conflict when parent and child disagree about **what country to live in**. In the most extreme situation, the parents may want to live in the U.S. and the child wants to live abroad, or vice versa. In the leading case on the subject (set forth in the following example), the court held that if the minor child seeks *political asylum* in the U.S. over his parent(s)' objection, **both** the parent(s) and the child have a due process interest in receiving a hearing, at which each party's interest must be considered.

> **Example:** When C is 12 years old, he, his two siblings and his parents emigrate from the U.S.S.R. to Chicago. After a few months, the parents decide that they want to return to the Soviet Union. C, who does not want to go with them, leaves home. He is made a ward of the state. Then, without notice to or the presence of his parents, C applies for and receives political asylum, becoming a permanent resident alien. C's parents sue for a finding that the grant of asylum to C over their objection and without notice to them violated both their procedural and substantive due process rights. (By the time the case is finally heard on appeal, the parents have already returned to the Soviet Union.)
>
> *Held*, asylum was improperly granted. The parents had a strong constitutional interest in maintaining their parental rights over C, and it was a violation of procedural due process for these rights to be terminated (via the asylum hearing) without notice to or participation by the parents. However, any hearing on asylum should also

have considered C's own constitutional rights, including his political opinions about which country and system he wished to live in. The court should have balanced these two competing interests (with C's rights gaining more and more weight vis-a-vis the parents' rights as C got older). *Polovchak v. Meese*, 774 F.2d 731 (7th Cir. 1985).

F. **Zoning and the "non-nuclear family":** The government may not pass *zoning regulations* which *impair the ability of family members to reside together*, even if the family is an "extended" rather than a "nuclear" family. In *Moore v. East Cleveland*, 431 U.S. 494 (1977), the Court struck down a zoning ordinance which allowed only members of a single "family" to live together.

   1. **"Family" defined:** The ordinance's definition of "family" prevented the plaintiff from living with her two grandsons, who were first cousins. She would have been permitted to live with two grandsons had they been brothers rather than cousins.

   2. **Extended family protected:** A four-Justice plurality opinion concluded that the right of members of even a non-nuclear family to live together was a *liberty interest*, and that state impairment of that interest must be examined carefully. Although the state interests advanced in support of the ordinance were legitimate (e.g., preventing overcrowding, traffic congestion and burdens of the local school system), those interests were only marginally advanced by the ordinance.

III. INTRA-FAMILY IMMUNITIES IN TORT ACTIONS

A. **Definition of immunity:** An immunity is a defense to tort liability that is given to an entire *class* of persons based on their relationship with the prospective plaintiff, such as husband and wife. The common law created a number of virtually complete immunities, but all of these are beginning to break down at least to some extent, either by statutory reform or judicial overruling.

   1. **Privilege contrasted:** Where immunity is conferred the tort is not eliminated, but the liability for the otherwise tortious conduct is avoided if the tort occurs within the limits of the immunity. By contrast, a privilege *eliminates* the existence of the tort itself because the circumstances make it reasonable not to impose liability. For example, a parent has a privilege to discipline his child.

B. **Family immunity:** The common law recognized two immunities from suit growing out of family relationship: that between *spouses,* and that between *parent and child.*

   1. **Husband and wife:** At common law, the husband and wife were considered as one person. Because of this "legal identity" it was considered

illogical to allow the husband to bring a tort suit against his wife, or vice versa. Married Women's Acts, passed in the late nineteenth century, giving women property rights and legal identity, were held to allow at least suits between husband and wife regarding ***property interests.***

a. **Personal injury suits:** Inter-spousal immunity continued after Married Women's Acts with respect to suits for personal injury. This meant that a wife who was injured while a passenger in a car driven negligently by her husband could not sue him, nor could a battered wife recover for her abuse.

b. **Majority rule:** But two-thirds of the states have now completely ***abolished*** the inter-spousal immunity, even for personal injury suits. Clark, p. 372. In doing so, courts have rejected a number of arguments for continuing the immunity.

c. **Reasons for rejecting:** The Supreme Court of Washington, in *Freehe v. Freehe,* 500 P.2d 771 (Wash. 1972), rejected all the traditional reasons for the immunity, including the following:

   i. **Immunity of husband and wife:** First, the oneness of husband and wife clearly no longer exists under modern law.

   ii. **Peace and tranquility:** Second, it is not true that permitting suits between husband and wife would destroy the "peace and tranquility" of the home. "If a state of peace and tranquility exists between the spouses, then the situation is such that either no action will be commenced or that the spouses — who are, after all, the best guardians of their own peace and tranquility — will allow the action to continue only so long as their personal harmony is not jeopardized. If peace and tranquility is nonexistent or tenuous to being with, then the law's imposition of a technical disability seems more likely to be a bone of contention than a harmonizing factor."

   iii. **Flood of litigation:** A fear that abrogating the immunity would lead to a flood of litigation, involving trivial matrimonial disputes, has not materialized in other states that have abolished the immunity.

   iv. **Collusion:** It is true that there is some risk of ***collusion and fraud*** between the spouses, since the defendant spouse may carry liability insurance, and may intentionally put forward a weak defense so that the plaintiff can collect the insurance. But the solution for this is to make sure that the courts "ferret out the meritorious from the fraudulent in particular cases," not to bar all inter-spousal cases because of the possibility of fraud in some.

d. Partial abolition: In those states that have not completely abolished the immunity, a number of *limitations* on it are commonly applied. Clark, pp. 373-74.

   i. Termination of marriage: If the marriage has been *terminated* before suit, the immunity will usually not apply. This is true not only where there has been a divorce, but also where one spouse has died. For instance, the estate of a deceased spouse might sue the surviving spouse in a wrongful death action.

   ii. Tort before marriage: Similarly, if the tort occurred *before* the parties were married, some courts do not apply the immunity.

   iii. Intentional personal injury: If the personal injury derives from an intentional tort, such as assault or battery, some courts do not allow the immunity.

   iv. Automobile suits: A number of states have abolished the immunity, as to automobile accident suits. As a result, a "family exclusion clause" has been placed in some liability insurance policies providing that coverage does not apply to members of the same family living with the insured. However, one court has held that clause void as contrary to public policy. *Mutual of Enumclaw Ins. Co. v. Wiscomb*, 622 P.2d 1234 (Wash. 1980), adhered to on reconsideration 643 P.2d 441 (Wash. 1982).

e. Vicarious liability: Almost all states that have not abolished the immunity nonetheless permit a husband or wife to sue one who is *vicariously liable* for the other spouse's torts, even if the spouse himself could not be sued. Thus if a husband and wife work for the same employer, and the husband negligently injures the wife in a car crash while they are on a joint business trip, the wife may sue the employer under the doctrine of *respondeat superior* even though the inter-spousal immunity might bar her from suing her husband directly.

f. Minority view: Although the trend of decisions and legislation is to abolish or limit spousal immunity, trends do not bind courts. Each case must be examined with analysis of the principles underlying the immunity or the principles of *stare decisis.*

Example: One court noted that inter-spousal immunity is a judicial doctrine established to protect the family unit. Bringing "the full trappings of an adversary tort system into a family dispute" would be detrimental to the family and its resources. Although an intentional tort by one spouse against the other clearly shows marital disharmony, litigation would not be conducive to a reconciliaton. However, in a dissolution proceeding the trial judge may direct the offending spouse to pay necessary medical expenses and consider any permanent injury, disfigurement or loss of earning capacity caused by the intentional tort in setting alimony. *Hill v. Hill,* 415 So.2d 20 (Fla. 1982).

2. **Parent and child:** In the United States a common-law immunity also developed to bar suit by a ***child against his parents*** or vice versa. Except for the "oneness" of husband and wife, the same justifications for inter-spousal immunity were usually given to support the parent-child immunity.

    a. **Trend to abolish:** Most states have now ***abolished*** this immunity, like the spousal immunity, at least in automobile accident suits. One factor frequently stressed is that nearly everyone has liability insurance, and such suits usually are not between members of the family, but between the family and the insurance company. For instance, in *Gelbman v. Gelbman,* 245 N.E.2d 192 (N.Y. 1969), the court noted that in New York, there is compulsory motor vehicle liability insurance, so a suit whose real purpose is to recover against this insurance will not threaten family harmony.

    b. **Exceptions:** As in the case of inter-spousal immunity, a number of states that have not completely abolished the doctrine have developed exceptions to it. Frequent exceptions include the following:

        i.   **Emancipation:** If the child has been legally emancipated (*i.e.,* of legal age or where other circumstances indicate that the parent has renounced his right to the child's earnings);

        ii. *In loco parentis:* Where the defendant is a ***step-parent or guardian;***

        iii. **Relationship terminated by** *death:* Where the parent-child relationship has been terminated by the death of one or the other prior to the suit;

        iv. **Wrongful death of other spouse:** Where the plaintiff-child is suing his parent for the wrongful death of the other parent;

        v.   **Intentional or wilful:** Where the tort is ***intentional,*** or in some cases "wilful;"

        vi. **Property rights or pecuniary loss:** Where the action is for something other than personal injury, such as property torts or money loss.

        vii. **Business activity:** Where the injury occurred during the course of ***business activity*** by the defendant. See generally, Clark, pp. 375-80.

    c. **Intrafamily Offense Acts:** Statutes have been enacted in 37 states which provide civil and criminal remedies to victims of domestic violence. Intrafamily offenses may include: **threats of** physical harm, assault and battery, burglary, sexual abuse, false imprisonment, kidnapping, child stealing, and damage to property. Civil remedies may include: money damages, moving expenses, medical expenses, and restitution. Clark, p. 372.

3. **Siblings:** There is normally no immunity between ***brothers and sisters.*** *Emery v. Emery*, 289 P.2d 218 (Cal. 1955).

IV. CONTRACTS OF MINORS

A. **Capacity:** A minor may enter into a contract, but may disaffirm the contract before attaining the age of majority or within a reasonable period thereafter. The age of majority is a matter of statute, usually 18.

1. **Choices of minor:** The contract of a minor is said to be ***"voidable."***

   a. **Avoidance:** The minor may avoid the legal relations created by the contract by a manifestation of election to do so;

   b. **Ratification:** When the minor ***reaches adulthood*** he may ratify the contract and thereby extinguish the power of avoidance. Rest. 2d, Contracts §13.

2. **Effect of rescission:** If a minor disaffirms a contract and sues for restitution of the money or goods he gave, the minor must restore any consideration which he received, if he still has it. The burden of proof is on the minor to show that he squandered or otherwise disposed of the consideration he received, that it cannot be returned. *Whitman v. Allen*, 121 A. 160 (Me. 1923).

   a. **Quasi-contract:** Although a contract of a minor may be voidable, he may still be liable in quasi-contract to prevent unjust enrichment, for the ***reasonable value*** (as distinguished from the contract price) of the goods or services furnished to him.

3. **Unavoidable transactions:** There are certain exceptions in which liability is imposed on the minor for his contractual obligations. A minor is bound by and cannot disaffirm obligations imposed by law. These include:

   a. **Taxes:** Funds expended for sales taxes, for certificate of title to a motor vehicle, for transfer of license plates;

   b. **Penalties:** A recognizance in a felony case;

   c. **Bank regulations:** Rules and regulations of a bank with regard to a minor's funds are as binding on a minor as if he were of legal age;

   d. **Military:** Contracts of enlistment in the military service by an infant are valid;

e. **Necessaries:** Goods reasonably needed for subsistence, health, comfort or education are necessaries. Contracts furnishing these to the minor, his spouse or his children cannot be disaffirmed.

> **Example:** H and W marry and purchase a home. To finance the purchase H lies to L about his age. L loans H the money, and H gives L a note and a mortgage on the house. H and W separate and H sues L to recover payments made on the mortgage. L counterclaims to foreclose on the mortgage.
>
> *Held*, H may not recover the money paid. Under certain circumstances, age, maturity, fraud, estoppel, lack of restitution, emancipation and necessity will combine to preclude a minor from disaffirming a contract. Emancipation does not, by itself, operate to make an minor *sui juris*. It is, however, of practical importance in deciding questions under the law of necessaries. Here, the combination of facts is such that H should be held to the performance of the contract signed while a minor. *Merrick v. Stephens*, 337 S.W.2d 713 (Mo.App. 1960).

f. **Consent by guardian:** A statute may allow a child's guardian to contract for her when the child is a professional model or performer. These agreements may not be disaffirmed when the child reaches majority. Thus a child model could not prevent *future use* of photographs taken of her when she reached majority. *Shields v. Gross*, 448 N.E.2d 108 (N.Y. 1983).

V. TORTS OF MINORS

A. **Children:** In determining tort liability there is a special standard applicable only to children, not all "minors." That test is generally for children of "tender years," and it has "seldom been applied to anyone over the age of sixteen." Rest. 2d, Torts §283A, Comment a.

1. **Subjective test:** The test for *children* is primarily subjective, dealing with the capacity of a particular child to recognize and avoid risk and harm, taking into consideration this child's *age, intelligence* and *experience.* This test recognizes that children develop at different rates even in the same age group, and acquire capacity individually, and not in conformity to any presupposed pattern. *Kuhns v. Brugger*, 135 A.2d 395 (Pa. 1957).

2. **Fixed chronological test discarded:** Many older cases applied an irrebuttable presumption that a child under age seven could not be negligent, a rebuttable presumption that one between seven and fourteen was not negligent, and a rebuttable presumption that a child between fourteen and twenty-one was capable of negligence.

Example: A boy six years and eight months was found not to be contributorily negligent as a matter of law when he ran in front of a car. *Tyler v. Weed*, 280 N.W. 827 (Mich.1938).

   a. Discarded: Modern courts have nearly all **discarded** this arbitrary 7/14/21 system. For instance, *Tyler, supra,* was overruled in *Baker v. Alt*, 132 N.W.2d 614 (Mich.1965).

3. **Adult activity:** When children engage in activities normally pursued only by adults, such as driving a car or flying an airplane, they are held to the same standard as adults. Courts reason that if minors are acting in an adult world, they should be held to adult standards of care. In addition, the policy is to relieve adults of the continuing responsibility of determining whether the individual in such cases is a child or an adult. *Daniels v. Evans,* 224 A.2d 63 (N.H. 1966).

4. **Minor as employer:** If a minor employs other persons, he will be liable for the torts of his employees under the theory of **respondeat superior**, if an employee's act or omission is within the scope of the employment and in furtherance of the minor's (employer's) business.

VI. SPECIAL RULES GOVERNING MINORS

A. Disabilities: There are legal restrictions placed on the activities of minors besides those involving contracts and torts. The following summary shows the limitations on various activities in which a minor might engage.

1. **Property:** A minor may own property, real or personal. If a minor holds title to property, creditors of other family members, such as parents, cannot reach the minor's property.

   Example: F's three minor daughters receive sheep as a gift. The sheep are raised on F's farm where the daughters live. D, a creditor of F, obtains a judgment against F. The sheep are taken by the sheriff and sold in partial satisfaction of D's judgment. The children sue D for conversion. *Held*, for the children. The general rule is that property acquired by a child belongs to the child and not to her parent. D, as F's creditor, cannot have greater rights in the sheep than F. The sheep are owned by the children, who are entitled to a judgment for conversion. *Kreigh v. Cogswell*, 21 P.2d 831 (Wyo. 1933).

   a. Disaffirmance: Any **executory contract** one party to which is a minor may be **disaffirmed** by the minor. To assure third parties that their dealings with the minor on property will not later be disaffirmed (and to manage the minor's property in an orderly, legal fashion), a custodian or **guardian** may be appointed.

2. **Making a will:** Testamentary capacity is governed strictly by state statutes. Usually the age of capacity to make a will is eighteen.

3. **Agency:** Any person may act as an *agent* so long as he is able to perform the task of the agency. The fact that the agent may not have sufficient capacity to perform the act for himself is not controlling because the agent does not act for himself, but for his principal.

   a. **Acting as principal:** A minor is competent to be a *principal* although he has the power to disaffirm contractual obligations. *Goldfinger v. Doherty,* 276 N.Y.S. 289 (1934).

   b. **Partnerships:** Any natural person who has the capacity to contract has capacity to become a partner in a partnership. If a minor is a partner, the minor may disaffirm only contracts which are personal to him; he may not disaffirm partnership contracts.

3. **Employment:** Employment of minors is governed by the Fair Labor Standards Act, 29 U.S.C. §201 *et seq.* and state statutes. These laws set the minimum age and other conditions under which minors may be employed.

4. **Court actions:** A minor must be represented by a guardian if he is suing or being sued.

VII. RIGHTS OF JUVENILES IN CRIMINAL LAW

A. **Background:** Traditionally, it has been said of juvenile court proceedings that they are neither adversary in nature, nor are they criminal trials. The concept which underlies traditional juvenile court and delinquency law is that there is a need to *protect* and *rehabilitate* a wayward youth. Such a youth is not a defendant who is on trial for a crime for which he will be punished if he is found guilty. The court is seen as acting in the role of benevolent, understanding parents.

1. **Application:** Consistent with these ideas, an objective of juvenile procedures has been to "hide youthful errors from the full gaze of the public and bury them in the graveyard of the forgotten past." For this reason statutes have provided that findings against a child are not a "crime," to help protect the child's future.

2. **Common law:** The following presumptions were applied under the common law with respect to criminal responsibility.

   a. **Under age 7:** A child under seven years of age was *conclusively presumed* to be incapable of committing a crime.

   b. **Age 7-14:** One between the ages of seven and fourteen was *presumed* incompetent. The state had the burden of overcoming that presumption.

   c. **Over 14:** A youth over fourteen was *presumed capable* of committing a crime, but the defendant could overcome that presumption by showing either mental or physical incapacity.

Note: The common law presumptions extend only insofar as chronological age is concerned. Mental age or evidence of mental incompetency is generally admissible to prove that the accused did not have the required intent to commit the crime with which he is charged.

3. **Criminal responsibility:** A child is not criminally responsible for his acts or omissions unless he is old enough and has sufficient intelligence to be capable of having a *criminal intent* as to such acts or omissions. The test is whether the child understands the nature of the act and whether it is right or wrong.

4. **Jurisdiction of juvenile courts:** All states have statutes creating juvenile courts which may dispossess criminal courts of jurisdiction over persons up to 16 or 18 years of age. Model Penal Code §4.10.

   a. **English system:** About half of the states extend the old English Chancery jurisdiction to the juvenile courts, thus enabling the state to assume the protection of neglected children. Such statutes have for their purpose the *supervision and rehabilitation* of minors, and not their punishment. They are constitutional under the police power of the state.

   b. **Concurrent jurisdiction:** The jurisdiction of juvenile and criminal courts is concurrent in many states. In those states the juvenile court must waive jurisdiction before the juvenile can be tried as an adult in a criminal court.

      i. **Judge determines jurisdiction:** As to any given defendant, where concurrent jurisdiction exists, the juvenile court judge determines in his discretion, usually based upon statutory guidelines, whether to waive the jurisdiction of the juvenile court and have the juvenile tried as an adult.

      ii. **Waiver:** Before a juvenile is tried as an adult he is entitled to a hearing, including access by his counsel to the social records and probation reports which, presumably, are considered by the court, and to a statement of the reasons for the juvenile court's decision. *Kent v. United States*, 383 U.S. 541 (1966).

   c. **Restricted jurisdiction:** Some states give jurisdiction to criminal courts instead of juvenile courts in the case of all felonies or certain named felonies.

B. **Constitutional rights:** In practice, with respect to the same conduct, an individual may be subject either to the jurisdiction of a juvenile court or the adult criminal court. As a result, from the inception of the juvenile court system, wide differences have been tolerated, if not insisted upon, between procedural rights which are accorded to adults and those which are accorded to juveniles.

1. **State authority limited:** The leading case in the field of juvenile justice is ***In re Gault,*** 387 U.S. 1 (1967). In *Gault* the Supreme Court considered the claim by the juvenile that he had been deprived of basic constitutional rights in proceedings where a determination was made that he, a juvenile, was a "delinquent," as a result of his alleged lewd or indecent telephone call to a neighbor for which he was committed to a state institution until age 21. The Court held that ***at least four Bill of Rights safeguards apply*** to protect a juvenile on a charge under which he can be imprisoned for a term of years:

   a. **Notice:** ***Timely notice*** must be given sufficiently in advance of the hearings, of the specific issues to be heard, as required by the Sixth Amendment.

   b. **Counsel:** The child and his parent must be notified of the child's right to be ***represented by counsel*** retained by them, or if they are unable to afford counsel, that counsel will be ***appointed*** to represent the child, as required by the Sixth Amendment.

   c. **Self-incrimination:** The constitutional privilege against ***self-incrimination*** is applicable in the case of juveniles, as it is with respect to adults, as required by the Fifth Amendment.

   d. **Cross-examination:** The right to ***confrontation*** and ***cross-examination*** of witnesses against the juvenile must be afforded, as required by the Sixth Amendment.

   Note: Even though the Court imposed certain criminal procedural safeguards on juvenile proceedings in *Gault,* it made it clear that those proceedings were not being equated with criminal proceedings. The Court refused to repudiate the basic rehabilitative theories of juvenile law, and made it clear that the juvenile delinquent is not a convicted criminal.

2. **Standard of proof:** The Due Process Clause of the Fourteenth Amendment requires ***proof beyond a reasonable doubt*** in state criminal cases. This standard applies to the adjudicatory stage of a juvenile court delinquency proceeding in which a youth is charged with an act that would be a crime if committed by an adult. *Matter of Winship,* 397 U.S. 358 (1970).

3. **Double jeopardy:** Where a person is tried for an offense as a juvenile and found guilty of violating a criminal statute, the ***Double Jeopardy*** Clause of the Fifth Amendment, as made applicable to the states through incorporation into the Due Process Clause of the Fourteenth Amendment, bars a subsequent trial of the juvenile as an adult for the same offense. Even though the defendant never risked more than one punishment, he was twice put in jeopardy, which is unconstitutional. *Breed v. Jones,* 421 U.S. 519 (1975).

4. **Death penalty:** The Court has held that the death penalty may be imposed for a crime committed when the defendant was 16. So long as some consideration is given to the fact that the defendant was a minor, there is no violation of the Eighth Amendment's prohibition of cruel and unusual punishment. *Stanford v. Kentucky*, 492 U.S. 361 (1989).

5. **Other rights:** The Supreme Court has not ruled that all rights constitutionally assured to an adult accused are applicable to juvenile proceedings. Thus, a trial by jury is not constitutionally required in the adjudicative phase of a state juvenile court delinquency proceeding. *McKeiver v. Pennsylvania,* 403 U.S. 528 (1971).

DIVORCE: JURISDICTION AND GROUNDS

I. INTRODUCTION

A. Nature of divorce: Divorce procedures in the United States are a curious blending of English law, equity law, and statutory law. All are subject to an overlay of federal constitutional law.

1. **Divorce and separation distinguished:** A divorce *dissolves* the marriage relationship, usually as of the date of the divorce decree. A legal separation is a *partial suspension* of the marriage relationship. Older cases refer to this as a "divorce from bed and board."

B. Jurisdiction: All petitions for divorce are handled by **state courts.** Federal courts have no jurisdiction to grant divorces. A state has jurisdiction to grant a divorce where at least one spouse is domiciled in that state, and a minimum residency requirement is met.

1. **Interstate recognition:** Article IV, Section 1 of the United States Constitution provides: "Full faith and credit shall be given in each state to the public acts, records, and judicial proceedings of every other state."

    a. **Effect of Clause:** The Full Faith and Credit Clause requires all states to recognize divorce decrees of the forum state where the state had jurisdiction on the basis of **bona fide domicile** and the decree was otherwise valid, that is, free from extrinsic fraud.

    Note: There are situations where a divorce decree may not be challenged because of estoppel or *res judicata*. These must be differentiated from situations where the decree may be attacked collaterally. These cases are analyzed in the sections which follow (*infra,* pp. 89-90).

2. **Effective date of divorce:** The procedures for divorce are determined by the applicable state statute. In some states the divorce decree is final when issued. In other states an *interlocutory decree* is issued which does not immediately dissolve the marriage; the parties must wait a specified period. At the end of that period the divorce becomes final at the request of either party. Still other states prohibit remarriage for a certain period of time after the divorce is granted.

3. **Grounds:** Traditionally, legislatures and courts attributed the failure of a marriage to the *fault* of one or both spouses. Consequently, there were only fault-oriented grounds for divorce.

    a. **No-fault divorce:** Today, all states grant **"no-fault"** divorces, in at least some situations. However, most courts continue to have at least some fault-oriented grounds for divorce. Furthermore, even when the parties seek a no-fault divorce, fault or misconduct of one spouse may be relevant to issues of custody, support and property division. No-fault divorce law is discussed further *infra*, p. 98.

II. JURISDICTION

A. **Generally:** The basic fact pattern in a divorce involves a situation in which both parties are domiciled in the jurisdiction where the divorce action is instituted, both are before the court at the time of the hearing with personal service having been made upon the defendant, and with the court having jurisdiction over the issue of the marriage.

1. **Jurisdictional issues:** Over the years questions have arisen as to the extent to which this fact pattern can be altered and the contacts with the forum state "watered down", and still assume that the divorce decree and/or custody decree will receive the protection of the Full Faith and Credit Clause.

   Note: Jurisdiction in child custody and support cases is considered separately. See pp. 131-134 and 145-146, *infra*.

B. **General Principles:** A divorce action seeks to terminate the marital status of the parties. The marital status is the *"res"* or thing which "exists," and serves as a basis of jurisdiction in the state of the domicile of either party.

1. **Jurisdiction present:** A state in which *either* spouse is *domiciled* has jurisdiction through its courts to terminate the marriage by granting a divorce decree.

2. **Significance of personal jurisdiction:** A valid divorce decree, terminating the marital relationship, may be obtained *without personal jurisdiction* over the defendant spouse. However, if the court is to settle *property rights* and *support* issues, in addition to pronouncing the parties divorced, then personal jurisdiction over both spouses *is* necessary.

   a. **Mere presence sufficient for service:** By the way, where personal jurisdiction over a spouse is needed (because the court will be addressing property or support issues), that jurisdiction may be based even upon the defendant's *transient presence* in the forum state at the moment of service. Thus in *Burnham v. Superior Court of California*, 495 U.S. 604 (1990), W served H with a petition for divorce while H was briefly visiting California. The Supreme Court held that H's temporary presence in California at the moment of service was enough to give the California courts personal jurisdiction over H, so that all issues relating to the divorce could be heard in California.

b. **Minimum contacts:** Where property division or support issues are to be heard, the requirement that there be personal jurisdiction over both spouses means that each spouse must have *minimum contacts* with the forum state.

    i. **Child in state:** The fact that a *child* of the marriage is living together with one spouse in the forum state is *not* enough to automatically give the other spouse minimum contacts with the forum state. See *Kulko v. Superior Court*, discussed *infra*, p. 146.

3. **State where neither spouse is domiciled:** A state in which *neither* spouse is domiciled has *no jurisdiction to terminate the marriage,* even though both parties are before the court and consent to the decree.

    Example: H and W are domiciled in State A. While they are on a trip to State B, W files for divorce, and personal service is made on H. H moves to dismiss the suit in B on the ground that the court has no jurisdiction over the action. H's motion is sustained since the marital status of H and W constitutes a relationship in which A, their domicile, has an interest. Without that interest as a *res* before it, the court in B has no jurisdiction to terminate the relationship.

4. **Restatement view:** In Rest. 2d, Conflict of Laws, §§70-72, the following rules are given with respect to jurisdiction to grant a divorce:

    a. "A state has power to exercise judicial jurisdiction to dissolve the marriage of spouses, *both* of whom are domiciled in the state."

    b. "A state has power to exercise judicial jurisdiction to dissolve the marriage of spouses, *one of whom* is domiciled in the state."

    c. "A state may not exercise judicial jurisdiction to dissolve the marriage of spouses if *neither spouse* is domiciled in the state and neither has such other relationship to the state as would make it reasonable for the state to dissolve the marriage." (Emphasis added)

5. **Divisible divorce:** Because personal jurisdiction is required to settle property rights, but not to dissolve the marriage itself, the concept of a *divisible divorce* was developed. Under this concept a valid *ex parte* divorce dissolves the marriage, but may not affect the property rights of the spouse who did not appear in the proceeding.

    Example: H and W separate in California. W moves to New York and establishes her domicile there. H obtains a divorce in Nevada. W is not served with process and does not enter an appearance in the case. W now sues H in New York for alimony. H enters a special appearance and argues that B's court should treat the divorce decree as terminating the marriage and with it his duty of support.

Held, an *ex parte* divorce in a foreign state does not destroy the alimony rights of W in the state where she resides. Where W is not subject to the jurisdiction of a state court rendering a divorce decree, that court has no power to extinguish any rights W may have for support from H. A court cannot adjudicate a personal claim or obligation unless it has jurisdiction over the **person** of the defendant. To the extent that the Nevada court purported to do so, New York was not obligated to recognize Nevada's action. Nevada had *"in rem"* jurisdiction over the marital status, not the parties. *Vanderbilt v. Vanderbilt,* 354 U.S. 416 (1955).

C. Application of general principles: A decree of divorce granted by a court having jurisdiction over the plaintiff spouse who is a **bona fide resident** (domiciliary) of the state, is entitled to full faith and credit in every other state.

1. **Determining domicile:** The court of the forum may decide for itself whether a court in another state had jurisdiction to grant a divorce. Where the divorce-granting court had no jurisdiction because the plaintiff did not establish a *bona fide* domicile in that state, there is no requirement that the decree be recognized.

   Example: H and W, husband and wife, and X, a married man, are domiciled in State A. W and X go to State B, live there six weeks, and begin actions for divorce against their respective spouses. Service of process is made in A. Neither spouse appears in B. B's court finds that W and X have established a *bona fide* residence and grants each a divorce. W and X marry, and they return to A where they are prosecuted for bigamy. In defense they argue that A must recognize B's divorce decree under the Full Faith and Credit Clause. W and X are convicted and appeal.

   Held, assuming W and X are domiciled in B, its courts have jurisdiction to grant their divorces. Other states must recognize that divorce even though B's court does not have personal jurisdiction over their spouses. This is so because a divorce action is one *in rem* and not *in personam*. Jurisdiction exists whenever one of the spouses has a *bona fide* domicile. The Court assumed for purpose of its decision that W and X had *bona fide* domiciles in B. In those circumstances B's court had jurisdiction to grant the divorce which must be recognized in other states. *Williams v. North Carolina,* 317 U.S. 287 (1942), *overruling Haddock v. Haddock,* 201 U.S. 562 (1906).

   Note: In reaching its decision the Supreme Court assumed that B had jurisdiction to grant the divorces. The issue of whether B's jurisdiction could be attacked in A when jurisdiction had not been litigated in B was not ruled upon. However, that was the issue in a subsequent case involving the same parties and the same facts (*Williams II, infra*).

Example: After the decision in *Williams I, supra,* W and X are retried for bigamy. The facts are the same, but the prosecution contends that the divorces are invalid because W and X never established a *bona fide* domicile in State B. That issue was litigated, and the jury concluded that no domicile had bee established in B. W and X are convicted of bigamy and appeal.

Held, the convictions are upheld. If W and X established a *bona fide* domicile in B, then State A must give full faith and credit to B's divorce decree. However, the issue of domicile may be litigated in A, for otherwise, A would be compelled to submit to the governing of its internal affairs by B with respect to a marital status in which A has a vital interest. A may find that W and X were not domiciled in B, and B's court had no jurisdiction over their marital status. *Williams v. North Carolina,* 325 U.S. 226 (1945) (*Williams II*).

Note: In the first *Williams* decision, the existence of the domicile of the plaintiff spouse in the divorce action was *not* questioned. Thus, assuming domicile, the Supreme Court precluded collateral attack. However, on remand, the domicile of W and X in B was successfully attacked.

2. **Residency:** A state may impose minimum residency requirements before entertaining a petition for divorce.

Example: H and W are married and live in State A. After a separation W moves to State B and files for divorce. H is served when he travels to B to visit his children. H makes a special appearance to contest jurisdiction. W's petition is dismissed because B has a one year residency requirement before filing for divorce. W appeals, contending that the residency requirement is unconstitutional.

Held, the residency requirement is valid. A divorce decree is of concern to both spouses as well as to the state. A residency requirement furthers the state's interest in avoiding intermeddling in matters in which another state has a paramount interest, and in decreasing the chance that its own divorce decrees will be subject to collateral attack. A state "may quite reasonably decide that it does not wish to become a divorce mill for unhappy spouses who have lived there as short a time as [W] had when she commenced her action." The fact that some states may establish a constitutionally permissible shorter period does not compel other states to do the same. Finally, it should be noted that the residency requirement does not deny W access to B's courts, but only delays it. *Sosna v. Iowa,* 419 U.S. 393 (1975).

3. Estoppel: One who procures a void divorce decree or who uses a void divorce decree to his or her advantage by remarrying is estopped from attacking that decree at a later time. A party will also be ***estopped*** from later attacking a divorce decree if the attack is inconsistent with the position taken at the time of the divorce, or the party upholding the divorce has relied upon the decree.

> **Example:** H1 and W live in State A. H1 becomes totally and permanently disabled. W procures a "paper Mexican divorce" through a Mexican court. She makes no appearance in Mexico and no service of process is made on H1. W then marries H2. Upon H1's death, W claims part of the estate as H1's widow.
>
> *Held*, W's claim is denied. The Mexican divorce is void, so H1 and W were still husband and wife at H1's death. Because of that fact W's marriage to H2 is bigamous. However, since W procured the Mexican divorce and remarried, W is estopped to claim later that the divorce was valid for one purpose and invalid for another. *Rediker v. Rediker,* 221 P.2d 1 (Cal. 1950).

> **Example:** In a Mexican divorce proceeding W appears personally and H appears by an attorney. The divorce decree awards custody of their child, C, to H. Subsequently, W petitions for divorce from H in the Virgin Is., and seeks custody of C. W contends that the Mexican divorce is invalid because neither W nor H was domiciled in Mexico at the time of the divorce.
>
> *Held*, W's petition is dismissed. W may not collaterally attack the validity of the Mexican divorce since she is the spouse who sought and obtained the divorce. W obtained the divorce by representing to the Mexican court that she resided in Mexico. Under these circumstances W is ***estopped*** to deny later that the Mexican divorce is invalid. That court had jurisdiction to award custody of C when it dissolved the marriage, so no marriage remains to give this court jurisdiction over the custody proceeding. *Perrin v. Perrin,* 408 F.2d 107 (3d Cir. 1969).

4. *Res judicata:* A spouse who has the opportunity to contest the jurisdiction of the court when suit for divorce is filed and does not do so, may not later collaterally attack the jurisdiction of the first court.

> **Example:** H and W have their matrimonial domicile in State A. W goes to State B, and after the requisite period to establish residence, files for divorce. H enters a general appearance and contests the divorce. H has an opportunity to raise the question of W's domicile, but he does not do so. A divorce is entered in W's favor. Later in A, H serves W and attacks the decree on the ground that W was not domiciled in B at the time of the divorce.
>
> *Held* H's petition should be dismissed. When H entered a general appearance in B, the question of W's domicile was a proper issue to

be raised. Although it was not raised and litigated, it became *res judicata* when the decree was issued. Under the Full Faith and Credit Clause a state must recognize the decree of another state where all the issues of the case are contested and decided or where there was *full opportunity* to do so. *Sherrer v. Sherrer,* 334 U.S. 343 (1948); *Coe v. Coe,* 334 U.S. 378 (1948).

Note: The state of domicile has a vital interest in the marital status of the couple seeking a divorce in another state. However, the interests or *justified expectations* of the couple who obtain a divorce in another state are considered more important, and may be a reason for the *Sherrer* decision.

D. Limiting the requirement of domicile: Rules have developed, both by court decision and statute, under which the requirement of domicile has been weakened.

1. **"Limited" divorce:** The jurisdictional rules pertaining to divorce do not always apply to "divorce from bed and board." A state has jurisdiction to grant such a divorce if the parties are before the court, even though neither party is domiciled in the state. Such a "divorce" does not terminate the marital status of the parties; it only terminates their personal rights and obligations to one another, and allows them to live apart.

   Example: H and W are domiciled in State A. W sues H in State B seeking a decree permitting her to live separate and apart from H, but not an absolute divorce decree. Service of process is made on H personally in B. H's defense that neither party is domiciled in B is not valid.

   Note: Local statutes, however, often require the plaintiff to be domiciled in the state to maintain such an action.

2. **Servicemen:** Many states have passed statutes for the benefit of servicemen and women which permit a local divorce based upon their having been stationed in the state for a significant period of time, such as six or twelve months, even though they are legally domiciled elsewhere. Although those statutes do not take domicile into account, they have been held valid since more than "presence" is required. *Wood v. Wood,* 320 S.W.2d 807 (Tex. 1959); *Wallace v. Wallace,* 320 P.2d 1020 (N.M. 1958).

   Note: For servicemen and servicewomen in many cases "domicile" is not relevant due to the transient nature of their vocation. Therefore, these statutes do not change the domicile of servicemen, but constitute an exception to the normal jurisdictional requirements.

3. **Foreign country:** In some circumstances the rule concerning domicile of either spouse is further limited. The most important limitation con-

cerns divorces in Mexico or another foreign country. They comprise a "watering down" of requirements for out-of-state divorce jurisdiction.

Example: One type of Mexican divorce is a "paper divorce" in which *neither* spouse makes an appearance in Mexico. This type of divorce will not be recognized in the United States.

Example: A second situation is one where *one spouse* makes an appearance in Mexico without being domiciled there. This type of divorce will generally not be recognized.

Example: Another situation occurs where one or both spouses actually live in Mexico for a short period of time. If the time period is long enough to obtain a Mexican domicile, the divorce will be held valid in the United States. Clark, pp. 431-33.

a. **Legal precedents:** The law concerning the validity of Mexican divorces is scanty, and even if one finds a case, it is not clear that the holding will be followed in other jurisdictions.

Example: H and W, who reside in State A, obtain a Mexican divorce. Mexican jurisdiction is based on the plaintiff's having met the Mexican formalities of establishing residence by a one-day presence and on the defendant's filing of a pleading along with an appearance by his Mexican attorney. The divorce was recognized because H established residence and W was represented by counsel, thus giving the Mexican court jurisdiction over the marital *res.* The court reasoned that to disallow such divorces where jurisdictional requirements were met would be inconsistent with the recognition of divorces obtained in other states on similar grounds. *Rosensteil v. Rosensteil,* 209 N.E.2d 709 (N.Y. 1965).

Note: Since a state is not required to recognize a divorce obtained in a foreign country, the Full Faith and Credit Clause does not apply, and a state may ignore such a divorce in order to follow its own policies. The holding in *Rosensteil* has received much criticism, and it appears that many jurisdictions would not follow it. See Clark, pp. 432-33.

III. FAULT-ORIENTED GROUNDS FOR DIVORCE

A. **Statutes:** Due to the interest of a state in the marital status of its residents, all state legislatures have passed laws governing the grounds on which a divorce will be granted.

1. **Divorce complaint:** If the action which forms the basis of the complaint for the divorce *does not* constitute a ground under the divorce statute of that jurisdiction, the divorce will not be granted. This is so because divorce is controlled strictly by statute.

2. **Specific grounds for divorce:** A divorce will be granted for reasons which are enumerated separately in the statutes of each jurisdiction. Typically, they include the following:

    a. *Adultery;*

        i. **Circumstantial evidence:** *Circumstantial evidence* is sufficient to prove adultery. For instance, P can establish adultery by showing that D and X had a *mutual affection*, coupled with an *opportunity* to commit adultery.

            Example: In a divorce proceeding H contends that W committed adultery. A private investigator testifies that a man visited W at her home on a number of occasions from early evening to 1:00 or 2:00 a.m. Sometimes they went out, and W had her arm around the man. In addition, a calendar date book kept by W contains statements which appear to be admissions of adultery. *Held*, these facts collectively establish adultery. Therefore, H is not required to pay alimony. *Leonard v. Leonard*, 259 So.2d 529 (Fla.Dist.Ct.App.1972).

    b. *Habitual drunkenness;*

    c. *Non-support;*

    d. *Insanity;*

    e. *Criminal conviction;*

    f. *Drug addiction;* and

    g. *Desertion* or *abandonment*.

        i. **Definition:** Desertion or abandonment is the voluntary separation of one spouse from the other with *intent to desert*. The desertion must continue for the statutory period, frequently one year.

        ii. **Older statutes:** Some statutes provided that the husband may choose and fix a reasonable domicile for his wife. If the wife refused to follow the husband and cohabit with him, her conduct would constitute desertion. *Toth v. Toth*, 178 A.2d 542 (Conn.Supp. 1962).

        iii. **Present statutes:** These older statutes have been held unconstitutional by more recent decisions. They discriminate against women on the sole basis of gender by arbitrarily forcing them to follow husbands wherever they choose to live, in violation of the Equal Protection Clause. *Crosby v. Crosby*, 434 So.2d 162 (La. 1983).

        iv. **Constructive desertion:** This doctrine developed by court decisions. Under it the *conduct* which caused the spouse to leave is deemed to be desertion. Thus constructive desertion is both a *defense* to an allegation of desertion and a *ground for divorce* by the spouse who leaves.

v. **Conduct:** Any acts which make continued cohabitation impossible with safety, health or self-respect, are sufficient. The conduct need not be by itself a specified ground for divorce.

Example: H and W are husband and wife. W becomes intoxicated frequently, quarrels with H and insults H in public and private by calling him a homosexual. H brings an action for divorce for desertion.

Held, H is granted a divorce. A pattern of behavior which is persistent and intolerable to the other party of the marriage will warrant a finding of constructive desertion. Here, W's persistent behavior is detrimental to H's health, and her accusations are so demeaning that they amount to constructive desertion. *Liccini v. Liccini,* 258 A.2d 198 (Md. 1969).

3. **General grounds for divorce:** In addition to the specific grounds outlined *supra,* many statutes contain more general grounds such as *physical cruelty, mental cruelty* or *gross neglect.* Some court decisions use only the word "cruelty" without distinguishing between physical cruelty and mental cruelty.

a. **Development of cruelty grounds:** Originally, physical cruelty involved some danger to life, limb or health. As divorce laws became more liberal, *mental cruelty* became the more common ground used to obtain a divorce.

Example: W seeks a separation on the ground of cruelty. W's credible testimony is that H is habitually intemperate, threatens her and forces her to leave the family home. They separate for a year, and W returns only after H promises to correct his behavior. After one month H resumes his abusive treatment of W, including cursing, denying that he loves W, and making physical threats. W leaves the house and files this action for divorce. *Held,* H's conduct constitutes mental cruelty sufficient to render continued cohabitation insupportable. *Hughes v. Hughes,* 326 So.2d 877 (La.Ct.App. 1976).

i. **Must be more than one episode:** Courts generally hold that for physical or mental cruelty to constitute grounds, there must be more than one episode, unless the incident was particularly shocking or dangerous. Areen, p. 323.

b. **Criteria for cruelty:** What constitutes cruelty differs from jurisdiction to jurisdiction, and depends on whether the action is contested or uncontested. The criteria include:

   i. Acts and conduct of the defendant;

  ii. Motivation of the defendant; and

 iii. Effect of the acts and conduct on the plaintiff.

> **Example:** W seeks a divorce from H on the ground of **extreme cruelty.** H is addicted to heroin and refuses all aid in overcoming the habit. As a result there has been an attrition of H's sexual power and he refuses to have intercourse with W.
>
> *Held,* W is entitled to a divorce. "Rejection of sex, however it may be accomplished, can turn marriage from a benediction and a fulfillment into a nightmare of frustration, despair and decay. That has been plaintiff's tormented experience....The touchstone of extreme cruelty is its impact upon the victim." In this case the denial of sexual relations was more than transitory, and W has shown its detrimental effect on her physical and mental health. *Melia v. Melia,* 226 A.2d 745 (N.J.Super. 1967).

> **Example:** W is granted a default judgment for divorce on the ground of cruelty. W gave evidence that H stayed away from home, used abusive language to her, and visited another woman's apartment. Such evidence is corroborated. H moves to vacate the judgment, contending that the evidence is insufficient.
>
> *Held,* H's motion is denied. The evidence shows more than mere incompatibility, which is not sufficient for divorce under state law. H's conduct is a long, continued course of ill-treatment which resulted in injury to W's health. This is "cruelty" even though there was no actual or threatened violence. *Swenson v. Swenson,* 101 N.W.2d 914 (Minn. 1960).

> **Example:** Courts in some states have ruled that homosexual conduct of one spouse constitutes cruelty, and is grounds for divorce. *H. v. H.,* 157 A.2d 721 (N.J.Super. 1959).

  c. Proof: The degree of proof as to the behavior which constitutes physical or mental cruelty or gross neglect also varies depending on whether the divorce is contested or uncontested.

    i. Contested action: The issues are sharply joined, and the court must make a specific decision as to whether or not certain conduct falls within the statutory definition.

   ii. Uncontested action: The plaintiff's statement with respect to the defendant's conduct is unquestioned, and presents no factual or legal issue in terms of whether or not it falls within the statutory definition.

4. **Relation to annulment:** In some jurisdictions a divorce will also be granted for grounds that are the same as those for an annulment. These grounds include fraud, duress, impotence, and bigamy.

   a. **Divorce preferred:** Often divorces will be petitioned for and granted in cases where an annulment action would be proper. This procedure is followed to prevent a financial hardship for one spouse. If an annulment is granted, the marriage terminates retroactively and alimony may not usually be awarded. By contrast, if a divorce is granted, the marriage is terminated as of the date of the decree and alimony may be awarded.

5. **Applicable law:** In circumstances involving more than one state, the law of the domicile of the plaintiff at the time the divorce action is commenced determines the grounds available for the divorce.

   Example: H and W are domiciled in State A where mental cruelty is not a ground for divorce. W moves to State B where she establishes residence and sues for divorce from H on the ground of mental cruelty. Mental cruelty is a ground for divorce in B. W may be granted the divorce since she is a ***bona fide resident*** of B and has grounds for divorce. It is immaterial where the cause of action arose. Rest. 2d, Conflict of Laws, §285.

IV. TRADITIONAL DEFENSES TO DIVORCE

A. **Specific defenses:** There are a number of defenses generally available in fault-oriented divorces. These defenses are ***not*** available in no-fault jurisdictions.

1. **Collusion:** The defense of ***collusion*** is recognized in all jurisdictions. It is an ***agreement*** between the parties to a marriage that one of them will appear to commit an act that will constitute grounds for divorce in order to obtain a divorce. The act will not actually be committed. Thus there is an element of fraud required.

   Example: H and W are married. While H is in the army, W lives with A and has a child by A. W informs H of the situation and H agrees to a divorce so W can marry A. H files for divorce on the grounds of adultery and abandonment. W files an answer requesting that the divorce be granted. The lower court dismisses the suit because of collusion.

   Held, the divorce should be granted. Collusion is an agreement to defraud or to obtain an object otherwise forbidden by law. Here, W merely stated that she had no objection to the divorce since she had no defense. There was no collusion. *Conyers v. Conyers*, 224 S.W.2d 688 (Ky. 1949).

2. **Condonation:** *Condonation* is the voluntary resumption of the marital relationship by spouses, after one commits an act that constitutes grounds for divorce, with knowledge of the act by the other party. ***Forgiveness,*** and ***restoration of the marital relationship*** are the two important aspects of condonation.

> **Example:** H and W are married and W commits adultery. H learns of the incident, but forgives W and cohabits with her when she promises to be faithful. Subsequently, W commits adultery on additional occasions while cohabiting with H; he is unaware of W's adultery at that time. H now sues for divorce for adultery, and W raises the defense of condonation.
>
> *Held*, the divorce is granted. H had no knowledge of W's subsequent acts of adultery, so he could not have condoned them. Condonation of specific past acts of adultery does not affect subsequent acts. *McKee v. McKee,* 145 S.E.2d 163 (Va. 1965).

  a. **Division of authority:** The various states are divided with respect to the necessity of the two elements for condonation.

    i. **Either** forgiveness or the resumption of sexual relations constitutes condonation in some jurisdictions.

    ii. **Only** resumption of the ***marital relationship*** will constitute condonation in other jurisdictions.

    iii. **Both** forgiveness and the resumption of sexual relations are necessary in other states.

Note: Condonation is a *factual issue* to be determined at trial.

3. **Connivance:** *Connivance* is the consent of one of the parties to a marriage, to an act by the other that constitutes grounds for a divorce, and the commission of the act. This is usually found only in actions based on adultery.

> **Example 1:** H believes that W is unfaithful and wants to divorce her. H hires a detective agency that sends an agent to entertain W. The agent has sexual relations with W. H brings suit for divorce, and W raises the defense of connivance.
>
> *Held*, the defense is valid. H is not entitled to a divorce since connivance may be implied from his acts, which in a positive manner tended to bring about W's adultery, and which amounted to H's consent thereto. *McAllister v. McAllister,* 137 N.Y.S. 833 (Sup.Ct. 1912); *Rademacher v. Rademacher,* 70 A. 687 (N.J.Eq. 1908).
>
> **Example 2:** H sues for divorce on the ground of habitual drunkenness of W. W raises the defense of connivance. W states that H, knowing of her problem, made liquor available to her. Specifically, H brought liquor home, took W to social affairs where liquor was served, and drank with her.

Held, the divorce is granted. An essential element of connivance is the corrupt (deliberately wrongful) *intent* on the part of the spouse bringing the divorce action that the other spouse commit the act complained of. H did not intend that W become an alcoholic. Undoubtedly, H could have taken precautions to protect W from her own weakness, but as a matter of law he is not obligated to forego his own pleasures at the risk of being charged with corrupt intent to make W an alcoholic. *Muir v. Muir,* 86 A.2d 857 (Del. 1952).

4. **Recrimination:** The defense of *recrimination* bars a divorce to either spouse where *both* spouses have committed acts which are grounds for divorce.

   Example: W brings suit for divorce against H, who files a cross-complaint for divorce. H had physically injured W on several occasions, was often intoxicated, and boasted of having sexual relations with other women. H showed that W wrote letters to different persons falsely accusing H of homosexuality. The court denied a divorce to either party on the ground of recrimination, reasoning that W's actions should bar her from obtaining a divorce even though H's actions were grounds for divorce. W appeals.

   Held, reversed and remanded for further consideration. Whether or not mutual cruelty results in recrimination depends on the circumstances of the case. This includes the *comparative fault* of the parties, the *prospects for reconciliation,* and the *effect of the marital strife* upon the parties, their children and the community. The lower court did not consider all aspects of recrimination. *DeBurgh v. DeBurgh,* 250 P.2d 598 (Cal. 1952).

   a. **Modification by statute:** Some states passed legislation or developed special doctrines permitting divorces in cases of fault by both spouses.

      i. **Less guilty spouse:** In some jurisdictions the spouse committing the less serious act is granted the divorce. This is known as the doctrine of *comparative rectitude.*

      ii. **Dual divorce:** Other jurisdictions grant a divorce to each party *(dual divorce)* where both spouses are at fault.

         Example: H petitions for a divorce because of cruel and inhuman treatment. W files a counterclaim seeking a divorce on the same grounds. The court did not determine whether H or W was ultimately at fault for the breakdown of the marriage. Instead, the court found that both H and W had grounds for divorce, and granted a divorce to each spouse. *John W. S. v. Jeanne F. S.,* 367 N.Y.S.2d 814 (N.Y.App.Div. 1975).

      iii. **Significance of decision:** The decision is important because it rejected traditional policy considerations of preserving a marriage which was no longer viable, and it recognized the difficulty of determining which spouse was ultimately at fault for the breakdown of the marriage.

V. NO-FAULT DIVORCE

A. **Background:** Traditionally, divorces were granted based on fault. That is, one spouse committed an act which, under a state statute, was grounds for divorce by the other spouse. The concept of no-fault divorce developed because:

1. **Fault-oriented system:** There was recognition that divorces based solely upon fault failed to prevent the breakup of marriages; and

2. **Perjury:** Fault-oriented grounds for divorces encouraged perjury to obtain a divorce.

B. **No-fault:** All states, at least in part, have some form of no-fault divorce statute. Where it is not necessary to show fault, the issue is what evidence is required to show that there has been a marital breakdown or otherwise meet the statutory criteria.

1. **Statutory interpretation:** Statutory criteria for no-fault divorces are intentionally broad in most states. The purpose is to give much discretion to the court which decides whether to grant the divorce. Statutes and court interpretation of them vary from state to state.

   a. **Basis for no-fault divorce:** Some statutes require that the parties be living *"separate and apart in different habitations"* or that there be "voluntary separation from bed and board."

   Example: H leaves W to live with his mother. H goes to W's house daily, performs chores, and attends social events with W, but they do not have sexual intercourse. The court held that the "separate and apart" standard was not met because of these associations. Suit for divorce was dismissed. *Ellam v. Ellam,* 333 A.2d 577 (N.J. 1975).

   Example: W agrees to a separation after learning that H is having an affair with another woman. W's consent is *not voluntary,* so the mutuality required by the statute is lacking. Both parties must consent to the voluntary separation. Where one party is guilty of some misconduct, the "consent" of the other party to the separation is not voluntary. *Wife S. v. Husband S.,* 375 A.2d 451 (Del. 1977).

   b. **Irreconcilable differences:** The no-fault divorce statute in California requires *"irreconcilable differences,* which have caused the *irremediable breakdown* of the marriage." Cal. Civ. Code §4506 (1970). A case interpreting that phrase stated that it meant "substantial marital problems which have so impaired the marriage relationship that the legitimate objects of matrimony have been destroyed and as to which there is no reasonable possibility of elimination, correction or resolution." *In re Marriage of Walton,* 104 Cal. Rptr. 472 (1972).

   c. **Irretrievably broken:** A Delaware statute provides for divorce where the marriage is *"irretrievably broken."* This may be shown by *voluntary separation,* or a separation caused by *mental illness, misconduct of one spouse or incompatibility* where reconciliation is improbable.

2. **Defenses eliminated:** Traditional divorce defenses of condonation, collusion, recrimination, etc. are not applicable to no-fault divorces because they are founded, in varying degrees, on a fault finding system of divorce. They are not compatable with the spirit of no-fault divorce. *Flora v. Flora,* 337 N.E.2d 846 (Ind. 1975).

3. **Issues at no-fault hearing:** One spouse may seek a no-fault divorce and assert that the marriage is broken. In defense the other spouse, who does not want to be divorced, may argue that the marriage can be saved. Most courts in this situation grant the divorce because a marriage requires the consent and cooperation of both spouses. "This is the inevitable consequence of abandoning the fault grounds for divorce and adopting marriage breakdown as the ground." Clark p. 517.

   Example: H petitions for divorce on the ground that his marriage is irretrievably broken. W denies H's allegations. H moves for summary judgment, and submits an affidavit stating that their present separation is permanent. H states that he is unwilling to live with W at any time in the future, and that there is no possibility of a reconciliation. W submits an affidavit which *denies* that the marriage is irretrievably broken, and states her *willingness to reconcile* and continue the marriage.

   Held, the divorce is granted. It takes two consenting parties to make a contract, and it takes two consenting parties to make a reconciliation. There is no issue of fact as to the irretrievable brokenness of the marriage. H refuses to cohabit with W, and the fact that W desires a reconciliation will not support a finding by the trier of fact that there are prospects for a reconciliation. *Manning v. Manning,* 229 S.E.2d 611 (Ga. 1976).

   Example: W asks H to leave their home because H is an alcoholic, and H leaves. Attempts at reconciliation fail because H refuses treatment for alcoholism. H files for divorce. In defense W contends that the marriage can be saved if H is treated for alcoholism.

   Held, the divorce is granted. The test is the existing state of the marriage. The evidence shows serious marital discord and irretrievable breakdown. *Hagerty v. Hagerty,* 281 N.W.2d 386 (Minn. 1979).

4. **Constitutionality:** No-fault divorce laws have been attacked on constitutional grounds, but they have withstood all challenges.

   a. **Illustrative case:** The constitutionality of no-fault statutes is illustrated by *Ryan v. Ryan,* 277 So.2d 266 (Fla. 1973). In *Ryan,* a statute provided that the sole grounds for divorce were irretrievable breakdown or insanity. In a suit under the statute, its constitutionality was challenged on the grounds that: (a) It impaired the rights and obligations of the parties to the marriage contract; (b) It was unconstitutionally vague and uncertain; and (c) It operated retroactively to marriages entered into before its enactment. But the court rejected all of these contentions, and found the statute constitutional.

5. **Fault considered as to custody and property division:** Even though a state has adopted no-fault as the principal or sole grounds for divorce, fault concepts may still play a role in other issues.

   a. **Custody:** For instance, some states allow fault to be considered in determining who shall receive *custody* of minor children of the marriage. See, e.g., Cal. Civ. Code §4509.

   b. **Property division:** Similarly, many state still permit the court to consider marital misconduct when it decides how the parties' property should be divided upon divorce. Areen, pp. 713-14.

6. **Model statute:** The principal model divorce statute, the Uniform Marriage and Divorce Act, provides for no-fault divorce. UMDA §302 provides for the granting of a divorce if:

   "(2) the court finds that the marriage is *irretrievably broken,* if the finding is supported by evidence that (i) the parties have *lived separate and apart* for a period of more than 180 days next preceding the commencement of the proceeding, or (ii) there is *serious marital discord* adversely affecting the attitude of one or both of the parties toward the marriage; [and]

   (3) the court finds that the conciliation provisions of Section 305 either do not apply or have been met."

Section 305 provides:

   "(a) If both of the parties by petition or otherwise have stated under oath or affirmation that the marriage is irretrievably broken, or one of the parties has so stated and the other has not denied it, the court, after hearing, shall make a finding whether the marriage is irretrievably broken.

   (b) If one of the parties has denied under oath or affirmation that the marriage is irretrievably broken, the court shall consider all relevant factors, including the circumstances that gave rise to filing the petition and the prospect of reconciliation, and shall:

(1) ***Make a finding*** whether the marriage is irretrievably broken; or

(2) Continue the matter for further hearing not fewer than 30 days nor more than 60 days later, ... and may suggest to the parties that they seek ***counseling***. The court, at the request of either party shall, or on its own motion may, order a conciliation conference. At the adjourned hearing the court shall make a finding whether the marriage is irretrievably broken.

(c) A finding of irretrievable breakdown is a determination that there is ***no reasonable prospect of reconciliation.***" (Emphasis added)

DIVORCE: FINANCIAL ASPECTS

I. INTRODUCTION

A. Matters to be resolved: Generally, a divorce decree does more than terminate the marriage status of the parties. It does the following:

1. **Grants the divorce;**

2. **Divides the marital property;**

3. **Awards alimony;**

4. **Awards custody** of any minor children of the marriage; and

5. **Awards child support.** Child custody and support are discussed in a separate chapter *infra*, pp. 125-152.

B. Area of controversy: In many instances the financial aspects of a divorce constitute the focal point of the controversy. For both parties the financial aspects have emotional and practical implications.

1. **Motives of parties:** The husband may attempt to evade or minimize his support responsibilities in order to show contempt for his wife and to retain as much income as he can for his new life. Similarly, the wife may use the divorce proceedings as a device to vent her emotions as well as seek legal redress for wrongs to her, and she may seek to secure ample resources for her new life.

2. **Constitutional aspects:** Starting in the 1970's, a number of United States Supreme Court decisions have applied the Equal Protection Clause of the Fourteenth Amendment to traditional Family Law concepts. This has brought about many changes. For instance, men are entitled to alimony in appropriate cases because decisions may not be based on sex-oriented criteria.

C. Community Property laws: Eight states have these laws which may change the distribution of property upon divorce. Community property laws define the interests of spouses in property acquired *during* marriage. Generally, both the husband and wife are deemed to have an undivided, *equal,* present, vested interest in each item of community property. Property acquired *before* marriage or *after the dissolution* of a marriage is separate property and *not* community property.

1. **Source:** The source of property acquired during marriage is also a determining factor in the classification of an asset as community property or separate property. Property acquired through gift or inheritance is separate property. See Chart III, *infra* p. 103.

CHART III. ALIMONY AND DIVISION OF PROPERTY COMPARED

	<u>Alimony</u>	<u>Division of Property</u>
1. Change in circumstances	Can be modified.	Usually may not be changed.
2. Remarriage	Terminates obligations	Does not end obligation where paid in installments
3. Contempt	Remedy available for non-payment	Remedy not available in some states
4. Bankruptcy	Does not discharge obligation.	May discharge obligation.
5. Taxes	The payer may deduct payments, and they are taxable to the payee. The payments must meet the statutory definition of alimony (e.g., they must not be child support, and must terminate on the recipient's death.) See Clark, pp. 693-98.	Transfers of property incident to divorce result in no taxable gain or loss to either the transferor or the transferee. The transferor gets no deduction. See Clark, pp. 699-700.

II. PROPERTY DIVISION IN DIVORCE

A. **Noncommunity property states:** Almost all states which do not have community property laws divide property according to equitable distribution laws which allow the courts to divide property equitably between the spouses. To aid in that division of property, certain classifications are used.

   1. **Separate property:** This is property acquired before the marriage or by gift or inheritance during the marriage.

      a. **Distribution:** Separate property is not divided upon divorce; it is considered the sole property of the person who received it.

   2. **Marital property:** This is all property acquired by either spouse during the marriage, except gifts and inheritances.

      a. **Distribution:** An equitable division of property is based on factors such as age, health, length of the marriage, occupation and income of the parties; the needs and contributions of the parties in acquiring and maintaining the property; and the alimony awarded.

      Note: Recent cases view the services of a full time housewife as a substantial contribution to the marriage and often divide the property equally regardless of which spouse earned the money to buy the property. That policy is consistent with the reasons for no-fault divorce. *DiFlorido v. DiFlorido,* 331 A.2d 174 (Pa. 1975); *In re Marriage of Dietz,* 527 P.2d 427 (Or.App. 1974).

   3. **Commingled property:** This is property which is purchased with a combination of separate funds and marital funds. This usually occurs when land is purchased before the marriage and payments are made during the marriage.

      a. **Source of funds theory:** Many courts use this theory which looks to the source of payments for the property. The spouse who contributed separate property is entitled to a proportionate interest in the property which is not subject to division. The balance of the property is deemed marital property and is subject to equitable distribution.

      Example: H purchases land on an installment sales contract one year before his marriage to W. H and W build a house on the land where they live. H holds title to the land and provides most of the money for payments, but W makes substantial nonmonetary contributions as a mother and wife for 29 years.

      Held, the land and house are marital property. Title does not control. H is entitled to the proportion of his contribution of separate property. Relying on these principles the court ordered the house and land sold, with the proceeds divided equally. *Harper v. Harper,* 448 A.2d 916 (Md. 1982).

b. Transmutation theory: Under this theory used by some states, property cannot be both separate and marital as in the source of funds theory. When separate and marital funds are commingled, the property becomes marital property subject to division.

4. **Increased value of separate property:** Real property purchased before the marriage may appreciate in value during the marriage. Courts deal with this "profit" using different approaches.

   a. Source of funds theory: If the increased value is attributable to the direct and significant efforts of the other spouse, then it is marital property. Otherwise, it remains separate property. The burden of proof is on the non-owning spouse to show the substantial contribution made.

   b. Transmutation of funds: There is a *rebuttable presumption* that the entire property is marital and subject to division. This shifts the burden of proof to the spouse who claims the property is separate to show that the increased value is due to inflation or some other cause rather than the efforts of the non-owning spouse.

B. Community property states: Eight states derive their property law from the civil law system of Spain instead of the common law. Those states are: Arizona, California, Idaho, Louisiana, New Mexico, Nevada, Texas and Washington. Under this system there is equality of ownership unless control of some property can be distinguished.

1. **Commingled property:** Most community property states use the *inception of title* theory. Under this theory, property purchased with separate funds before marriage remains the separate property of the spouse who made the initial investment.

   Note: Inception of title should be distinguished from perfection of title. Title is perfected when the mortgage or other lien is paid off.

2. **Increased value of separate property:** Community property states have used both the inception of title and source of funds theories to distribute such property.

3. **Harsh results avoided:** Most courts, regardless of the theory used to divide property, emphasize equity and fairness in determining whether property is marital and thus subject to division.

   Example: W buys a house before her marriage to H. H makes improvements valued at $5,000. The court held that the house was W's separate property, but it granted H an equitable lien for the value of his improvements. *In re Elam,* 650 P.2d 213 (Wash. 1982).

   Example: H purchases a house before his marriage to W. The house was deemed H's separate property, but insofar as the increased value of the house was due to home improvements made during the marriage and W's nonmonetary homemaking efforts, the enhanced value of the house could be considered marital property. *Honnas v. Honnas,* 648 P.2d 1045 (Az. 1982).

4. **Other criteria:** Some courts recognize the distinction between separate and marital property to be significant, but not controlling because the distribution must be just and equitable.

   a. **Factors:** In *Friedlander v. Friedlander,* 494 P.2d 208 (Wash. 1972), the court stated: "First, the court must consider the necessities of the wife and the financial ability of the husband. Then, it should take into account the age of the parties, their health, physical condition, education, their employment history....It should likewise consider their training and business or occupation experience, as well as their future earning prospects. The court should give regard to the date the parties accumulated in property, the party through whom it was acquired, the kinds of property involved, as well as the value of the parties' respective contribution to the community."

C. **Intangible property:** Intangible assets are considered by the court in connection either with a division of property or alimony. The principal areas concern professional degrees and licenses, the goodwill of a business, and pension rights.

   1. **Professional or educational degree:** The most frequently-litigated issue is whether a *professional degree*, or an *advanced educational degree* earned by one spouse during the marriage, may be counted as marital property (and thus subject to property division).

      a. **Majority view:** Most courts have concluded that such degrees should *not* be treated as marital property, and thus should *not be subject to equitable distribution.*

         Example: During the six years that H and W are married, H finishes his B.A. and earns an M.B.A. During this period, he works only part-time, so that he can pursue his education. W, meanwhile, works full-time as a flight attendant to help put H through school. The couple do not accumulate any financial assets during the marriage. They divorce soon after H receives his degree and gets a good job. W asserts that H's enhanced earning value from his M.B.A. degree should be treated as a marital asset, some part of which should be equitably distributed to her.

         Held, H's M.B.A. degree is not marital property. The degree "does not have an exchange value or any objective transferrable value on an open market. It is personal to the holder. It terminates on death of the holder and is not inheritable. It cannot be assigned, sold, transferred, conveyed or pledged.... It may not be acquired by the mere expenditure of money. It is simply an intellectual achievement that may potentially assist in the future acquisition of property." Therefore, the degree simply has none of the attributes of property in the usual sense of the word. (A dissent argues that W's earnings have been "invested" in H's education, so that equity demands treating H's increased earning power from the degree as a distributable asset.) *In re Marriage of Graham*, 574 P.2d 75 (Col. 1978).

b. Compensation to working spouse: However, most courts that follow the majority rule that a professional license or advanced degree is not distributable marital property nonetheless recognize the unfairness of denying all compensation to a person who has put his or her spouse through school. Most of these courts therefore *award some compensation* in lieu of treating the degree as property. Courts commonly apply one of two theories to compensate the non-degreed spouse.

i. Reimbursement: Some courts order the degreed spouse to *"reimburse"* the non-degreed spouse for the latter's contribution to the degree. Under this reimbursement theory, if H's degree had a "cost" of, say, $40,000 (measured by both the cost of tuition and the earnings that the couple sacrificed by having H study rather than earn), the non-degreed spouse could receive a reimbursement of half this amount (on the assumption that H and W each contributed half the cost or "sacrifice" for the acquisition of the degree). The leading case allowing reimbursement is *Mahoney v. Mahoney*, 453 A.2d 527 (N.J. 1982).

ii. Maintenance: Other courts consider the non-degreed spouse's contribution to the degree in determining the amount of *maintenance* (alimony) to be awarded. See, e.g., *In re Marriage of Olar*, 747 P.2d 676 (Colo. 1987).

c. Minority (New York) view: But a few states *recognize an advanced or professional degree as marital property*. The most notable of these states is *New York*. See, e.g., *O'Brien v. O'Brien*, 489 N.E.2d 712 (N.Y. 1985), holding that H's medical license was marital property for equitable distribution purposes, and refusing to allow mere reimbursement of expenses as a remedy. (But the result in New York seems to be due mostly to that state's unusual language in its equitable distribution statute, by which the court is directed to consider each party's "direct or indirect contribution...to the *career* or *career potential* of the other party...." N.Y. Dom. Rel. L. §236.)

i. Celebrity status: In fact, the New York courts have treated as marital property not just professional degrees but also one spouse's *celebrity status* or other enhanced earning power.

Example: At the beginning of W's and H's marriage, W is a struggling young opera singer. During the marriage, W (Frederica von Stade) becomes an international opera star. During that time, H, who is himself a singer and voice teacher, travels with W to critique her performances and to photograph her for albums and magazines. In divorce proceedings, H contends that W's career and celebrity status increased in value during the marriage due in part to his contributions, and that he is entitled to equitable distribution of this marital property. W argues that since her career and status are not licensed, they are not things that can be "owned" and should thus not be treated as marital property.

Held, for H. "Things of value acquired during marriage are marital property even though they may fall outside the scope of traditional property concepts." Marital property may be intangible. During the marriage, H contributed to the increase in value of W's career. It is the extent of that contribution, not the nature of W's career, that has turned the career into marital property here. *Elkus v. Elkus*, 572 N.Y.S.2d 901 (N.Y.App.Div. 1991).

2. **Professional goodwill as an asset:** Even in the majority of courts that do not treat a professional degree as a marital asset, *"professional goodwill" is* a marital asset that may be equitably distributed. By "professional goodwill," the courts mean the enhanced earning capacity that comes from a professional's *reputation*, and *client or customer list*.

Example: For instance, whereas a newly-graduated neurosurgeon in most states has no career-related prospects that are to be treated as marital property, a neurosurgeon who has built up a practice and reputation and who has been earning large sums from that practice will usually be found to hold an asset — the practice — that can be valued and subjected to distribution. See, e.g., *Dugan v. Dugan*, 457 A.2d 1 (N.J. 1983) (law practice); *In re Marriage of Fleege*, 568 P.2d 1136 (Wash. 1979) (dentist's practice).

a. **Goodwill of non-professional business:** This rule that "professional goodwill" can constitute a marital asset is really just a special case of the more general rule that *business goodwill* is an asset. Thus if W owns, say, a candy store that has few if any tangible assets (e.g., it rents its space at market rents and has little inventory), the intangible "ongoing business value" of the store, measured mainly by the fact that it has an established clientele, will in all courts constitute an asset that can be distributed as marital property.

3. **Pension rights:** Where one spouse has worked for a particular employer for some years during the marriage, at the time of the divorce

that spouse may have certain *pension* rights. Whether and how these pension rights should be divided upon divorce is one of the most important and complex issues in family law. In general, courts hold that pension rights *are* a marital asset that can and should be divided.

a. **State vs. federal law:** The states are generally free to decide how to handle pensions upon divorce. However, because there are a number of federal statutes dealing with various types of pensions, the states do not have complete freedom in deciding how to divide pensions on divorce — under the Supremacy Clause of the U.S. Constitution, of course, Congress is always free to preempt state laws on particular pension issues, and Congress has frequently done so. For instance, the Supreme Court has held that Congress, when it enacted the Railroad Retirement Act, preempted a state's ability to divide a railroad employee's pension between the employee and his spouse; see *Hisquierdo v. Hisquierdo*, 439 U.S. 572 (1979).

   i. **Congress generally allows division:** However, Congress when it has legislated in the pension area has generally allowed the states to treat pensions as marital property, and to divide pension rights more or less as the state court or legislature sees fit. But see our discussion below of ERISA, a federal statute governing private-sector pensions, which establishes stringent procedures that state courts must follow to divide private pensions between the spouses.

b. **Vested and non-vested pensions:** At a particular moment (e.g., the moment of divorce), pension rights may be either *"vested"* or *"non-vested."* Pension rights are "vested" if the employee would be entitled to benefits even if he or she were, at that moment, to quit or be fired. Federal statutes usually govern when a pension must vest. The pension rights of a private-sector employee who has been with her present employer for more than *five years* are generally completely vested.

   i. **Division of vested rights:** The vast majority of states, whether they follow common-law or community-property rules, treat vested pension rights as being *marital property* that is subject to distribution upon divorce. This is true even though the employed spouse is still working, and will probably not be entitled to receive the pension payments until some or even many years in the future. (Issues of how the court should *value* these "intangible" but vested rights to receive payments in the future are discussed below.) Clark, p. 613.

   ii. **Division of non-vested rights:** Where pension rights are *non-vested*, courts are split. Here, too, however, most courts treat the rights as being marital property subject to division. Clark, pp. 613-14.

c. **Valuation of rights:** In the usual case where the employee with pension rights is still working at the moment of divorce, the pension rights (whether vested or non-vested) will not turn into actual payments until sometime in the future. How, then, is the court to value and apportion this present possibility that there will be pension payments in the future? In general, courts adopt one of two sharply differing approaches:

i. **Present division:** Courts sometimes use the *"present division"* method. Under this method, the court attempts to determine the *present value* of the pension rights. In making this valuation, the court considers the length of time until payments will start (using a discount percentage to convert future payments into equivalent present-value dollars), and also attempts to factor in the possibility that the working spouse will quit, be fired, die, or otherwise lose the chance to ever get the payments. Once the court places a present value on the pension rights, the court will then increase the non-pension property being given to the non-employed spouse, and will leave the pension rights with the employed spouse.

Example: Assume that the state is a community-property jurisdiction (where 50/50 division of marital property is required), or that in a common-law jurisdiction the court has already decided that all property in the case at hand should be divided 50/50. The court now decides that H's vested pension rights have a net present value of $100,000. Assume further that the value of all other marital property is $400,000. The court will award $250,000 of the $400,000 of other property to W. H will retain $150,000 of non-pension property, plus the $100,000-value pension rights. Thus H will collect all pension money if and when payments become due.

Note: Observe that under this "present division" approach, the entire risk of *forfeiture* due to quitting, being fired, etc., rests upon the employed spouse. This can be unfair to that spouse, especially where there is a substantial risk that the pension rights will never in fact turn into real payments. Accordingly, courts generally use the present division method only where the rights are vested, there are not too many years remaining until retirement, and all factors make it quite likely that the payments will really be made. (A court is free to choose the present value method in one situation and the alternative "reserve jurisdiction" method in another case.)

ii. Reserve jurisdiction: The second method for valuing and dividing pensions is the *"reserve jurisdiction"* or "future division" method. Under this approach, the court does not try to make a present valuation and division of the pension. Instead, the court *retains jurisdiction* to divide the payments when they become due in the future. This method is the preferable one where the pension is non-vested at the time of divorce, where there are many years before payments will begin, or where for some other reason the pension is difficult to value or at high risk of not being paid.

Example: W, who has worked for Employer for a number of years, is still 20 years from retirement. Although W has vested rights (which if W quit today would entitle her to a $50,000 lump-sum payment), W may not receive this money while she continues on the job, and the amount that W eventually receives when she does retire or quit cannot be precisely estimated today. Therefore, dividing property between H and W, the court may choose to disregard W's rights for the moment, and divide the other property as if there were no pension rights. Simultaneously, the court will retain jurisdiction. If W quits or, eventually, retires, at that time the court will order Employer's pension plan administrator to divide the payments between W and H as the court at that time shall determine. See, e.g., *Laing v. Laing*, 741 P.2d 649 (Alas. 1987) (retaining jurisdiction until H's non-vested rights become vested).

d. ERISA and QDRO's: Where the court follows the "present division" method (the first alternative discussed above), no cooperation from the pension plan administrator is needed — the non-employed spouse simply gets extra assets to compensate for the fact that he or she is not getting any part of the pension. But when the court uses the "reserve jurisdiction" approach, normally the court expects to order the pension plan to *split the payments* between the two former spouses when the payments begin sometime in the future. (That is, the court does not allow the working spouse to collect the full payment, under orders to disgorge some part of the money to the other spouse each month. This approach creates too big a risk that the non-pensioned spouse will not in fact receive the monthly payments.) Instead, the court *orders the pension administrator to send two separate checks* to each of the former spouses.

i. ERISA places limits: An important federal statute, the Employee Retirement Income Security Act of 1974 (ERISA) imposes complex procedural rules that a state court must follow before its order to a pension plan that payments be split will be legally binding on the plan. Essentially, the state-court order must be a Qualified Domestic Relations Order (QDRO) in order to be binding on the pension plan. A court order only becomes a QDRO by complying with precise rules for notifying the plan administrator, receiving the approval of that administrator, etc. (The purpose of the whole QDRO system is to make sure that the orderly administration of the pension program is not disrupted. C&G, p. 823.) See 29 U.S.C. §1056(d).

D. Other issues: There are other considerations with which courts must deal in the division of property. The same principles are applied in both non-community and community property states.

1. **Enforcement:** Although the failure to make alimony payments is generally punishable by *contempt*, this is not always true regarding property settlements. In some states the failure to comply with a property settlement, where it involves money payments, is not punishable by contempt because it would be imprisonment for a debt.

    Note: Enforcement by contempt is discussed *infra*, p. 118.

2. **Bankruptcy:** Ordinarily *bankruptcy proceedings* do *not discharge* alimony or support obligations. This rule sometimes applies to property settlements as well.

    Example: H and W obtain a divorce decree under which H is given title to their house, but H is to pay W $29,208. This is secured by a lien on H's real property (including the house). H files for bankruptcy before any money is paid to W. In the bankruptcy petition H claims a homestead exemption, which if allowed would defeat W's lien in the house. W claims that the exception cannot be used to divest her of her interest in the marital home.

    Held, for W. The bankruptcy code does not allow a debtor to avoid a lien granted to a former spouse to secure her interest in property under a divorce decree. The divorce decree extinguished W's half interest in the real estate and conveyed it to H. At the same moment it gave a lien to W to secure her half interest. H cannot avoid the lien, since the lien fastened to W's preexisting interest. Therefore, the lien survives in bankruptcy, so W will take the first $29,208 of proceeds from the bankruptcy sale of the house. *Farrey v. Sanderfoot*, 111 S.Ct. 1825 (1991).

3. **Misconduct of spouse:** Courts are *split* as to whether the *misconduct of one spouse* should be considered in dividing property.

    a. **Rationale for not considering:** Courts that do not consider marital fault in making the property division reason that the concept of fault is simply not relevant to property division, since the purpose of division is to recognize the contribution of each spouse during the marriage. See, e.g., *Chalmers v. Chalmers*, 320 A.2d 478 (N.J. 1974).

4. **Indebtedness:** Debts of the parties are not property, so it is not necessary to divide them equally. If there are obligations remaining after a division of property, or if there are only obligations and no assets, the court has discretion to order payment in a manner that is *just and equitable.* This division of debts depends on the earning capacity of the parties and other relevant factors. *In re Marriage of Eastis,* 120 Cal.Rptr. 861 (1975).

III. HISTORICAL BACKGROUND OF ALIMONY

A. **Definitions:** Alimony is the legally imposed allowance paid to one spouse (or former spouse) by the other spouse for maintenance and support. The prerequisite to the granting of alimony is the existence of a marriage.

1. **Temporary alimony:** If the financial conditions of the parties warrant, support may be awarded while the *litigation is pending* [so long as the spouse awarded the payments, does not contend the marriage is invalid (subject to annulment)], because the existence of the marriage is still in controversy.

2. **Permanent alimony:** This may be awarded at the conclusion of the litigation. However, it will not be awarded, in the absence of statutory authorization, in annulment actions, since the existence of a marriage has been adjudicated and denied.

B. **Historical basis:** Alimony in the United States has been influenced by English law. In England alimony was utilized to provide support for wives living apart from their husbands, but still married to them. In the United States the concept of alimony has been expanded, and includes the wife who is separated from her husband as well as a spouse who is divorced.

1. **Purpose:** Historically, it was justified for the following reasons:

   a. **Support:** It was a continuation, after divorce, of the support which a wife had received during marriage;

   b. **Damages:** It was a measure of damages for breach of the marriage contract; and

   c. **Penalty:** It was a penalty levied upon a guilty husband.

2. **Modern basis:** Today, alimony awards are generally based upon the *needs and abilities* of each party. The following factors are considered:

   a. **Age** of the parties;

   b. **Health** and physical condition of the parties;

   c. The *earning capacity* of the parties;

   d. **Present income** of the parties; and

e.   The *duration of the marriage* (in some jurisdictions).

3.   **Other basis:** When divorce statutes were fault-oriented, there were two additional factors which courts considered in awarding alimony:

  a.   **Degree of fault:** Courts reasoned that the party at fault in causing the breakdown of the marriage should be punished, and the innocent party should be compensated for the wrong done to him or her. *Melny v. Melny,* 203 P.2d 588 (Cal.App. 1949).

  b.   **Maintenance of status:** The wife should be permitted to continue the lifestyle which she had during the marriage. This criterion was a reflection of the husband's continuing duty to support his wife. *Radandt v. Radandt,* 140 N.W.2d 293 (Wis. 1965).

  Note: Although the reasons for the criteria above may be somewhat inconsistent with the theory of no-fault divorce, some courts continue to apply them in no-fault cases. *Magruder v. Magruder,* 209 N.W.2d 585 (Neb. 1965); *In re Marriage of Williams,* 199 N.W.2d 339 (Iowa 1972).

4.   **Rehabilitative alimony:** This is defined as alimony to support the spouse during a period of retraining or re-education for entry into the work force, and to enable that spouse to become self-supporting. The award of rehabilitative alimony has been allowed in recent court decisions where the wife had the potential to earn a livelihood, but required support from the time of the divorce to the realization of her potential as a wage earner. *Dakin v. Dakin,* 384 P.2d 639 (Wash. 1963); *Morgan v. Morgan,* 366 N.Y.S.2d 977 (1975).

  a.   **Reason:** In contrast to traditional alimony which imposes the burden of support on the defendant spouse, rehabilitative alimony assumes that the other spouse is ultimately responsible for his/her own support, but needs temporary assistance in becoming able to do so. Accordingly, a number of states have placed *limits* on the *length of time* during which alimony can be awarded.

  Example: A state statute limits alimony awards to three years where there are no minor children, but permits an extension of the period if justice so requires. W petitions for an extension beyond the three years. *Held,* for H. The purpose of alimony is not to provide a "life-time profit-sharing plan" for one spouse, but rather, to provide support for a limited period until the spouse can obtain employment and become self-supporting. The burden of proof is on W to show that justice requires an extension of the alimony period. *Calderwood v. Calderwood,* 327 A.2d 704 (N.H. 1974).

5.   **Husband's alimony:** Prior to 1970 most states did not permit an award of alimony to the husband. Most state laws were changed in the

1970's so that husbands could be awarded alimony in appropriate cases. *Pfohl v. Pfohl,* 345 So.2d 371 (Fla.App. 1977).

   a. Constitutional issue: In ***Orr v. Orr,*** 440 U.S. 268 (1979), the Supreme Court held that an Alabama statute which provided that a husband, but not a wife, could be required to pay alimony, violated the Equal Protection Clause of the Fourteenth Amendment. The Court recognized that the statute helped serve an important governmental objective: compensating women for discrimination during marriage. But an outright ban on alimony awards against women was ***not substantially related*** to that objective.

   i. Rationale: The Court observed that the relative financial need of the parties was already required to be considered as part of the divorce process, so that there was no need to use sex as an automatic "proxy for financial dependence." Furthermore, the only women who would be given extra protection by the statute were those who were ***not*** financially needy; thus the statute's main effect was at odds with its stated purpose.

   ii. Sexual stereotypes: The Court in *Orr* also sounded another note which has been repeated in other reverse-sex-discrimination cases. The Court warned that even sex-based statutes which were designed to mitigate past discrimination carried the "inherent risk of ***reinforcing stereotypes*** about the ***'proper place'*** of women...." Here, a gender-neutral statute under which both needy men and needy women could be given alimony, was a superior way of protecting all parties.

   Note: A number of courts have been sympathetic to alimony awards or property settlements where an ***unmarried couple*** separated after living together. See, e.g., *Marvin v. Marvin, supra,* p. 45.

IV. TEMPORARY ALIMONY

   A. Availability: A decree for temporary alimony, or alimony ***pendente lite,*** is a decree ***in personam,*** and consequently, it must be based upon personal service within the jurisdiction or on a personal appearance of the defendant.

   1. Basis of award: The award or denial of temporary alimony lies within the discretion of the court. The amount, absent a statute, depends upon the circumstances of each situation. *Hempel v. Hempel,* 30 N.W.2d 594 (Minn. 1948).

   a. Facts: When H and W return from their honeymoon, H leaves W. H is wealthy, but W earned $180 per month prior to her marriage. W uses H's car and refuses to leave H's home. W files for divorce and temporary alimony.

b. **Contentions of the parties:** H maintains that he should pay only $200 per month temporary alimony; he should receive the return of his car; and W should vacate his home. W claims that she should receive sufficient temporary alimony to enable her to live according to the station in life of the parties.

c. **Trial court:** W is awarded temporary alimony of $750 per month; attorney's fees; and use and control of the car. H is enjoined from disposing of his other property during the litigation, except as necessary to maintain himself. H receives sole possession of his home.

d. **Appeal:** H contends that the trial court abused its discretion in making the award. *Held*, there is no abuse of discretion.

e. **Reasoning of court:** Where W has no separate means of her own, temporary alimony should furnish W with means of support consistent with H's means and the station in life of the parties during the marriage. In determining the ability of H to pay, his income and property of all types must be considered. The amount awarded for attorney's fees is also within the court's discretion; the same factors that are applied in the award of temporary alimony should be applied there. Voluntary litigation by the parties to a marriage of their respective property rights, places the issue before the court and allows the court to determine the question raised irrespective of whether or not the court would otherwise have had jurisdiction to do so.

2. **Duration:** The right to enforce an award of temporary alimony expires when the divorce action upon which it is based, terminates.

3. **Modification:** The amount of temporary alimony awarded is subject to modification as the circumstances of the parties change.

V. PERMANENT ALIMONY

A. **Types:** Permanent alimony awarded to a spouse after a divorce may take different forms, such as periodic payments, a lump sum payment, annuity purchase or an alimony trust. The particular form that alimony takes depends on the circumstances and *needs* of the parties; the *statutes* of the jurisdiction; the *negotiations* between the parties; and the *discretion* of the court.

1. **Periodic payments:** Periodic payments allow a spouse to pay a generally large sum in alimony over a period of time. The spouse receiving these payments obtains support over a time span. The court retains jurisdiction over the decree to prevent hardship on either spouse.

2. **Lump sum payment:** One spouse may discharge his obligation totally and not contend with a continuing liability, by means of a single *"lump*

sum" payment. The spouse receiving that payment has a large sum with which to plan a new life.

3. **Other forms:** *Annuities and alimony trusts* provide security and flexibility to both spouses.

4. **Court discretion:** The trial judge has ***broad discretion*** in determining alimony. For instance, Ohio Revised Code §3105.18, provides in part:

> "(B) In determining whether alimony is necessary, and in determining the nature, amount, and manner of payment of alimony, the court shall consider all relevant factors, including:
>
> (1) The relative ***earning abilities*** of the parties; (2) The ***ages,*** and the physical and emotional conditions of the parties; (3) The ***retirement benefits*** of the parties; (4) The ***expectancies and inheritances*** of the parties; (5) The ***duration of the marriage;*** (6) The extent to which it would be inappropriate for a party, because he will be custodian of a minor child of the marriage, to seek ***employment*** outside the home; (7) The ***standard of living*** of the parties established during the marriage; (8) The relative extent of ***education*** of the parties; (9) The relative ***assets and liabilities*** of the parties; (10) The ***property*** brought to the marriage by either party; (11) The ***contribution*** of a spouse as homemaker." (Emphasis added)

Example: W obtains a divorce from H after 25 years of marriage. W never worked during her marriage and at the time of the divorce was ill, requiring much medical attention. W is awarded alimony in the amount of $225 per month. H earns between $833 and $916 per month. W appeals the alimony award, claiming that it is inadequate.

Held, W's appeal is dismissed. In fixing alimony a court must look to all the circumstances of the case and fix an amount equitable to both parties. Courts should not force a husband to pay such an amount of alimony as to destroy his incentive to work and to pay any alimony. On the basis of the facts it cannot be said as a matter of law that the lower court erred in its alimony award. Such awards will not be overturned unless they are clearly inadequate. *Bramblette v. Bramblette*, 448 S.W.2d 44 (Ky. 1969); *Canady v. Canady*, 197 N.E.2d 42 (Ill. 1964).

B. **Modification of amount:** The amount of permanent alimony awarded may later be ***modified*** by the court, or even terminated completely, under certain circumstances. For instance, if the wife's needs increase dramatically, courts generally have authority to increase the amount of alimony. Conversely, if the wife remarries, courts generally ***terminate*** the alimony. Modification and termination of alimony is discussed more extensively *infra*, p. 119.

C. Contempt proceedings to enforce alimony and support decrees: Suppose that a spouse or parent does *not comply* with a court order of alimony or child support. There are a number of ways of *enforcing* the order. One of the most important is the use of *contempt* proceedings. If the defendant is found in contempt for failing to obey a support order, the court may impose *imprisonment* and/or *fines*.

1. **Civil vs. criminal proceedings:** Before we discuss the use of contempt proceedings to enforce support orders, we must first understand the key distinction between *"civil"* contempt proceedings and *"criminal"* proceedings.

    a. **Criminal proceedings:** A contempt proceeding is *criminal* if its purpose is to *punish* the defendant for refusing to comply with the court's order. The clearest indication that a proceeding is criminal is that the sentence imposed by the court is *unconditional* — nothing the defendant does after imposition of the sentence will undo the effect of the contempt conviction.

    b. **Civil proceedings:** By contrast, contempt proceedings are *civil* in nature if the judge's purpose in imposing the sentence is to *compel the defendant to do some act*. (In the context of alimony and child support proceedings, of course, the purpose is to compel the defendant to pay the arrearages, and to comply with the support order in the future.) The sentence in a civil contempt proceeding is therefore generally *conditional* in nature: the defendant is sentenced to a term of, say, 30 days in jail, but with jail time to end as soon as the defendant complies with the support order.

    See generally *Hicks v. Feiock*, 485 U.S. 624 (1988), the leading Supreme Court case describing how to distinguish between civil and criminal contempt proceedings in support actions.

    c. **Civil usually used:** Where the problem is that the defendant has not complied with an alimony or child support order, *civil* proceedings are used far more frequently than criminal ones. The reason, of course, is that the court is generally interested in making the defendant comply prospectively with the support order, not in punishing him for past violations.

2. **Inability to pay:** The defendant in contempt proceedings to enforce child support will frequently defend on the grounds that he was *unable to pay*.

    a. **Must be allowed as defense:** It is clear that inability to pay *must* be allowed as a defense to contempt proceedings. This is true whether the proceedings are civil or criminal. In the case of criminal proceedings, the Due Process Clause prevents punishing a defendant for something he had no control over. In civil cases, the constitutional prohibition on *imprisonment for debt* similarly means that a defendant who is unable to pay may not be imprisoned as a means for compelling payment.

b. **Burden of proof:** Most statutes allow the state to require that the defendant *prove* his inability to pay (rather than requiring the plaintiff to prove that the defendant *can* pay). So long as the proceedings are civil, this shifting of the burden of proof is allowable (as is discussed further below).

c. **What constitutes inability:** In general, courts take a narrow view of what constitutes "inability" to make payments. It is not enough that the defendant would find it *inconvenient* or *burdensome* to make the payment — he must show that it is *virtually impossible*. Clark, pp. 675-76.

i. **Full disclosure:** The defendant must normally make *full disclosure* of his finances in order to show inability — general, conclusory claims by the defendant that he cannot make the payments are not enough. *Id.*

ii. **Could pay some but pays none:** Similarly, if the defendant could pay *some* (though not all) of the amount ordered, and instead pays *none*, the defendant will not be found to have established inability to pay, and may be punished. *Id.*

iii. **Refusal to work:** And if the defendant *could earn* the money, but has chosen not to do so (e.g., the defendant refuses to take available jobs because they are for work he doesn't like), the defendant will not be treated as unable to pay, and may be punished.

3. **Due process protections:** If the contempt proceedings are found to be criminal in nature, the protections of the *Due Process* Clause apply. Most significantly, this means that the defendant may not be put to the burden of proving inability to pay. Instead, the burden is on the state to prove beyond a reasonable doubt that the defendant *can* pay. This is one of the reasons why contempt proceedings in alimony and support cases are generally brought as civil proceedings (thus allowing the state to shift onto the defendant the burden of showing inability to pay). See *Hicks v. Feiock, supra,* holding that the state's "burden of proof on the defendant to show inability" rule would be constitutional if the proceedings were civil, but a violation of due process if the proceedings were criminal.

VI. MODIFICATION OR TERMINATION OF ALIMONY

A. **Basis:** Normally, once alimony has been fixed by the court, the obligation to pay it continues, and at the same rate, until the recipient remarries. However, most states, by either statute or common law, hold that the court may *modify* the amount of alimony (in either direction) where *justice so requires*. When the court issues a divorce decree, the court often implicitly or explicitly reserves jurisdiction to modify the amount of the payments.

1. **Alimony vs. property division:** Whereas an award of alimony is generally modifiable by the court, a *division of property* by the court usually is *not modifiable*. This is true even if the circumstances of one or both parties later change dramatically. Therefore, it can be quite important (as well as difficult) to distinguish between an award of alimony and a property division.

    Example: Suppose that the court orders H to pay W four equal annual installments of $50,000 each. The court does not make it clear whether this is alimony or property division. After the first annual payment has been made, W falls ill, loses her job, and needs extra money, both to replace her lost income and to pay for her medical bills. If the award is found to have been a property division, most states hold that the award may not be modified even in light of changed circumstances. Clark, p. 657. If, on the other hand, the award is found to have been alimony (which is not so unlikely — recall that more and more courts are now viewing alimony as a short-term "get on your feet" solution rather than as a permanent income to the recipient), most states would allow the judge to increase the amount or duration of the required payments.

B. **Procedure:** *Either party* may petition to have the alimony decree modified.

    1. **In original court:** Usually, the petition to change the amount will be filed in the court that rendered the original decree. Even if the defendant no longer has any current minimum contacts with the state, the court is deemed to have continuing jurisdiction to modify the decree (assuming, of course, that it had personal jurisdiction over the defendant at the time the original decree was entered, a constitutional prerequisite for that decree in the first place. See *supra*, p. 86).

    2. **Second court:** The situation is more complicated if the petition for modification is made in a *different court* than issued the original decree.

        a. **Personal jurisdiction required:** The second court may not modify the first court's decree unless the second court has *personal jurisdiction* over the defendant at the time the modification proceeding begins.

            Example: H and W are divorced in California, where they are both domiciled. The California court orders alimony of $2,000 per month. W moves to Kansas, and H has no contact with her or with Kansas. W now petitions the Kansas court for an increase in the alimony rate. The court may not modify the California decree (or issue its own conflicting decree), because a state may not order a defendant to pay alimony (or change the amount to be paid) without personal jurisdiction over the defendant.

    i. Modifiable: Now, let's assume that the second court *does* have personal jurisdiction over the defendant. The next question the second court must ask is, "Was the original alimony decree modifiable, under the law of the state that rendered it?" If the original decree would not be modifiable in the state that rendered it (either because of an unusual statutory or common law provision, or because the parties explicitly so agree), then the second court may not modify that decree. A modification in this circumstance would violate the Full Faith and Credit Clause. The same would be true if the first court made a final decision that there should be *no* alimony payments, merely a property division — here, too, the second court would not be permitted to award alimony.

    ii. First decree modifiable: But if the second court finds that under the law of the first state, the first decree *is* modifiable, then the second court *may* modify the first decree (assuming, of course, personal jurisdiction over the defendant). Clark, p. 660. This is also true if the alimony recipient uses the special enforcement procedures given by the URESA or RURESA (discussed *infra*, p. 147).

C. Changed circumstances: The basic rule is that the amount of alimony may not be modified except where this is required by a *substantial change* in the *circumstances* of either the payor or the payee.

    1. Substantial and unforeseen change: It is not enough that the circumstances of the payor or the payee have changed somewhat. Most courts hold that the change must be a *substantial* one. For instance, the Uniform Marriage and Divorce Act §316, allows the amount to be changed "only upon a showing of changed circumstances *so substantial and continuing as to make the terms unconscionable.*" (That section also provides that provisions regarding property disposition may not be revoked or modified even where the circumstances have changed in this way.)

        a. Not contemplated: Most courts further hold that only changes that were *not contemplated* by the original decree may be considered. For instance, if it was clear to the original court that H was within two years of retiring (so that he would have less money to spend on alimony), H probably will not be able to come back into court and argue, now that he has retired, that his payments should be reduced.

b. Only as to unaccrued obligations: Most courts hold that a modification may take effect only as to installments that have *not accrued* as of the date the motion for modification is made. See, e.g., UMDA §316.

Example: At a time when H is required to pay W $2,000 per month in alimony, W loses her job on Jan. 1. W does not bring a motion for modification until August 1. Most courts would hold that they do not have power (no matter how compelling the circumstances) to increase, retroactively, the amount owed by H for January through July.

2. **Recipient's needs and resources:** A substantial and unforeseen increase in the *recipient's needs* (or decrease in her resources) will be grounds for *increasing* the alimony owed. Conversely, a decrease in the recipient's needs, or an increase in the recipient's other resources, will result in a lowering of the amount.

   a. Ill health: For instance, if the recipient suffers *ill health*, this may be grounds for increasing the alimony amount, either to replace income that the recipient can no longer earn herself, or to help her pay the costs of treatment.

   b. Inflation: Similarly, a substantial increase in the *cost of living* will frequently be grounds for an increase in alimony.

   c. Employment: If the recipient loses a job that she had at the time the original decree was granted, this, too, will be grounds for an increase.

   i. Obtains job: Conversely, if the recipient was unemployed at the time of the original decree, and has now gotten a job, this is likely to be grounds for a reduction (assuming, of course, that the first court did not set the amount of the decree on the assumption that the recipient would find a job like the one she has in fact found). Recall that the present tendency is to strongly encourage the recipient of alimony to become self-supporting; therefore, a modern court may well hold that the fact that the recipient now has a stable job is enough to cause alimony to be not only reduced but in fact terminated.

   d. Remarriage or cohabitation: The recipient's remarriage or cohabitation presents special issues, which are discussed below, p. 123.

3. **Payor's needs and resources:** On the other side of the scale, a substantial change in the personal needs of the payor, or in his *resources*, may similarly be grounds for a change in the amount of alimony.

   a. Job change or retirement: Traditionally, courts have been unsympathetic to a husband's claim that because he has *retired*, or taken a ***lower-paying job***, he should be allowed to pay lesser sums. But courts today are not so hostile — as long as the court believes that the husband has been motivated by reasons other than the desire to harm his ex-wife, and is convinced that the husband has made a good-faith career decision similar to the one he would have made had the divorce not occurred, the court is likely to grant the relief. Clark, p. 662.

    b. Remarriage by payor: Similarly, the fact that the payor has ***remarried*** may be grounds for reducing his obligation. But this is not necessarily so. For instance, the new wife may have income of her own; if so, the court will certainly consider this in determining how much money the husband really has available with which to support the first wife. *Id.*

    c. Payor becomes richer: Suppose the income or wealth of the payor ***increases*** dramatically after the marriage. In general, this will ***not*** be grounds for increasing the amount of alimony. The recipient is merely entitled to support on the scale that was enjoyed by the parties during their marriage; as one court put it, the recipient is ***not entitled to a "lifetime profit-sharing plan."*** *Calderwood v. Calderwood, supra,* p. 114. (But if the initial award was less than the recipient really needed, because the husband at the time simply could not pay more, then an improvement in the husband's ability to pay *would* justify an increase.) Clark, pp. 662-63.

D. Remarriage by recipient: All states agree, at least as a general matter, that alimony shall be ***terminated*** if the recipient ***remarries***.

    1. How termination occurs: In about 12 states, the payor ***automatically*** has the right to stop paying, without any court action, once the recipient remarries. Clark, p. 663, n. 84. See also UMDA §316(b). Other states require the payor to get a court order before stopping payment.

    2. Termination almost always allowed: Even in states where a court order is necessary before the payor can stop payment, granting of the order is virtually ***automatic***. Except for the special case where the second marriage is annulled (discussed below), practically no courts continue alimony after remarriage, even if the recipient remains needy (e.g., she has married one who is unemployed or otherwise unable to contribute to her support). A few cases say that alimony may continue in "extraordinary circumstances," but even these cases very rarely find that the requisite extraordinary circumstances exist; see, e.g., *In re Marriage of Shima,* 360 N.W.2d 827 (Iowa 1985) (W's 18 years of service to H and their children as a homemaker are not the kind of "extraordinary circumstances" justifying alimony after W's remarriage).

3. **Annulment:** If the recipient's new marriage is *annulled*, some courts treat it as never having happened. Therefore, these courts frequently permit the first spouse's obligation of alimony to be restored. But even in this annulment situation, a substantial number of courts hold that the alimony obligation is *not* restored. Clark, p. 664.

E. **Cohabitation by recipient:** The fact that the alimony recipient is *cohabiting* with another person may be grounds for terminating the obligation to pay alimony.

   1. **Statutory authorization:** About 10 states have statutes either requiring or at least authorizing the court to reduce the alimony award if the recipient lives with a person of the opposite sex. Clark, p. 665, n. 98.

   2. **Common law approach:** Even in the majority of states that do not have a statute on the subject of cohabitation, most courts will reduce the alimony if there is evidence that the cohabitation arrangement has *reduced the costs* borne by the recipient. Thus if H can show that W and her new companion (let's call him X) are living together, and that X is paying part of the monthly rent or mortgage, the court is likely to reduce H's alimony obligation by some amount.

      a. **Homosexual cohabitation:** Occasionally, a *homosexual* cohabitation has been used as a basis for terminating alimony. See, e.g., *Anonymous v. Anonymous*, 5 F.L.R. 2127 (Minn.Dist.Ct. 1978) (W's homosexual cohabitation has made her remarriage substantially less likely, thus creating a change of circumstances not considered when the court originally ordered alimony; therefore, alimony is terminated).

   3. **Separation agreement:** Since in most states cohabitation does not automatically entitle the payor to reduce or terminate alimony, an attorney representing the husband in negotiations for his *separation agreement* should obviously attempt to obtain a clear provision that cohabitation will entitle the husband to terminate payments.

F. **Death of payor:** The obligation to make alimony payments generally terminates upon the *death* of the payor. That is, the receiving spouse usually does not have a claim against the payor's *estate* for payments accruing after the payor's death. Clark, pp. 669-70.

   1. **Extraordinary circumstances:** Some states have statutes providing that unless the parties otherwise agree or the court explicitly so provides in the original divorce decree, alimony terminates automatically upon the payor's death. In states not having such statutes, court very occasionally hold that extraordinary circumstances (e.g., the exceptional need of the former spouse, and the estate's ample ability to pay) justify the court in ordering post-death alimony. But these cases are rare. *Id.*

CHILD CUSTODY
AND SUPPORT

Introductory note: The children of a couple being divorced are innocent parties who are vitally affected. It is the interests of the innocent children which underlie the traditional rules as to child custody in a divorce. Although modern courts have adopted new criteria in the granting of divorces, they have been reluctant to deviate from traditional principles in determining child custody.

I. CHILD CUSTODY

A. **Standard used by courts:** Child custody is determined by courts according to the *best interests of the child.*

   1. **Factors considered:** State statutes set criteria for courts to evaluate in determining the best interests of the child. Typically, they include:

      a. The *age* of the child;

      b. The physical and mental *health* of the child;

      c. The parent's *fitness* to care for the child, including the parent's *emotional stability* and his or her possible *misconduct*;

      d. The *financial situation* of the parents; and

      e. The *desires of the child*; most jurisdictions provide that at a certain age the child may elect the custodial parent or that the preference of the child is to be considered.

   2. **Gender:** Traditionally many courts applied a *presumption* that custody of a child of *"tender years"* should be awarded to the mother in the absence of evidence that she was not fit or suitable.

      a. **Abolished:** Today, most states have abolished the tender years presumption, and *disregard the parent's gender completely* in deciding custody. Some states have reached this result by statute, and others by case-law. Some decisions have even held that use of the presumption to favor women violates the Equal Protection clause of the federal Constitution (though the Supreme Court has never decided this issue).

      Example: In a divorce proceeding H and W each seek custody of their two children of tender years. Both H and W are fit and proper persons to be granted custody of the children. There is no clear preponderance of the evidence favoring either party regarding child custody. Therefore, the court awards custody to W based on a presumption that when dealing with children of tender years the natural mother is the proper person to be vested with custody. H appeals, contending that the presumption violates the Equal Protection Clause of the Fourteenth Amendment.

Held, for H. The gender-based presumption is unconstitutional. The presumption is based on sex, and is therefore subject to scrutiny under the Fourteenth Amendment. The presumption is not related to any significant state interest. Further, the presumption discriminates against H by requiring him to prove the unfitness of W. *Ex parte Devine*, 398 So.2d 686 (Ala. 1981).

3. **Sexual activities:** Courts are not in agreement as to the effect that a parent's non-marital *sexual activities* should have on the custody issue. In general, courts are far more tolerant of non-marital sex (and therefore less likely to consider it to be a disqualification for custody) than they used to be.

   a. **Heterosexual out-of-wedlock relationships:** Where the sexual activities are *heterosexual*, the vast majority of courts give much less weight to the activity than they did 10 or 20 years ago. Nearly all courts today hold that the mere fact that a parent has a sexual relationship outside of marriage, or even is part of an adulterous relationship, does *not in itself* constitute grounds for denying custody. Clark, p. 804. Only where there is a showing that the non-marital relationship has a *negative impact* on the child will most courts explicitly consider it on the custody issue. (Of course, many courts may *silently* consider what they believe to be a parent's "sexual immorality" in making the custody determination, but few will say so explicitly anymore.)

   Example: After H and W are divorced, W (who has custody of the couple's two minor children) begins dating X, who as W knows is married. X and W advertise in *Screw* Magazine for "other ... couples or groups ... for fun & games." They keep copies of the magazine (as well as letters and explicit photos sent in response to the ad) around the house. H argues that this conduct makes W unfit to retain custody.

   Held, for W. "Immorality, sexual deviation and what we conveniently consider aberrant sexual practices do not ipso facto constitute unfitness for custody." Unless there is evidence that a parent's sexual activities involve or affect his or her minor children, these activities may not constitutionally be considered by the court. Here, there is no evidence that W's activities have affected the children in any way. *Feldman v. Feldman*, 358 N.Y.S.2d 507 (App.Div. 1974).

      i. **Initial decree vs. modification:** Observe that a court is much less likely to consider evidence of a parent's alleged sexual immorality where the issue is whether a custody decree should be *modified* than where custody is at issue for the first time. Thus the court in *Feldman, supra,* attached weight to the fact that the minor children there had already been living under W's custody for several years before the modification proceeding was brought.

b. Homosexuality: A similar, though slower, shift in judicial opinions has occurred with respect to a parent's *homosexuality.*

    i. Traditional view: Thus traditionally, courts have frequently regarded a parent's homosexuality as a virtually automatic grounds for denying custody, or even visitation. Clark, p. 805. Courts following this view have made a number of arguments, including "if gay parents have custody, they will molest the children; if gay parents have custody, they will turn the children into homosexuals; if gay parents have custody, they will perform sex acts in front of the children; if gay parents have custody, the children will be harmed because of the immoral environment." 11 U. Dayton L. Rev. 275, 324 (1986). See, e.g., *Roe v. Roe,* 324 S.E.2d 691 (Va. 1985) ("the father's continuous exposure of the child to his immoral and illicit [homosexual] relationship renders him an unfit and improper custodian as a matter of law").

    ii. Modern/progressive view: But many if not most courts have fortunately adopted a more progressive and enlightened view of what significance a parent's homosexuality should have in the custody decision. These courts reason that a parent's homosexuality — even the parent's carrying out of an open homosexual relationship — should not without more even be a factor in the custody decision. Only if the homosexual relationship is shown to *adversely affect* the child do these courts treat it as grounds for granting custody to the other parent. Furthermore, many courts in this more forward-thinking group discount the argument that the child will be harmed by teasing or derision from friends and classmates who learn that the parent is gay.

    Example: H and W are divorced. W receives custody of their three children, including B, a son, now 12. W has been hospitalized over 80 times in the past 10 years with various serious health problems. W has also been unable or unwilling to keep B in professional counseling that he needs. H is a homosexual who has lived for eight years with a male partner, seeks custody of B. W contends that if custody were given to H, B would be subjected to taunting, teasing and ostracism.

    Held, for H. The court here applies the "nexus test," by which "the homosexuality of a parent should only be an issue insofar as the parent's sexual orientation can be proven to have harmed the child." Here, no proof of harm to B has been shown. It is true that B will have genuine social pressure stemming from the fact of H's homosexuality, but this is not the same thing as showing that H's homosexual *conduct* has had an adverse affect upon B. H has been a caring, worthy father, and his behavior has been discreet. (Furthermore, W may not move from New York to Florida with the other two children, since this would deprive H as their non-custodial parent of regular access, and no exceptional circumstances justifying the move have been shown.) *M.A.B. v. R.B.*, 510 N.Y.S.2d 960 (Sup.Ct. 1986).

4. **Race:** A court may *not* use *race* as the determining factor when awarding custody of a child.

> **Example:** H and W are both white. When they are divorced, custody of their child, C, is awarded to W. W marries a black man, and H petitions for custody of C because of changed conditions. The court finds that both H and W are devoted to C, have adequate housing and the new spouses of H and W are respectable. However, the court awards custody of C to H to avoid "social stigmatization." W appeals.
>
> *Held*, child custody may not be denied because of a racially-mixed household. "A core purpose of the Fourteenth Amendment was to do away with all governmentally-imposed discrimination based on race." The hypothetical effects of private racial prejudice may not be used to deny equal protection of the law to anyone. Whatever problems a racially mixed marriage may pose for C, they cannot justify removing C from W's custody where W is found to be an appropriate person to have custody. *Palmore v. Sidoti*, 466 U.S. 429 (1984).

> **Note:** The Supreme Court decision in *Palmore* did not require that custody revert to W. The decision only held that custody may not be predicated upon W's association with a black man. While that case is pending in the Supreme Court, H and his second wife move from Florida to Texas with C. After the decision W files a motion in Florida to compel return of C. H applies for a temporary restraining order in Texas. The Florida court defers to the Texas court to determine permanent custody. It noted: (1) H's original petition also sought custody because of W's inattention to C's nutrition and schooling; and (2) the Court decision does not require immediate custody reversion to W. The best interests of C are most important. There is no need for a substantial upheaval in the child's life as the Texas court's determination of custody can be made expeditiously. *Palmore v. Sidoti*, 472 So.2d 843 (Fla.1985).

5. **Religion:** Where custody determination involves inquiry into the consequences of *religious* practices of one of the parents, the court must be alert to the impact of its order on the constitutional right of freedom

of religion of the parent. If a religious practice poses an ***immediate and substantial*** threat to the child's well-being, the court may issue an order to protect the child. But such an order must make the ***least possible intrusion*** upon the religious practice of the parent. See, e.g., *Osier v. Osier*, 410 A.2d 1027 (Maine 1980) (Lower court may consider the fact that W as a Jehovah's Witness would not consent to any blood transfusions that might be required for the child; but the court must consider alternative remedies to a denial of custody, such as an order eliminating any requirement for W to consent to any necessary blood transfusions.)

6. **Handicap and illness:** A ***handicap*** which only affects a parent's ability to participate with children in physical activities is not sufficient to deny custody. *In re marriage of Carney*, 598 P.2d 36 (Cal. 1979).

B. **Standards for modifying custody:** Where one party wants to ***modify*** an existing custody decree, a different and much tougher standard applies than for the original decree. When the court is considering as an initial matter who should receive custody, the court begins with a presumption that either party is equally fit. But once the court has ordered custody in favor of one parent, and that arrangement has persisted for a while, then the court requires the other parent to show a ***substantial change in circumstances*** before the decree will be modified.

1. **Rationale:** The child's interest in ***stability*** dictates that, as one court has put it, custody be changed only where "circumstances affecting the welfare of the child have been ***so greatly altered*** that there is a ***strong possibility*** [that] the child will be ***harmed*** if he continues to live under the present arrangement." *Perreault v. Cook*, 322 A.2d 610 (N.H. 1974).

2. **Liberal interpretation:** But notwithstanding this general rule that substantially changed circumstances are required, courts in practice frequently accept something less than a cataclysmic change of circumstances as being sufficient for modification.

> **Example 1:** H receives custody after he and W divorce. H remarries, but later divorces his second wife.
> *Held,* H's second divorce is a sufficiently great change of circumstances that (coupled with the fact that W has remarried and now has a stable household with her new husband and their two children) custody should be shifted to W. *Perreault v. Cook, supra.*

> **Example 2:** S is eight years old when H and W divorce. Physical custody is awarded to W except on weekends. When S turns 12, H seeks custody. S testifies that he wishes now to live with H.
> *Held,* the four-year increase in S's age, together with his stated desire to live with H now, justify changing custody to H. *King v. King*, 333 A.2d 135 (R.I. 1975).

C. **Joint custody:** An increasing number of courts now provide for *joint custody* of children, rather than the traditional award of sole custody to one parent.

   1. **Presumption:** Many states now in fact impose by statute a *presumption* in favor of joint custody.

   2. **Joint custody allowed:** Of the states that do not impose a presumption that joint custody is desirable, most *allow* the trial judge to award joint custody. Some states allow joint custody to be imposed only if *both parents agree*. But most states permit the judge to award joint custody even over the objection of one parent. Areen, p. 635.

   3. **Different types of joint custody:** Observe that "joint custody" is a vague concept, and can apply to at least two different kinds of arrangements.

      a. **Joint legal custody:** In "joint *legal* custody," both parents have an equal say in important matters of child-rearing (e.g., where the child will attend school, or what religion the child will follow).

      b. **Joint physical custody:** In "joint *physical* custody," by contrast, the parents typically share the actual day-to-day living arrangements (e.g., the child spends three days of the week at one parent's residence and four days at the other parent's home).

      c. **Preference:** Courts are more inclined to award joint legal custody than joint physical custody, because of the extremely large effort and commitment required for the latter.

D. **Custody dispute between natural parent and a non-parent:** When a custody dispute is between the two parents, as we have seen, nearly all courts apply the "best interests of the child" standard. But where a custody conflict is between a *parent* and a *non-parent*, this standard does *not* apply. Instead, nearly all courts recognize that the parent has some sort of "right" to custody of the child, and hold that the parent "may only be deprived of the custody of his child if he is shown to be *unfit* to perform the duties that custody imposes." Clark, p. 823. So even if the non-parent would be a "better" custodian (e.g., because the child has lived with that non-parent for a long time, and has come to regard him or her as a "psychological parent"), the general rule is that custody will still be given to the parent unless the parent is shown by *clear evidence* to be *neglectful*, *abusive*, or otherwise unable to provide even a reasonable upbringing. *Id.*

   1. **Voluntary relinquishment to non-parent:** The issue arises most commonly where the parents' marriage breaks up (or the parents were never married in the first place), and one of the parents *relinquishes* the child to a *friend or relative*. Sometimes the relinquishment is explicitly stated to be temporary, in which case the parent will clearly have the right to reclaim the child. But other times the parent indicates to the friend or relative that the latter should *permanently*

bring up the child. In this "permanent relinquishment" situation, what happens if the parent years later seeks to reclaim custody of the child? In general, courts have applied the rule stated above, that the parent is **entitled to regain custody** unless he or she is shown by clear evidence to be an unfit parent.

> **Example:** Two months after C is born, his parents, H and W, separate. Because neither parent is able to care for the child, H places the child with his sister, S, who lives in another town with her husband and two teenage daughters. S keeps custody of C until C is four years old. H visits C frequently, and regularly sends money to S for C's support. C develops a child-parent relationship with S and her husband, but also comes to recognize H as his father. When C is four, H seeks to regain custody of him, and S objects. A state statute allows "any person*(D3who has established emotional ties creating a child-parent relationship with the child" to begin or intervene in child custody proceedings.
>
> *Held*, custody should be returned to H. "A natural parent has the right to the custody of his or her children, absent a compelling reason for placing the children in the custody of another. The 'best interests of the child' standard applicable to custody disputes between natural parents in a marriage dissolution proceeding is not applicable to custody disputes between natural parents and other persons." Although the state statute allows S (as one who has a "child-parent relationship" with C) to intervene in the proceedings, the statute was not intended to give the intervener the substantive rights of a parent, merely a procedural opportunity to be heard. Here, although S might the "better" parent for C (in the sense that C will suffer some psychological harm from being removed from the home he has had for nearly his whole life), H has not been shown to be unfit or unable to love and care for S, so there is no "compelling reason" for denying custody to H. *Matter of Marriage of Hruby*, 748 P.2d 57 (Ore. 1987).

E. Jurisdiction over custody disputes: A very frequently litigated question is, "Does a particular court have **jurisdiction** to make a custody decree in a particular situation?" If there are no custody decrees outstanding or custody proceedings pending, and both parents and the child reside in the same state, then the matter is easy — the state of residence, and only that state, has jurisdiction to issue a custody decree. But where a state has issued a decree and then one or both parents has moved (with or without the child), or where a court is asked to make an initial decree at a time when the parents and the child are not all residents of that state, or where a court is asked to modify the custody determination of another state, problems arise. The sorting out of custody jurisdiction in a multistate context is probably the most intricate and confusing area in all of family law. We can only touch the surface here.

1. **UCCJA and PKPA:** To begin with, there are two statutes that are of supreme importance in the area of custody jurisdiction. The first is the Uniform Child Custody Jurisdiction Act (UCCJA), which has been adopted by *all 50* states and the District of Columbia. The second is the federal Parental Kidnapping Prevention Act (PKPA), which despite its name deals with all cases where one state is asked to enforce or modify another state's custody decree, not merely with cases of parental kidnapping.

    a. **Function of UCCJA:** The UCCJA sets the ground rules in each state for determining whether a state has jurisdiction to issue a decree, if custody proceedings are not pending in any other state at the time and no other state has already issued a custody decree. In this "first state to hear the matter" situation, the PKPA plays no role, so the case can be decided solely on local state law, which as noted is in all states the UCCJA.

    b. **Function of PKPA:** The PKPA, by contrast, deals with those situations where a state is asked to either: (i) issue a custody decree at a time when another state already has custody proceedings pending; or (2) modify a custody decree previously issued by another state. (In either of these situations, the UCCJA purports to set down rules that are sometimes the same as and sometimes different from the PKPA's rules; because of the U.S. Constitution's Supremacy Clause, the PKPA takes priority, and ends up pretty much setting the rules for either of these situations.)

    c. **Combined function:** Taken together, the UCCJA and PKPA require a state to *enforce the custody decree of a sister state without modification*, unless the court that issued the original decree no longer meets certain jurisdictional tests and the forum state does meet those tests.

    d. **Framework of discussion:** We consider below first the "initial custody proceedings" situation, and then the "subsequent proceedings" situation.

2. **Initial custody proceedings:** Where a state is asked to issue a custody decree at a time when there are no outstanding custody decrees from any other state, and there are no other pending proceedings in another state that were begun before the present proceeding was started, as noted the UCCJA sets out the ground rules. Under the UCCJA, the forum state will only be deemed to have jurisdiction if *at least one* of the four following conditions is satisfied. (The first two are overwhelmingly the most important.)

    a. **"Home state":** First, the forum state qualifies if it was the *"home state"* of the child at either of two dates. First is the date the proceedings were commenced. The second possible date is any date within *six months* before the proceedings were commenced, but only if the child is *now absent* from the forum state "because of his removal or retention by a person claiming his custody or for other reasons, and a parent or person acting as parent continues to live in" the forum state. UCCJA §3(a)(1).

    i. Home state defined: *"Home state"* is, in turn, defined in §2 of the UCCJA as "the state in which the child immediately preceding the time involved lived with his parents, a parent, or a person acting as parent, for *at least six consecutive months*, and in the case of a child less than six months old the state in which the child lived from birth with any of the persons mentioned." So assuming the child was more than six months old at the time the proceedings were commenced, a state could only be the child's "home state" if the child lived there for at least six consecutive months, *and* had not been away from the forum state for more than six months (even if the absence from the forum state was due to abduction by the other parent not residing in the state.)

    ii. Illustration: Suppose Father abducts Son from Forum State, where Son and Mother lived together. Mother must bring suit within six months — otherwise Forum State will no longer be deemed to be Son's "home state."

b. "Best interests": Second, the forum court can have jurisdiction if "it is in the *best interest* of the child" that a court in the forum state assumes jurisdiction because: (i) the child and his parents, or the child and at least one contestant, have a *significant connection* with the forum state; and (ii) there is available in the forum state *"substantial evidence* concerning the child's past or future care, protection, training and personal relationships. ..." UCCJA §3(a)(2).

c. Abandonment or emergency: Alternatively, the forum state will have jurisdiction if the child is physically present there, and has either been *abandoned* or there is an *emergency* requiring protection of the child against mistreatment, abuse or neglect. UCCJA §3(a)(3)).

d. No other state: Finally, the forum state will have jurisdiction if *no other state* has jurisdiction (or is willing to exercise jurisdiction), and it is in the *child's best interest* that the forum state hear the matter. UCCJA §3(a)(4).

Note 1: Observe that *physical presence* of the child by itself is *not* enough to confer jurisdiction on a state. The purpose of this rule is to avoid giving a parent an incentive to "snatch" a child and bring the child to a state where the snatching parent thinks the court will be more sympathetic to him or her. (*Example:* H and W have lived in California with S for 10 years. Just before H is to commence divorce and custody proceedings in California, W takes S to Oregon, and asks a judge to issue a divorce and give her custody. Oregon certainly does not have "home state" jurisdiction, because S has not lived there for six consecutive months; unless W can convince the Oregon court that S and W now have a "significant connection" with Oregon, and that it is in S's "best interests" to have the case heard in Oregon, the Oregon court does not have jurisdiction. Meanwhile, the California court continues to have jurisdiction for at least six months after the snatching, because California remains the "home state" for that period.)

Note 2: Conversely, physical presence of the child in the forum state is *not* a *prerequisite*. As the example in the above note demonstrates, even after one parent has removed the child, the child's original state of residence will continue to have jurisdiction so long as the proceeding is begun less than six months after the child's removal.

Note 3: Observe that the UCCJA does *not* explicitly require that the forum state obtain *personal jurisdiction* over the absent parent, in order for the court to have jurisdiction over the custody dispute. The Supreme Court has never explicitly decided whether the Due Process Clause prevents a state from issuing a custody decree when the court does not have personal jurisdiction over the absent parent. (Under *Kulko v. Superior Court of California, infra*, p. 146, if a parent does not have minimum contacts with the forum state and is thus not subject to personal jurisdiction in the forum state, the state may not issue an award of *child support*; but *Kulko* does not deal with custody determinations.) Most lower courts have held that personal jurisdiction is *not* necessary for the issuance of a custody determination (usually on the theory that all that is being decided is the "status" of custody). In any event, the UCCJA does deal somewhat with due process concerns by requiring that the absent parent be given *notice* and an *opportunity to be heard*. See UCCJA §5.

3. **Action in second state for modification:** Now, let us consider the circumstances in which a second state's court may jump into the fray by either: (1) beginning proceedings at a time when custody proceedings are *already pending* in another state; or (2) *modifying* another state's previously-issued custody determination. Here, the rules, as noted, are mainly set forth in the federal PKPA, not the UCCJA. In either of these situations, the court must proceed through a multi-step analysis.

In the following discussion, the court that has already issued a decree, or in which proceedings were first begun that are still continuing, is referred to as "State One." The present, forum state, which is being asked to either disregard proceedings pending in State One or modify State One's prior custody decree, is referred to as "State Two."

a. **Did State One have jurisdiction:** First, State Two must ask, "Did State One have jurisdiction?" The court will answer this question by looking at State One's version of the UCCJA. (There are some small variations from state to state in the precise wording of the state's implementation of the UCCJA, but the differences are not usually significant.) The rules for making this determination are, of course, those set forth in paragraph (2) above. Note that the question here is whether State One *did*, at the time proceedings there were commenced, have jurisdiction, *not* whether State One would *still* have jurisdiction if proceedings were commenced there today.

   i. **State One had jurisdiction:** If the court in State Two decides that State One did have jurisdiction, the State Two court should shift its analysis to that given in step (b) below.

   ii. **State One without jurisdiction:** If State Two decides that State One did *not* have jurisdiction (i.e., State Two decides that State One simply misapplied State One's version of the UCCJA), the analysis should shift to that given in step (c) below.

b. **If State One had original jurisdiction:** This step applies if State Two concludes that State One had jurisdiction when State One commenced the original custody proceedings. State Two's analysis now depends on whether State Two is being asked to issue an initial decree while proceedings are still pending (but have not yielded a decree in) State One, or is instead being asked to modify a decree previously issued by State One.

   i. **State One proceedings are continuing:** If proceedings in State One are continuing, and have not yet yielded a custody decree, then State Two *must not exercise* jurisdiction. See 28 U.S.C. §1738A(g). That is, the PKPA imposes a rule that "the first valid proceeding commenced is permitted to continue to its end."

   Example: H and W live in California with their son, S. H files for divorce in California, and seeks custody. These proceedings are pending and have not yet yielded any sort of custody decree. W takes the child and moves to Arizona. Since the Arizona court must conclude that California has jurisdiction (since under all forms of the UCCJA, California was the "home state" of S at the time proceedings there were commenced), Arizona must decline to exercise jurisdiction over the custody issue as long as California is continuing to hear that issue.

ii. **State Two has jurisdiction to modify:** If State One has already issued a custody decree, and State Two is being asked to *modify* that decree, then State Two must ask, "Does State Two now have jurisdiction over custody?" This question is to be answered under a provision of the PKPA, 28 U.S.C. §1738A(c)(2), which lists essentially the same four possibilities for jurisdiction as does the UCCJA (see *supra*, pp. 132-133). In most situations, this means that unless State Two is now the "home state" of the child, or there is a "significant connection" between the child and State Two making it in the child's best interest that State Two hear the case, State Two must go no further, and may *not* modify the State One decree. If State Two concludes that State Two *does* now have jurisdiction, then the analysis shifts to step (d) below.

c. **If State One didn't have original jurisdiction:** If State Two concludes that State One did *not* originally have jurisdiction (even though State One purported to have it), then:

i. **State Two has jurisdiction:** If State Two concludes that it how has jurisdiction (under the same tests as described in step (b) above), then the State Two court may *issue its own decree*. If the State One proceedings are pending but have not yielded a decree, then the State Two decree will of course be the first decree. If State One entered a decree (which, by hypothesis, State Two has decided State One did not have jurisdiction to enter), then State Two will probably say that it is *"modifying"* the State One decree, but essentially State Two is deciding the custody matter on its own.

ii. **State Two doesn't have jurisdiction:** If, however, State Two concludes that it does *not* now have jurisdiction (even though it has also concluded that State One did not have jurisdiction), State Two must *decline to hear the case*. That is, State Two may not enforce State One's decree, since neither State One nor State Two have jurisdiction.

d. **If State One had original jurisdiction, and State Two now has jurisdiction:** Now, we consider the remaining possibility, that (State Two has decided) State One had original jurisdiction, but State Two *now* has jurisdiction. Here, State Two's duty depends on whether State One has *continuing* jurisdiction.

i. **State One has continuing jurisdiction:** If State Two determines that State One has continuing jurisdiction, then State

Two ***must enforce*** State One's decree. See 28 U.S.C. §1738A(f)(2). This situation can certainly arise, because it is quite possible under the UCCJA for two states to simultaneously have jurisdiction for custody matters over the same child (e.g., State One remains the "home state," and State Two has significant connections with the child and the controversy, making it, in the State Two court's opinion, in the child's "best interest" to have the case heard there). In this "both states have jurisdiction" situation, the PKPA requires that State Two ***not modify*** State One's decree — State Two must, in fact, ***enforce*** State One's decree. See 28 U.S.C. §1738A(a).

ii. **State One's jurisdiction no longer continues:** If, however, State Two concludes that State One ***no longer*** has jurisdiction over the matter, then State Two ***may modify*** the State One decree. The same is true if State Two has indicated that it no longer wishes to ***exercise*** its jurisdiction to reconsider the decree. 28 U.S.C. §1738A(f)(2).

Example of the operation of the UCCJA and the PKPA: H and W reside with their two sons in North Dakota. In 1983, the North Dakota courts issue a divorce decree, and award custody to W. H moves to his parents' home in Pennsylvania in 1985. In June 1986, the children come to Pennsylvania for an extended visit with H (which W agrees upon). In March 1987, H refuses to return the children as agreed, and instead starts a Pennsylvania proceeding for custody. Both Pennsylvania and North Dakota have enacted the unmodified form of the UCCJA. W continues to reside in North Dakota.

The Pennsylvania court should refuse to grant H custody. Applying step (a) above, the court should find that the North Dakota court had jurisdiction when it issued the decree in W's favor, since North Dakota was clearly the "home state" of the children at that moment. Proceeding to step (b), the Pennsylvania court should determine that it does have jurisdiction to modify, because Pennsylvania is now clearly the home state of the children (since they have lived there with H for more than six months prior to commencement of the Pennsylvania proceedings).

Now, the court should proceed to step (d) above, which deals with the situation where the first court had jurisdiction and the second court now has it. The Pennsylvania court must now determine whether, under North Dakota law, the North Dakota courts would have continuing jurisdiction if the second proceeding (instituted by H) had been started in North Dakota instead of in Pennsylvania. North Dakota should not find that it was the "home state" at the time the second proceeding was begun, since the children had been away for more than six months. But North Dakota probably would have found that it was in the "best interest" of the child that the North Dakota courts assume jurisdiction, because all the parties had a significant connection with North Dakota (H and W lived there throughout their marriage, the children resided there until nine months ago, and W still lives there); there is also clearly available in North Dakota "substantial evidence" concerning the children's present or future care, protection, etc. The fact that the North Dakota courts heard the evidence concerning custody the first time around adds to the likelihood that that state would find that it had continuing jurisdiction under UCCJA §3(a)(2).

If the Pennsylvania court concludes, as suggested above, that the North Dakota courts have continuing jurisdiction over the custody issue, then under UCCJA §14(a)(1) and 28 U.S.C. §1738A(f)(2), the Pennsylvania court must not modify the North Dakota's decree, and must in fact enforce that decree. (The facts and holding are suggested by *Barndt v. Barndt*, 588 A.2d 320 (Pa.Super.Ct. 1990).)

4. **No federal court jurisdiction:** The *federal courts* do *not* have jurisdiction to grant divorces, award alimony, or decide child custody in the first instance. This is known as the "domestic relations exception" to the exercise of federal jurisdiction.

   a. **No jurisdiction to decide between two states:** Furthermore, the federal courts do not even have jurisdiction to decide which of two conflicting custody decrees issued by state courts is valid. *Thompson v. Thompson*, 484 U.S. 174 (1988). So if two state courts should come up with inconsistent custody decrees, the litigants must continue fighting the matter out in state court, rather than asking the federal courts to settle the matter.

5. **Federal Extradition Act:** By the way, if a parent "snatches" a child from State One and removes him to State Two, and if this act is a crime (e.g., kidnapping) under the laws of State One, it may be possible to use the *federal Extradition Act*, 18 U.S.C. §3182, to force officials of State Two to send the parent back to State One to face the criminal charges. This is true even if the courts of State Two believe that the charges in State One are meritless (e.g., because, State Two believes, State One is misinterpreting the federal PKPA by erroneously asserting jurisdiction over the custody issue). So long as charges in State One are "formally" correct (i.e., the extradition papers follow necessary procedures), State Two must remand the parent to face the State One charges without any inquiry into the merits of the State One charges. *California v. Superior Court of California*, 482 U.S. 400 (1987). This possibility of extradition gives the early victor in an interstate custody dispute additional potential leverage.

II. VISITATION

A. **Visitation generally:** After custody is decided, contact between the child and the non-custodial parent must be considered. The court will generally order ***reasonable visitation rights*** unless this would ***seriously harm*** the child. Clark, p. 812.

B. **Restrictions:** The court may decide that while visitation should be allowed, it should be subject to special ***restrictions*** for the child's best interest.

C. **Child refuses to visit:** Frequently, the non-custodial parent (typically the father) complains that his visitation rights are being interfered with by the mother, and the mother retorts that what is really happening is that the ***child does not wish*** to visit the father.

   1. **Child's wish:** Where the court is convinced that this is truly the child's wish, and that this desire has not been orchestrated by the mother, the court may well decide that it cannot or should not order visitation over the child's strong objections.

   2. **Mother's wish:** But if the court concludes, as it often does, that the child's lack of desire to see the father is due to the child's not wanting to anger the mother, or is due to the mother's repeated efforts to fan the child's resentment against the father, then the court is likely to hold that visitation must occur even over the child's supposed objections. See, e.g., *Smith v. Smith*, 434 N.E.2d 749 (Ct.App.Ohio 1980) ("[T]he plaintiff must do more than merely encourage the minor children to visit the defendant. Until the children can affirmatively and independently decide not to have any visitation with the defendant, the plaintiff must follow the court order that she deliver the children to the defendant for purposes of visitation").

   3. **Older child:** Obviously, the older the child is, the more weight the court will give to the child's own wishes in deciding whether to order visitation over the apparent objections of the child. For instance, by the time the child is a teenager, a court is unlikely to order visitation if the child clearly does not want it.

D. **Means of enforcement:** Where the custodial parent has repeatedly thwarted the non-custodial parent's court-ordered visitation rights, a number of remedies are possible.

   1. **Contempt:** Occasionally, courts have issued a sentence of ***civil contempt*** against the custodial parent, until the visitation order is complied with. See, e.g., *Smith v. Smith, supra* (P ordered to go to prison for five days, sentence to be suspended if P complies with the visitation order).

2. **Change of custody:** In the most extreme case, courts have sometimes dealt with a custodial parent who thwarts the other parent's visitation rights by *changing custody* to the latter. In theory, this remedy is not so much punishment as it is an attempt to produce a situation where the custody/visitation rights of both parents will be better observed. See, e.g., *Egle v. Egle*, 715 F.2d 999 (5th Cir. 1983) (Where W repeatedly interfered with H's visitation rights, moved the children without letting H know their whereabouts, successfully turned one of the children against H, and started a separate action against H in W's new state of residence merely to harass H, the trial court was justified in shifting custody of both children to H, who was more likely to honor the other parent's visitation rights).

E. **Out-of-state move by custodial parent:** Suppose the non-custodial parent has been granted liberal visitation rights, and the custodial parent then decides to *move far away*. What, if anything, can or should the court do to prevent the inevitable interference with the non-custodial parent's visitation rights?

1. **Prohibit move:** Courts occasionally in effect *prohibit* the move. The judge, of course, cannot prevent the custodial parent from moving her own residence. But the court can and occasionally does say, "You may not move the child with you, and you must give custody to the other parent if you do make the move." The court is of course most likely to take this extreme action where the judge believes that the move is being made in bad faith for the *purpose* of defeating visitation rights.

2. **Good faith move:** Where the judge believes that the proposed move is a good faith one made for better job opportunities, for the needs of the custodial parent's new spouse, or for other substantial reason, the court is not very likely to block the move. Clark, p. 813. As one court put it, "To establish sufficient cause for the removal, the custodial parent initially must show that there is a *real advantage* to that parent in the move and that the move is not inimical to the best interests of the children. Removal should not be allowed for a frivolous reason. The advantage, however, need not be a substantial advantage but one based on a sincere and genuine desire of the custodial parent to move and a sensible good faith reason for the move." *Cooper v. Cooper*, 491 A.2d 606 (N.J. 1984).

F. **HIV-infected parent:** As noted, courts generally award visitation unless it would pose serious harm to the child. One issue that courts have begun to struggle with is whether to order visitation with a parent who has *AIDS* or is HIV-positive. Early indications are that most courts will not deny or restrict visitation rights to AIDS-infected or HIV-positive parents. See, e.g., *Stewart v. Stewart*, 521 N.E.2d 956 (Ct.App.Ind. 1988) (in light of strong medical evidence that AIDS is not transmitted through everyday household contact, trial court should not have cut off visitation rights of the HIV-positive father). A judge might, however, condition visitation rights on the parent's observation of standard health procedures for reducing the already-small danger of contagion (e.g., wearing of rubber gloves where an exchange of bodily fluids is likely, such as bandaging a cut on the child).

G. **Visitation by grandparents or other non-parents:** Nearly all states have enacted statutes that give visitation rights to *non-parent* in certain circumstances. Clark, p. 828.

   1. **Grandparents:** Nearly all of these statutes give visitation rights to *grandparents*. But some states have added other categories (e.g., siblings, great-grandparents, etc.).

      a. **Any interested person:** A few states (Alaska, California, Connecticut and Maine) have given their courts the power to grant visitation rights to *any person*, regardless of relationship, if the court finds that this is in the child's best interest. See, e.g., Cal. Civ. Code §4601 (court has discretion to order reasonable visitation rights to "any other person having an interest in the welfare of the child").

   2. **Family breakdown:** Most of the statutes apply only where the child's parents have been or are being *divorced* or *separated*, or where one or both parents have *died*. Clark, p. 828. In this "broken family" situation, the case for granting visitation rights to the grandparent (or other person with a close tie to the child), even over the objection of the custodial parent, is the strongest.

      a. **Intact family:** But in the minority of states whose statute allows visitation even where the nuclear family is intact, courts occasionally will order visitation for, say, a grandparent, even over the objections of *both parents*. Clark, p. 832.

II. CHILD SUPPORT — GENERALLY

A. **Post-divorce child support:** After the parents have been divorced or separated, each parent must contribute to the *financial support* of the couple's minor children. This duty is not really any different from the duty both parents have to support the child while the parents are living together. However, disputes between the parents about who will pay what towards child support are obviously much more common once the parents are no longer together.

   1. **Award against non-custodial parent:** Typically, child support orders are issued against the *non-custodial* parent. That is, the court orders that the non-custodial parent pay a specified amount each week or month to the custodial parent. The custodial parent, of course, is effectively paying child support in the sense that he or she is directly

purchasing goods and services that are for the child's benefit (e.g., groceries or rent).

    a. Shared custody: In a shared physical custody situation (e.g., the child lives half of the time with the mother and half with the father), the court will generally order the higher-earning spouse to make a payment to the lower-earning one.

B. Amount of support: In general, courts will order that the non-custodial parent pay an amount that is sufficient to cover the child's *needs* (after subtracting a reasonable amount representing the implicit contribution of the custodial parent). However, a court will attempt not to order the non-custodial parent to pay more than that parent is *able* to pay.

    1. Independent income of child: In determining the minor child's needs, may the court take into account *independent income* or *assets* that the child himself may possess? In general, courts do so only to a limited extent. If the non-custodial parent has the ability to pay for a reasonable standard of living for the child, that parent will typically be ordered to do so, in order that the child's assets or income need not be used for this purpose. But if the non-custodial parent is simply unable to pay for all that the child needs, then the court will assume that the child's income will be used. Clark, p. 720. See, e.g., *Armstrong v. Armstrong*, 544 P.2d 941 (Cal. 1976) (where two children have income from a trust set up for them by their grandfather, Father must pay for their basic needs, but will not be required to pay for expensive discretionary matters like education and travel, since the trust income can be used for this).

    2. Parent's income includes what she could, not merely does, earn: When the court computes the amount that the non-custodial parent must pay, the judge of course takes into account the amount that the custodial parent can pay. As to both parents' payments, courts typically consider what that parent *could reasonably earn* on the job market, not merely what that parent *does in fact* earn. Thus if the court is convinced that either parent is failing to take advantage of readily-available opportunities, the court is likely to order a higher payment (or, in the case of a custodial parent who does this, order a lower payment from the other spouse) than that parent's actual present income would warrant.

        Example: When H and W divorce, H earns $17,400 per year and W earns $130 per week. Several years later, H is earning $29,500 a year, but W's wages have been reduced to $90 per week. W petitions for an increase in child support.

        Held (on appeal), the lower court should increase the child support to be paid by H. However, in computing the appropriate amount, the court must take into account the fact that W insists on working very locally, rather than earning a higher wage by working in a nearby city. In deciding how much H should pay, therefore, the lower court should first determine how much W could reasonably earn, not merely what she is in fact earning. (But the child is entitled to benefit from H's increased earnings as well.) *Commonwealth ex rel. Kaplan v. Kaplan*, 344 A.2d 578 (Pa. 1975).

3. **Increased earnings:** An alimony award, as noted *supra* (p. 123), will normally **not** be increased merely because the income of the payor has increased dramatically after the divorce. But the same is **not** true of child support awards: nearly all courts agree that, at least up to the point where the child's reasonable needs have been satisfied, the support order should be **increased** to reflect any material increase in the non-custodial parent's income. See, e.g., *Commonwealth ex rel. Kaplan*, *supra*.

4. **Discretion of trial judge:** Child support awards are left largely to the *discretion* of the trial judge, and are usually not reversed on appeal.

   a. **Federal child support guidelines:** However, a federal law requires each state to enact non-binding *child support guidelines*, which are frequently followed. The guidelines are discussed immediately below.

C. **Child Support Guidelines:** Under federal law, each state is required to maintain *"Child Support Guidelines,"* which specify a precise method for computing the amount of child support that the court should order. See 42 U.S.C. §667, and 45 C.F.R. §302.56. Although the state is required to enact such guidelines, the state is **not** required to make these guidelines **binding** on the judge. Therefore, most states have enacted the guidelines, but have allowed trial judges considerable discretion in deciding whether and how much to deviate from them.

   1. **The "income shares" approach:** Most states have adopted the *"income shares"* approach to computing child support. Essentially, this approach uses two types of information: (1) the combined income of the two parents; and (2) the estimated cost of caring for a child, on the assumption that the cost per child increases as family income increases and decreases for each additional child in the family. After computing the cost of child care for a family of a particular size and a particular combined parental income, the judge then splits the amount owed in proportion to the incomes of the two parents (with the non-custodial parent writing a check to the custodial parent for the former's share).

      Example based on Colorado law: Here is a very simplified example of the "income shares" approach, as this approach is embodied under Colorado law. Assume that Father has an "adjusted gross income" (as defined below) of $3,000 per month, and Mother has an adjusted gross income of $2,000 per month. There are three minor children in the family, and they live exclusively with Mother, except for brief visitations. First, we would consult a schedule or grid, part of which looks like this:

Combined Gross Income	1 Child	2 Children	3 Children	4 Children	5 Children	6 or more Children
$4,000	$540	$838	$1,050	$1,183	$1,292	$1,380
[entries omitted]						
$5,000	$620	$959	$1,201	$1,354	$1,476	$1,577
[entries omitted]						
$6,000	$700	$1,080	$1,352	$1,525	$1,660	$1,774

This table tells us that for a combined gross income of $5,000 per month, the total cost of child care for three children is $1,201. Now (after some adjustments), the court will order Father, as the non-custodial parent, to pay three-fifths of this amount, or $720.60 per month. Because what is counted is "adjusted" gross income: Father would be permitted to subtract from his gross income: (i) the estimated cost of supporting any other children, such as those he is now living with or those from a different prior marriage; (ii) any spousal support paid to Mother or to any other former spouses; and (iii) the cost of health insurance coverage covering the children.

Under Colorado law, the court is not bound to apply these guidelines slavishly; however, the amount produced by the above chart "shall be used as a rebuttable presumption" for setting the amount, and the court may deviate from the guideline only where its application would be "inequitable." Any deviation must be "accompanied by written or oral findings by the court." In deciding what would be equitable, the court may consider (apart from the above grid) the financial resources of the child, the standard of living the child would have enjoyed had the marriage not been dissolved, the physical and emotional condition of the child and his educational needs, and the financial resources and needs of each parent (but *not* the *marital misconduct* of either parent). See generally C&G, pp. 902-12, extensively excerpting the Colorado guidelines.

D. **Support for adult child:** Ordinarily the obligation to support children continues until they reach the age of majority. However, the obligation of support may continue after the child reaches the legal age of majority if circumstances require.

1. **Statutes:** Some states have statutes which authorize court orders for education or maintenance of children after they reach majority. Such statutes have generally been held not to discriminate against divorced parents or to deny them equal protection of the law, even though parents who are not divorced do not have such a legal obligation. The support laws relate reasonably to a legitimate legislative purpose, which is to minimize the economic and educational disadvantages suffered by children of divorced parents. See, e.g., *Kujawinski v. Kujawinski*, 376 N.E.2d 1382 (Ill.1978).

2. **Illness:** If a child is mentally or physically unable to support himself, the general rule is that the parents must continue support after majority. Thus, where a child suffered from dyslexia, a brain defect requiring in this case psychiatric care and prescription drugs for life, the duty of support and maintenance continued after the child reached majority. *Elkins v. Elkins*, 553 S.W.2d 34 (Ark. 1977).

3. **College education:** Most persons begin college about age 18, when child support payments normally end. Court decisions are divided on whether to include a college education in child support orders. Most courts and commentators today seem to believe that a college education should be treated as a "necessary," towards which the parents should be required to contribute whatever financial support they can afford. See Clark, p. 723.

   a. **Disobedient child:** But a child who refuses to comply with the reasonable demands of a parent may be found to lose her right to support. See *supra*, p. 65.

   b. **Graduate school:** A few states permit the court to order a parental contribution toward ***graduate school***, if the student is qualified. See, e.g., *Ross v. Ross*, 400 A.2d 1233 (N.J.Super.1979).

D. **Jurisdiction:** Whether a state may exercise jurisdiction over a nonresident spouse in a child support matter depends on the contacts of the nonresident spouse with that state. The test is whether there is ***sufficient contact*** with the state to make it ***fair and reasonable*** for the court to adjudicate the claim against the nonresident.

   Example: H and W execute a separation agreement in New York, after which W moves to California. Under the agreement their two children, A and B, are to live with H for nine months each year while attending school, and live with W for the other three months. The agreement also provides for child support while A and B are living with W. Subsequently, W obtains a divorce which incorporates the terms of the separation agreement. Thereafter, A asks to live with W during the school year and with H during vacations and H agrees. Later W arranges with B to move to California without H's knowledge. W then brings an action against H in California to increase H's child support. H moves to quash based on lack of personal jurisdiction.

Held, California lacks jurisdiction. The Due Process Clause of the Fourteenth Amendment limits the power of state courts to assert personal jurisdiction over nonresidents. A defendant must have sufficient purposeful contact with the state to make it fair and reasonable for the court to adjudicate the claim. Here jurisdiction was based on H's consent to have A live with W. H's decision was based on his personal, domestic relations and he derived no financial benefit from it. Furthermore, H could not reasonably anticipate that his consent to A's living with W would be the basis of having to litigate the child support claim 3,000 miles away. Thus, H had insufficient purposeful contacts to provide a constitutional basis for exercise of personal jurisdiction over him. *Kulko v. Superior Court of California,* 436 U.S. 84 (1978).

1. **Procedure suggested by Court:** In a situation like that of *Kulko*, how can the forum state further its substantial interest in protecting the rights of resident children and in facilitating child support actions on their behalf? The Supreme Court in *Kulko* asserted that California could apply the Uniform Reciprocal Enforcement of Support Act (see *infra*, p. 147). By use of the Act, W could file a petition for support in California, and have the petition's merits adjudicated in New York without either W or H having to leave their own state. This would allow W to vindicate her claimed right to additional child support. See 9 Uniform Laws Ann. 476 (Supp. Pamph. 1977); Cal.Code Civ.Proc. §1650 *et seq.*; N.Y. Domestic Relations Law §30 *et seq.*

2. **Contacts required:** It is frequently difficult to determine whether a person has sufficient meaningful contacts with a state for personal jurisdiction, and specific rules cannot be formulated. One court held that *sexual intercourse* within the state was sufficient to assert jurisdiction for support of the child conceived. *Lake v. Butcher,* 679 P.2d 409 (Wash. 1984). In accord, Uniform Parentage Act § 8(b); 9B Unif.L.Ann. 309 (1987).

IV. CHILD SUPPORT — ENFORCEMENT

A. **Introduction:** For the custodial parent, obtaining a court order awarding child support is likely to be only the first step. Even with such an order in hand, actually collecting the money frequently proves difficult. The U.S. Government has estimated that of parents (generally women) who have been awarded child support, only 51% receive the full amount due, 25% receive partial payment, and 24% receive nothing at all. Areen, p. 797.

1. **Reasons:** Some of the reasons why it is difficult to enforce child support orders are:

    a. Lawyers' fees: The amount at stake is often too small to permit the parent to *pay for a lawyer*. If the lawyer wants an hourly fee, the parent seeking enforcement usually does not have the resources to advance the money, and the lawyer generally does not want to perform the services now in the hopes that the defendant parent will ultimately be required to pay the plaintiff parent's legal bill for enforcement. As for contingent fee arrangements, in some states these are illegal when applied to child support, and even in those states where they are allowed, the lawyer is likely to conclude that any contingent recovery will not be large enough to make the matter worthwhile. (But under federal law, states are required to make prosecutors or other public officials available to represent a parent seeking to collect court-ordered child support.)

    b. Mobility: The two parents will frequently now be living in ***different states*** (e.g., the non-custodial parent moves away from the state where the custodial parent and children live). Consequently, the custodial parent must locate the other parent, and pursue him in a possibly distant jurisdiction. (Two uniform statutes, URESA and RURESA, discussed below, p. 147, make this somewhat easier.)

    c. Judicial delay: To the extent that the parent seeking enforcement is using the court system to gain enforcement (e.g., use of civil contempt proceedings, see *supra*, p. 118, the ***delays*** which plague the judicial system make the enforcement process worse.

    See generally Clark, pp. 734-35.

B. The two-state problem (URESA and RURESA): Where the two parents live in different states, the custodial parent's burden of collecting support is made easier by two uniform statutes, the ***Uniform Reciprocal Enforcement of Support Act*** (***URESA***) and its new version, the ***Revised*** Uniform Reciprocal Enforcement of Support Act (***RURESA***). Either URESA or RURESA is in force in every state. Furthermore, the two statutes are sufficiently similar to each other that there is essentially a uniform national method for allowing a custodial parent located in State A to collect support from a non-custodial parent located in State B. For simplicity, the discussion below refers only to RURESA, but is equally applicable to states in which the statute in force is URESA.

    1. Alimony as well child support: RURESA can be used for interstate enforcement of ***alimony*** (spousal maintenance) awards, not just child support awards. The procedure is the same for the two types of support obligations.

    2. Procedure only: RURESA is a ***procedural*** statute only, not a substantive one. That is, it says nothing at all about when a parent must support his child or the other parent, or about how much that support should be. Instead, RURESA merely furnishes a mechanism by which the courts of two states can ***collaborate*** in enforcing whatever support order is justified under the non-RURESA substantive laws of the states.

3. **Two types of actions:** There are two quite different types of enforcement action that may be brought under RURESA.

    a. **Registration of pre-existing decree:** The first method can be used where there is already an existing decree issued by the courts of one state (let's call it State A), and the obligor (the parent owing the duty of support) resides in another state (let's call it State B). Under this method, State A is ignored completely, and the parent seeking enforcement merely ***registers*** the State A decree ***in the courts of State B***. See RURESA §§35-40. The parent seeking enforcement then is entitled to have the courts of state B enforce the judgment as if it had originally been entered by a State B court.

    b. **Two-state proceeding:** The more versatile method for using RURESA is as a ***two-state*** system. This two-state method can be used regardless of whether State A (the state where the parent seeking enforcement resides) has issued a formal support order.

        i. **Initiating state:** Under this method, the RURESA action begins when the claimant files a "petition" in the ***"initiating state."*** This is the state where the person seeking support resides (the state we've referred to as State A). Normally, the petitioner is the custodial parent, but the proceeding can be brought by the child for whose benefit child support is to be paid (typically, represented by a guardian) or by a state welfare agency trying to recover reimbursement for welfare payments made to the custodial parent. The initiating state does ***not*** decide on the merits whether support is due — the initiating state merely decides whether there is ***probable cause*** to believe that the defendant owes a duty of support. No notice is given to the out-of-state defendant at this point, and no adversary hearing is held.

        ii. **Responding state:** If the initiating state finds that there is probable cause to believe that D owes or will be found to owe support, and also probable cause to believe that D can be found in another state (the ***"responding state,"*** which we have been calling State B), the initiating state will ***transfer*** the case to the responding state. The court in the responding state must then try to locate the defendant so that jurisdiction can be exercised over him.

        iii. **Trial in responding state:** If D is found in the responding state, then the issue of support is tried like any other support case, except that the parent seeking enforcement need not appear in the responding state (and can submit affidavits). If the responding court finds that D owes support, any sums collected are remitted to the court in the initiating state and thence to the obligee. Clark, p. 280.

Note: The steps involved in this two-state type of RURESA proceeding are summarized in Chart IV on p. 150.

4. **Can be first proceeding for support:** Courts are split as to whether RURESA can be used to enforce a duty of support that has not already been embodied in a court order. Some courts hold that only where the person seeking enforcement has already obtained a formal order of support may the responding court grant enforcement under RURESA. But other courts hold that so long as the person seeking support establishes that she has a common-law or statutory right to support, the fact that there is no pre-existing court order makes no difference. See, e.g., *State of Iowa ex rel. Petersen v. Miner*, 412 N.W.2d 832 (Neb. 1987); C&G, p. 962.

5. **Whose law controls:** Which state's law controls in a RURESA proceeding, the law of the initiating state or that of the responding state? Remember that RURESA itself does not supply any substantive rules establishing whether and how much support is due — these issues are left to "other" state law. Section 7 of RURESA says that the duties of support being enforced under the act are "those imposed under the laws of any state where the obligor was *present* for the period during which support is sought." The next sentence says that the obligor is "presumed to have been present in the ***responding state*** during the period for which support is sought until otherwise shown." So in the usual situation where the father has resided in the responding state during the time for which support is sought, it is ***the responding state's law*** that will apply.

> **Example:** During all of 1992, Mother lives in California and Father lives in New Jersey. Late in 1992, Mother starts a RURESA proceeding in California (the "initiating state"). In early January, New Jersey (the "responding state") hears the petition. Assume that there is no outstanding order of support at the moment the New Jersey court hears the petition in early 1993. Assuming that New Jersey is one of the states that will allow RURESA to be used even though there is no pre-existing support order (see *supra*, p. 148), the court will decide whether Father owes support, and if so, how much, based on the law of New Jersey, since that is the state in which Father resided during the year (1992) for which support is now being sought.

6. **Modification of earlier decree:** Suppose that the initiating court (or some other court) has previously made a support order, and that either the parent seeking support or the parent against whom support is

CHART IV. PROCEDURAL OUTLINE OF AN ACTION UNDER THE REVISED UNIFORM RECIPROCAL ENFORCEMENT OF SUPPORT ACT (1968)

Step 1 — Filing of a complaint by the plaintff, usually a wife or child, which sets forth the names of the parties and their addresses as well as the facts on which the action is based. Such complaint is filed with a court of competent jurisdiction in the plaintiff's domicile.

Step 2 — The court then ascertains whether: (i) the complaint sets forth facts from which the duty of support may be imposed on the defendant and (ii) a court in another state (the "responding state") may obtain jurisdiction over the defendant.

Step 3 — If the court can so ascertain, then it certifies such a decision and transmits three copies of the complaint with such certification to an appropriate court in the responding state.

Step 4 — The court in the responding state then dockets the case and attempts to obtain jurisdiction over the defendant or his property, usually through service of summons.

Step 5 — If jurisdiction is obtained, a trial is then held in the responding state. The defendant may raise defenses, which may pose procedural problems since the plaintiff is usually not present. A counterclaim for divorce cannot be made by the defendant since the Act covers support only, and public officials, who usually represent the plaintiff, cannot litigate a divorce.

Step 6 — The responding state may order the defendant to furnish support if it finds such a duty.

Step 7 — If an order of support is issued, the defendant pays the amount due under such order to the court in the responding state, which forwards it to the court in the plaintiff's domicile.

See Revised Uniform Reciprocal Enforcement of Support Act (1968); §§ 11-14, 18-29.

sought wishes to have the responding court *modify* the earlier order. At least where under the law of the state that issued the order the order could be modified, all courts apparently agree that the responding state may similarly modify the decree. Some states even seem to hold that the responding state may modify the earlier order even if that order would be final under the law of the state that issued it.

> **Example:** Consider the facts of the above example, but now assume that California, in 1991, issued an order granting Mother $500 a month for child support, and $500 a month for spousal maintenance from Father. If this decree was modifiable in California under California law (which it would almost certainly be as to the child support part, and might or might not be as to the spousal support part), then clearly New Jersey, as the responding state in a RURESA proceeding, could also modify the order by making it either larger or smaller. To the extent that the decree was not modifiable under California law, courts are split as to whether the responding court (New Jersey) may modify the decree. See, e.g., *Elkind v. Byck*, 439 P.2d 316 (Cal. 1968) (even though child support order was not modifiable under the laws of Georgia, the state where the order was issued, California as the responding state in a RURESA proceeding could increase the amounts payable for child support). See also Clark, pp. 281-83.

C. **Federal statutes aiding in enforcement of support:** Because child support is so hard to collect, Congress has enacted legislation designed to make it easier. The main relevant statute is the Child Support Enforcement Amendments of 1984, as modified by the Consolidated Omnibus Budget Reconciliation Act. Here are some of the most important weapons that a parent seeking enforcement of a child support order (or a state that has received an assignment of support rights in return for making welfare payments) is given under these statutes:

   1. **Automatic withholding:** The parent seeking enforcement (or the state welfare agency) is entitled to *automatic withholding* of the obligor's *wages*, even if the payments are not in arrears. (The parent seeking support must pay a small fee to gain this automatic withholding.) This withholding is done under state law (since the states are required to enact such withholding laws if they want to benefit from various federal funds, which they all do).

   2. **Tax refund intercepts:** The parent or the state agency may require that both *state* and *federal tax refunds* owed to the obligor be *intercepted,* and forwarded to the agency or the parent seeking support instead of to the obligor.

   3. **Liens:** The parent or the agency may obtain a *lien* on the obligor's real and personal property.

4. **Federal Parent Locator Service:** Either the parent seeking support or the agency may obtain assistance in *locating* the obligor by means of the federal Parent Locator Service. This service, operated the Department of Health and Human Services, uses all of the records of the federal government (including the I.R.S. and the military) to locate a "missing" parent.

5. **Spousal support:** Even though the principal statute is called the "Child Support" Enforcement Amendments, the enforcement procedures of the Act can be used to collect *spousal* support, so long as collection is being sought in conjunction with child support.

6. **Health insurance:** If the obligor has access to low-cost health insurance, state courts are required to order that this insurance be made available to any child as part of a child support order.

See generally 42 U.S.C. §§651 at seq.

SEPARATION AGREEMENTS

Introductory note: Before the actual divorce the parties usually separate. Frequently at the time of the separation the spouses agree on some financial aspects of divorce such as a division of their real and personal property and support. This is called a separation agreement. They may intend this to be a temporary arrangement until a final divorce decree, or they may intend the agreement to be final. This chapter considers the significant aspects of separation agreements.

I. INTRODUCTION

A. **Generally:** Parties to a marriage may agree to live separately. This may be done *without* obtaining a divorce or instituting any legal action. Customarily, the rights and obligations of the parties are provided for in a separation agreement between them. The basis of all separation agreements is the ***discontinuation of cohabitation*** by the parties.

1. **Definition:** A separation agreement is a written document voluntarily entered into by the parties to a marriage which sets forth their rights and obligations. Like other contracts, separation agreements vary as to form and content. The following are typical subjects covered in a separation agreement:

   a. *Separation* of the parties;

   b. *Division of property,* real and personal;

   c. Amount of *alimony*;

   d. Amount of *child support*;

   e. *Custody and visitation rights*;

   f. *Medical* and dental expenses of any children;

   g. *Educational expenses* of any children;

   h. *Dependency claims* with respect to children for tax purposes;

   i. *Insurance* to guarantee payments contained in the agreement; and

   j. *Legal fees* and expenses.

2. **Enforceability:** Courts generally *enforce* separation agreements, even if the agreement handles an issue differently from how the court would handle it. Thus an agreement's provisions governing division of property or spousal support will almost always be enforced by the

court, so long as the agreement meets the standard requirements for contracts (e.g., that it is not the product of fraud or duress, and is not unconscionable).

    a. Child support and custody: But agreements as to *custody*, and as to the amount of ***child support,*** are ***not binding*** on the court, since these items involve the welfare of a third person (the child) who is not a party to the contract.

    b. Enforceability: The enforceability of separation agreements is discussed more extensively *infra*, p. 156.

3. When to make an agreement: Under older decisions any separation agreement entered into by parties who were still ***living together*** as husband and wife was void. This was so because spouses who were living together could not contract for support, and because such separation agreements were thought to promote divorce. Today many courts — perhaps most — would not insist on the requirement that the parties no longer be living together at the time they sign the agreement.

4. Reconciliation: If the parties resume their full marital relationship (i.e., ***reconcile***), the separation agreement is normally ***terminated***.

    a. Exception: If the agreement contained a property settlement in which property was transferred from one to the other, that conveyance will not be affected. If the conveyance was made for a waiver of inheritance rights, that waiver may also survive.

    Example 1: During the pendency of a separation suit, H and W sign a property settlement agreement. Under the agreement W receives certain property and H and W agree not to contest each other's will. They also agree that any reconciliation will not affect the terms of their agreement. H and W live together as husband and wife, during which time H pays board to W. When H dies his will leaves W $5.00, since she had already received a property settlement under the agreement. W sues for a widow's portion of H's estate, claiming that the reconciliation of the parties abrogated the agreement.

    Held, W's suit is dismissed. A reconciliation of the parties with a resumption of marital relations operates to avoid the agreement for separation with all provisions remaining executory. This agreement contained no provisions concerning the separation of the parties, but merely their property rights. With the transfer of the agreed property, the contract was completely executed and no executory features existed. The evidence does not establish any intention by the parties to abrogate the agreement. *Simpson v. Weatherman,* 227 S.W.2d 148 (Ark. 1950).

    Example 2: H and W sign a separation agreement under which W relinquishes her right of support and H relinquishes all claims to

W's property. W dies and H sues for a portion of W's estate as the surviving spouse.

Held, H may not recover. W's release of her right to support was invalid. However, no purpose would be served by invalidating the agreement because H had the benefit of her release of support, and W fully performed her part of the agreement. *Laleman v. Crombez*, 127 N.E.2d 489 (Ill. 1955).

5. **Effect of agreement:** If a separation agreement is presented for approval to the court in a divorce action, the court, after reviewing its provisions, may *accept* it for incorporation into the divorce decree with or without *modification,* or *reject* it entirely.

   a. **Merger with divorce decree:** If a separation agreement is expressly incorporated into the decree, it will generally be deemed *"merged."* This means that the separation agreement no longer has an independent existence, and its provisions may be modified just as the provisions of any other alimony decree without the separation agreement.

      i. **Enforcement:** Where a decree directs one spouse to pay alimony, it is enforceable by contempt proceedings. By contrast, if the decree merely confirms a separation agreement without specifically directing the parties to comply with its terms, a party will not be subject to contempt for failure to perform.

         Example: In *Oedekoven v. Oedekoven*, 538 P.2d 1292 (Wyo. 1975), the court "ratified and confirmed" the property settlement of H and W. H refused to perform. The court *held* that H was not in contempt because there was no specific direction in the decree to comply with its terms.

   b. **No merger:** If the separation agreement is not merged, it retains its *independent validity.* In this situation it is not enforceable by contempt, and the alimony provisions are not subject to modification in most jurisdictions. *Davis v. Davis,* 268 A.2d 515 (D.C. Cir. 1970).

      Note: Child custody and support provisions are always subject to modification regardless of merger or provisions in the separation agreement because the interest of the child is a primary concern to the court, and the child is not a party to the separation agreement.

   c. **Intent of parties:** Courts consider and usually follow the intent of the parties expressed in the separation agreement concerning merger. If the separation agreement states that it may not be modified, most courts, but not all, refuse to modify the agreement regardless of merger and hold the parties to their agreement.

II. ENFORCEABILITY OF SEPARATION AGREEMENT

A. Validity of agreement: Separation agreements may be attacked on the grounds of *fraud and duress. Lack of full disclosure of financial circumstances* constitutes fraud, and will subject a separation agreement to attack.

> **Example:** Under a property settlement W receives a house and car. H receives everything else, the value of which substantially exceeds the value of property awarded to W. The court later finds that H concealed from W the true value of the property he received. *Held,* this deception is a fraud on W, and she is entitled to equitable relief. *Pilati v. Pilati,* 592 P.2d 1374 (Mont. 1979).

1. UMDA: The Uniform Marriage and Divorce Act provides that the separation agreement is binding unless the court finds that it is *unconscionable.*

2. Unilateral mistake: One party's *mistake* about a material fact underlying the separation agreement will generally *not* prevent enforceability of the agreement. Thus if a spouse who has equal access to information makes a serious miscalculation about an item's value, and relies on this mistaken assessment in agreeing how property will be divided, that spouse will normally not be able to avoid the agreement on grounds of mistake (assuming the other spouse was not aware of the mistake.)

> **Example:** Prior to their divorce, H and W sign a separation agreement. At that time H earns $1,800 per month and W earns $800 per month. W waives maintenance, but the property settlement provides that W will receive $60,000 when their house is sold and H will receive the balance. The house sells for much less than H expects, so that H receives only $10,000. H asks that the separation agreement be set aside because of his mistake as to the value of the house. H argues that his mistake makes the contract unconscionable.
>
> *Held,* the separation agreement is enforced. The agreement was a contract between H and W. Traditionally a contract may not be set aside because of a unilateral mistake as to value unless the other party knew of the mistake. There is no such evidence here. Nor is there evidence of overreaching, fraud, concealment of assets or sharp dealing inconsistent with the obligation of H and W to deal fairly with each other. Considering also all the economic circumstances of the parties, the contract is not unconscionable. *In re Marriage of Manzo,* 659 P.2d 669 (Colo.1983).

3. Support: Generally, a separation agreement under which one spouse relinquishes all claims for support or receives a *lump sum payment* *in lieu of support* will be **valid**. However, in a few jurisdictions such an agreement has been held invalid.

B. Applicable law: The law of the jurisdiction in which the separation agreement is **executed** governs the validity of the agreement. If the parties indicate that the law of a different jurisdiction is to govern, courts disagree as to whether or not such provision should be honored. *Reighley v. Continental Illinois Nat. Bank,* 61 N.E.2d 29 (Ill. 1945); *Gessler v. Gessler,* 273 F.2d 302 (5th Cir. 1959).

ADOPTION

I. INTRODUCTION

  A. Definition: Adoption is the legal procedure by which the status of parent and child is conferred upon persons who are not naturally so related.

  B. Historical development: The development of the law of adoption may be traced to antiquity.

    1. Ancient civilizations: Adoption was known in Ancient Greece and Rome where it was employed to ensure succession of property and title. It was this particular aspect of adoption that was stressed in modern civil law.

    2. France: In furtherance of this concept, the French 1804 Civil Code provided for adoption, but only with respect to persons who had reached their majority by persons who had attained fifty years of age and who had no legitimate lineal heirs. It was not until this century that French statutes provided for the adoption of a minor into a normal family situation.

    3. England: Adoption was not recognized at common law. It was not introduced by statute in England until 1926.

    4. United States: Since there was no common law background for adoption, procedures in the United States are governed by statutes specifying the conditions, manner, means and consequences of adoption, as well as the rights and responsibilities of all parties.

      a. Development: Although adoption legislation in the United States was late in development and enactment, all fifty states at present have statutes authorizing and governing adoption.

      b. Purpose: In contrast to European adoption laws, the focus of statutes has been directed toward the welfare of the adopted child rather than toward the adoptive parent and his line of succession. States have developed procedures whereby children, whose natural parents cannot or will not properly care and provide for them, are placed with persons who can suitably attend to them and their needs.

  C. Present status: Despite the legal procedures of adoption, social considerations are assuming an increasingly important role in the adoption process. Social welfare agencies charged with administration of adoptions have developed policy considerations and procedures for all parties.

    1. Trends: Sociological changes have affected the development of laws concerning adoption and raised new considerations. The number of children available for adoption in recent years has decreased drastically for some of the following reasons.

    a. Cohabitation: Many couples who live together and have children out of wedlock do not give up their children for adoption.

    b. Social pressure: The stigma of bearing and raising a child born out of wedlock has lessened considerably.

    c. Abortion: This is more widely accepted and utilized.

    d. Contraceptives: Birth control information and devices are readily available.

2. Race and religion as factors: Legislatures and agencies may generally permit *race* and *religion* to be considered as factors in adoption placements, but a placement decision may not be based solely on race and/or religion. These factors are discussed more extensively *infra*, p. 162.

3. Subsidized adoption: Adoption of "hard to place" children, such as those with handicaps, has been encouraged by giving financial assistance to the adoptive parents based on the special needs of the child.

4. Confidentiality: Traditionally, adoption records have been *sealed* to the child, the natural parents, and to the adopting parents. Litigation in this area is beginning, and courts appear more willing now than in the past to divulge such information if a *special need* can be shown. However, it is still difficult to meet the *"good cause"* standard required to unseal records. The topic is discussed further *infra*, p. 000.

5. Constitutional issues: Interpretations of the *Due Process and Equal Protection Clauses* have affected many state statutes regarding adoption. These Clauses guarantee the biological parents certain rights, including notice of hearings and the right to equal treatment under the law. In addition, statutes may not arbitrarily favor the mother over the father. See *infra*, p. 180.

II. ADOPTION PLACEMENT PROCEDURES

A. Adoption placement procedures: There are two basic types of placement procedures, both of which are governed by statute:

1. Agency placement: *"Agency placement"* is characterized by the following procedures:

    a. Agency services: Arrangements for the adoption of a child are made by a licensed public or private agency charged with the responsibility of placing children.

    b. Investigation: Generally, a thorough, detailed investigation is made with respect to the suitability of the adoptive parents and the background of the child involved.

   c. **Cost:** In most cases the adoptive parents pay a fee to the agency. That fee may depend upon the financial resources of the parents.

2. **Private placement:** The alternative to agency placement is *"private placement"* (sometimes called "independent placement.") Private placement is characterized by the following procedures:

   a. **Services:** Arrangements for the adoption of a child are made by an *individual,* either the natural parent or an interested intermediary party who may represent the prospective adoptive parents or the natural parents. Most often, the intermediary is a lawyer or physician.

   b. **Investigation:** Generally a thorough investigation, *unless required by statute,* is not made of either the natural parents or the adoptive parents.

   c. **Cost:** Usually the adoptive parents pay the *medical expenses* and fees of the natural mother as well as any *legal expenses* and fees.

      i. **Comparisons:** There are distinct, definite advantages and disadvantages of both the private and the agency placement, which are illustrated in Chart V, *infra*, p. 161.

3. **Private placement sometimes barred:** All states allow agency placements. Virtually all states also allow private placements where the arrangements are made directly by the natural parents or other relatives of the child. But a number of states have enacted *"Baby Broker Acts,"* which forbid a private person (as opposed to an agency) from serving as an *intermediary* in arranging the adoption, with an exception given for placements arranged directly by relatives of the child. The net result is that lawyers and physicians in these states may not arrange a private placement. Illinois, New York and New Jersey fall into this "no private placement" category. See Clark, p. 906, n. 8.

B. **Criteria for adoption:** The chief consideration in adoption is the *welfare of the child.* Some or all of the following factors are implemented in agency placements or in private placements where, under state law, the adoptive parents must be investigated to determine who are suitable adoptive parents.

   1. **Religion** (see *infra*, p. 165);

   2. **Race** (see *infra*, p. 162);

   3. **Economic status;**

   4. **Home environment;**

   5. **Age;**

   6. **Health;**

   7. **Physical and character defects** of the adoptive parents; and

CHART V. COMPARISON OF PRIVATE AND AGENCY PLACEMENTS

ADVANTAGES

Private Placement	Agency Placement
(a) permits adoption of a child by persons who might otherwise be subjected to a lengthy waiting period or who would not find a child available through the normal agency channels due to stringent requirements or nonavailability of children.	(a) provides a minimization of the risk of a non-healthy child; of discovery of the identity of the adoptive parents by the natural mother; of a change of mind by the natural mother regarding the adoption.
(b) provides a certain degree of privacy and anonymity for natural mother.	(b) provides a rigorous investigation of the background of the natural parents as well as that of the adoptive parents to ensure suitability.
(c) permits the payment of medical expenses by the adoptive parents in the situation where the natural mother does not have adequate financial resources of her own to pay such expenses.	(c) provides, in most cases, a minimization of fees and costs with respect to the adoption.

DISADVANTAGES

Private Placement	Agency Placement
(a) risks the natural mother not actually completing the adoption procedure.	(a) involves lengthy and rigorous requirements established by the agencies with respect to the suitability of the adoptive parents.
(b) risks the discovery by the natural mother of identity of the adoptive parents and an attempt by her to claim the child.	(b) results in a limited number of children available for adoption.
(c) risks the adoption of a non-healthy child.	
(d) risks the non-suitability of the adoptive parents.	
(e) risks that such a procedure, if not strictly controlled, might lead to a "black market."	

8. Emotional factors.

> **Note:** Statutes and agency rules concerning the suitability of adoption are relaxing in some jurisdictions while in others they are not.

> **Example:** If a person is willing to adopt a "hard to place child," rules are often waived, whereas strict requirements must be met if a person desires to adopt an easily placed child.

C. Race and religion as factors: Many states allow — and a few even require — consideration of the adoptive parents' *race* and *religion* in deciding on where the child shall be placed. The idea is that, all things being equal, the child is better off being placed with adoptive parents whose race and religion "match" the child's.

1. Race: With respect to the consideration of *race*, there are no Supreme Court decisions deciding whether or how the states may allow (or require) race to be considered in the adoption placement process. Lower courts have generally reasoned that (as is discussed more fully below) the states may not ban transracial adoption completely, or even make race a very overwhelming factor, but may allow race to be one factor among many.

a. General Supreme Court approach: In virtually every area outside the adoption context, the Supreme Court has held that race is a *suspect class*, which may only be used by government if this is necessary to achieve a compelling governmental purpose.

i. *Palmore case:* Although the Supreme Court has not decided any race-matching cases in the adoption context, in one child-custody case, *Palmore v. Sidoti*, 466 U.S. 429 (1984) (discussed *supra*, p. 128), the Court faced a somewhat analogous issue. There, the mother and father were white; after the divorce, the mother lived with a black man, whom she later married. The trial court awarded custody to the father on the grounds that racial bias and prejudice might make life difficult for the daughter if she were raised in a bi-racial household. But the Supreme Court held that a state could never use race to remove a child from the custody of a parent who was otherwise suitable, and that societal prejudices must simply be disregarded when the custody decision is made.

ii. Case disregarded: However, lower courts hearing adoption cases after *Palmore* have universally held that the case applies only to custody determinations, not to the adoption context.

b. Can't ban transracial adoptions: Virtually all the lower court cases on adoption have concluded that the state may *not* place an *absolute ban* on transracial adoptions. This is true even though the state policy "treats all races equally," in the sense that black parents are prohibited from adopting white children just as white parents are prohibited from adopting black children. (In point of fact, virtually all transracial adoptions involve white adoptive parents and minority children.)

   i. Equal protection grounds: Such total bans have been found to be a violation of the Fourteenth Amendment's Equal Protection Clause. Lower courts have frequently relied on *Loving v. Virginia*, 388 U.S. 1 (1967) (discussed *supra*, p. 000), which held that a ban on interracial marriage violates the Equal Protection Clause. See, e.g., *In re Gomez*, 424 S.W.2d 656 (Tex.Ct.App. 1967), relying on *Loving* in striking down a Texas adoption statute that provided that "no white child can be adopted by a negro person, nor can a negro child be adopted by a white person."

c. Race may not be "overwhelming" factor: Most lower court decisions have also concluded that even where there is no absolute ban on transracial adoptions, a racial-matching preference will violate equal protection if race is made too *"overwhelming"* a factor. Similarly, if a facially-neutral policy is carried out by public agencies (or by private agencies acting under public instructions) in a way that *in fact* gives extremely *heavy weight* to racial-matching, there may be an equal protection violation. For instance, if an agency routinely makes white parents seeking to adopt black children wait longer, or puts them in a different queue than black parents seeking to adopt black children, this would be likely to be an equal protection violation.

d. Race allowable as one factor among many: However, nearly all lower courts have held that race *may be* considered as *one factor among many* in allocating children to adoptive parents.

Example: C is born to a white mother and black father. When he is one month old, C is placed with H and W, a white couple, for temporary foster care. H and W care for C for two years, and then petition to adopt him. The state agency charged with adoption rates the care given by H and W as excellent. But the agency attaches significant weight to the fact that as C grows older, he will retain the characteristics of his black father; therefore, the agency concludes that it is in C's best interest that the adoption petition be denied. The agency also orders that C be removed from H and W's care and placed with a different, probably black, family (which has not yet been selected), in preparation for his eventual adoption by what will probably be a black family (again, one which has not yet been identified). H and W file suit, alleging that this decision has denied them equal protection of the law because of the extent to which race was considered in the process.

Held, there was no violation of the rights of H and W. The difficulties inherent in transracial adoption justified the agency in considering race as a relevant factor. The agency did not treat race as the sole factor, or as an automatically-dispositive factor. Furthermore, the use of race here did not suggest any racial slur or stigma — "it is a natural thing for children to be raised by parents of their same ethnic background." Agencies normally try to place a child "with adoptive parents who could actually have pronated him," and thus consider factors such as age, hair color, eye color and facial features. Race may be considered along with these other factors, without violating the equal protection clause. *Drummond v. Fulton County Dept. of Family and Children's Services*, 563 F.2d 1200 (5th Cir. 1977).

i. **No strict scrutiny:** Some courts, such as the court in *Drummond, supra*, seem to apply only "rational relation" review to the use of race as one factor among many. Under this approach, so long as the consideration of race is rationally related to the fulfillment of some legitimate state objective (e.g., the best interests of the child), that use will be upheld. In courts applying this low level of review, approval of race as one factor will be virtually automatic.

ii. **Strict scrutiny:** But other decisions, especially more recent ones, apply ***strict scrutiny*** to the use of race, even though such decisions have nonetheless usually upheld consideration of race as one factor among many. This strict scrutiny approach is probably the more correct one, in light of the Supreme Court's decision in *City of Richmond v. J.A. Croson Co.*, 488 U.S. 469 (1989), holding that strict scrutiny must be given to even "benign" race-conscious state action, such as affirmative action programs. See, e.g., *Petition of R.M.G.*, 454 A.2d 776 (D.C.Ct.App. 1982), applying strict scrutiny to the use of race as one factor among many, but concluding that this use survives strict scrutiny because "racial classification ... is, in a constitutional sense, necessary to advance a compelling governmental interest: the best interest of the child."

e. **Mandatory consideration of race:** There are even a few cases holding that the state may ***require*** that race be considered as one factor among many in the process of matching adoptive children and parents. Thus statutes such as those of Minnesota and Arkansas — specifying a preference for placement with a family having the same racial and ethnic heritage — are probably constitutional. See, e.g., Minn. Stat. §259.28(2) ("The policy of the state of Minnesota is to ensure that the best interests of the children are met by requiring due consideration of the child's race or ethnic heritage in adoption placements....") But see 139 U. Pa. L. Rev. 1163 (1991), arguing that the preference for racial matching as it is usually applied harms black children, by keeping them in institutional or foster care far longer than they would be, on average, if there were no preference.

2. **Religion:** Many states allow courts or agencies to consider *religion* as a factor in matching children and adoptive parents. Any use of religion as a factor runs the risk either of violating the Establishment Clause of the First Amendment (which prevents the states from preferring one religion over another, or preferring religion over non-religion), or of violating the Free Exercise clause of that amendment (by which each person is guaranteed the right to pursue whatever religious beliefs, or non-beliefs, she wishes, without penalty from the state). In general, use of religion as a factor in adoption placements has *not* been found to violate either of these clauses. However, religion can be considered in various ways depending on the context, so each context needs separate analysis.

   a. **Expressed preferences:** Many states allow or even require that the natural parents' stated *preferences* concerning the faith in which the child is to be raised *shall be observed* in the adoption placement where feasible. See, e.g., N.Y. Fam. Ct. Act §116(g), which provides that placement rules "shall, so far as consistent with the best interests of the child, and where practicable, be applied so as to give effect to the religious wishes of the natural mother, if the child is born out-of-wedlock, or if born in-wedlock, the religious wishes of the parents of the child...." This type of "respect the parents' expressed preferences" provision has almost always been upheld against either Establishment Clause or Free Exercise Clause attack.

   b. **Imputation based on heritage:** Somewhat more difficult problems are posed by statutes that say where the natural parents have *not* expressed any preference about religion, the preference shall be given to adoptive parents who are of the same religion as the natural parents. Thus the New York statute quoted in the prior paragraph goes on to say that "In the absence of expressed religious wishes ... determination of the religious wishes, if any, of the parent, shall be made upon the other facts of the particular case, and, if there is no evidence to the contrary, it shall be *presumed* that the parent wishes the child to be reared in the religion of the parent." Such statutes in effect *"impute"* to the child the religion of the natural parents.

      i. **One factor among many:** So long as this type of "imputation" provision merely makes religion *one factor among many* to be considered in the placement (rather than making it automatically dispositive), the provision is, again, likely to be upheld against either Establishment Clause or Free Exercise Clause attack. See, e.g., *Dickens v. Ernesto*, 281 N.E.2d 153 (N.Y. 1972), finding that the above New York statutory provision did not violate either the Establishment Clause or the Free Exercise Clause, in part because even a parent without any religious affiliation would be eligible to adopt a child of unknown religious background, or a child whose natural parents expressly stated that they were indifferent as to the child's religious placement.

    ii. Automatic rule: But if a state were to establish religious matching as a *sole* or *dispositive* factor, or even as a factor that was very heavily weighted in the process, then such a practice might well be found unconstitutional. The practice might violate either the Establishment Clause (on the grounds that the state was strongly favoring religion over non-religion, by giving religious natural parents a veto power over this one aspect of placement, while not giving a veto power on any other factor relating to placement) or the Free Exercise Clause (on the grounds that a prospective adoptive parent of the wrong or no religious affiliation was unduly burden by being completely foreclosed from adopting a particular child regardless of suitability on all other points).

  c. Requirement that parent show some religious belief: Apart from religious matching statutes, a few states have, by statute or practice, attempted to impose a requirement that prospective adoptive parents show that they have *some* religious beliefs. The theory behind such a requirement is that a parent who does not believe in a Supreme Being is less likely to be a suitable parent than one who does. But in the principal case on this issue, the court held that this type of weight given to religion violated both Establishment Clause and the Free Exercise Clause. See *In re Adoption of "E,"* 279 A.2d 785 (N.J. 1971), where the New Jersey Supreme Court reversed a lower court's denial of the plaintiffs' adoption; the lower court had acted on the grounds that the plaintiffs' lack of belief in a Supreme Being automatically made them unfit to be adoptive parents (despite evidence that in all other respects they were fit).

D. Sexual orientation of adoptive parent: In recent years, many *same-sex* couples have sought to adopt. Frequently, but by no means always, the child in question is the biological child of one member of the couple. Since adoption is very heavily governed by statutes, the result in such attempted adoptions by homosexuals has depended largely on what the state statute says about the topic.

  1. State statute is silent: In most states, the statute is *silent* on the subject of whether the homosexual orientation of the prospective adoptive parent(s) may be considered. Instead, the statute simply lists the classes of persons who may adopt, and, generally, lists "an unmarried person" as one of the classes. In this "statute is silent" situation, virtually all of the recent cases hold that: (a) the statute should be interpreted so as to allow adoption by members of a same-sex couple; and (b) the homosexuality of the adoptive parent(s) is not, by itself, evidence that the adoption would not be in the child's best interest (as virtually all adoption statutes require before an adoption may be granted). See, e.g., *Adoption of Tammy*, 619 N.E.2d 315 (Mass. 1993) (both members of a lesbian couple permitted to simultaneously adopt the biological child of one of them); *In re Adoption of Charles B.*, 552 N.E.2d 884 (Oh. 1990) (gay man permitted to adopt eight-year-old severely handicapped boy with whom he had lived for several years).

   a. **Termination of natural parent's rights:** Where the child in question is the biological child of one member of the same-sex couple, one unintended feature of most state statutes can complicate the efforts of the other member of the couple to adopt the child. The typical adoption statute provides that when an adoption occurs, the parental rights of the natural parent(s) are *terminated*; there is generally an exception to this rule where the natural parent and the adoptive parent are married (the step-parent adoption situation). Since the step-parent exception is not available to help a member of a same-sex couple who wishes to adopt the natural child of the other member, literal enforcement of the statute would mean that the natural parent member of the couple would lose his or her parental rights at the same time the adoption went through! Fortunately, those courts that have considered the issue have held that the statute should not be read literally, and that the adoption should not serve to terminate the rights of the biological parent who is part of the couple and who supports the adoption. See, e.g., *Adoptions of B.L.V.B. and E.L.V.B.*, 628 A.2d 1271 (Vt. 1993) (where Jane and Deborah have lived together as members of a long-term homosexual couple, Deborah may adopt Jane's biological sons, without this act serving to terminate Jane's parental rights).

2. **State statute forbids:** By contrast, two states, New Hampshire and Florida, have statutes that *forbid* homosexuals from adopting. See N.H. Rev. Stat. Ann. §§170-b:2 to b:4; Fla. Stat. §63.042. Such statutes are probably constitutional, because the Supreme Court has refused to treat sexual orientation as a suspect class. The one state court case concerning these total-prohibition statutes has reached this conclusion; *Opinion of the Justices*, 530 A.2d 21 (N.H. 1987).

3. **State statute allows:** Conversely, a few states provide that the sexual orientation of the prospective adoptive parent(s) may not be grounds for denying adoption. New York, for instance, has done this by regulation; see New York Times, Aug. 28, 1982, p. 27, col. 1.

E. Other factors: Statutes and agency procedures also frequently allow consideration of other factors. Two of the more troublesome ones are the adoptive parents' *age* and *marital status*.

  1. Age: In most jurisdictions, the agency may consider the prospective adoptive parents' *age* as a factor. Thus if both parents are so old that there is a good chance the child will be orphaned before reaching majority, this may be treated as a significant factor, one likely to tip the balance away from that couple. However, as with racial matching and sexual orientation, most courts do *not* permit advanced age to be an *automatic* ground for denying adoption, so that if a particular couple is clearly the best solution to the child's needs despite the parents' advanced age, the adoption will generally be permitted. See, e.g., *In re Adoption of Michelle T.*, 117 Cal.Rptr. 856 (Ct.App. 1975), holding that the plaintiffs (H was 70 and W was 54) must be permitted to adopt the child whom they had served as foster parents for the first two years of the child's life, where the alternative would be to put the child in some other foster home that had not yet been selected.

  2. Unmarried status: Similarly, the fact that the prospective parent is *unmarried* is a factor that courts and agencies take into account, but again, one that is usually not dispositive. Clark, p. 910.

D. "Black market" babies: In addition to the agency placement and legal private placement, there is an *illegal* "black market" in babies which affords childless couples a chance to obtain a child.

  1. Generally: The term "black market" encompasses a wide variety of methods by which a child is procured from its natural mother and subsequently adopted by the adopting parents. These methods, which are *illegal,* generally arise from the extensive delays, complicated procedures of the agencies and courts, and the relatively small number of adoptable children *vis-a-vis* the number of individuals desiring to adopt a child.

  2. Reasons for development: The black market provides *speed* in the adoption procedure since there is no investigation, and *secrecy* to the natural mother.

  3. Cost: Not infrequently the illegality of the "black market" adoption arises from the amount of payment which is made by the adopting parents to the natural mother. Although the natural mother may be reimbursed for the expenses of delivery and confinement, both prior to and subsequent to the delivery of the child, the mother may not receive a payment for the infant itself, since it is illegal to sell children. The chief characteristic of the "black market" in babies is the ability of the adoptive parents to *pay the price* demanded by the black market operator.

III. SUBSIDIZED ADOPTION

A. **Purpose:** States and the federal government have recognized the benefits of adoption as opposed to institutional care, but have often found it difficult to place children for adoption who have special needs. That includes children with physical, mental or emotional handicaps and children of various minority groups. In recognition of those unfortunate circumstances a program of *subsidized adoption* has been developed in some states.

1. **Subsidy:** Under a subsidized adoption program the adoptive parents receive monthly reimbursement from a social agency according to a prior agreement.

2. **Purpose of subsidy:** The subsidy is designed to meet the special needs of the child. It may allow for specific medical or other costs. It may continue for an indefinite period or be for a limited time only.

IV. PRIVACY OF ADOPTION RECORDS

A. **General rule:** The accepted rule is that adoption records are *sealed* to the child, the natural parents, and the adopting parents. *Good cause* must be shown to obtain access to adoption records.

1. **Interests considered:** Factors which courts must consider in litigation to unseal adoption records include the interests of:

   a. **The child;**

   b. **The natural parents;**

   c. **The adopting parents;** and

   d. **The adoption system** of the state.

2. **Showing "good cause":** Courts have shown more willingness to order the release of adoption records in recent decisions than in the past. However, it is still difficult to establish the required "good cause" necessary to obtain such records. The type of need most likely to be found to be "good cause" is where the adoptee has a specific need for *medical information* about her background (e.g., she has early-stage breast cancer, and treatment decisions would be influenced by knowing whether her natural mother or other relatives had the disease).

   a. **Constitutional attacks:** Adoptees have frequently attacked records-secrecy statutes on constitutional grounds. But virtually all such attacks have failed.

   Example: P seeks access to his adoption records, which are maintained under seal. State law allows the opening of such records only for good cause. P's search is not based on medical need (which might be good cause), but on a desire to know information pertaining to him as a person. P also contends that the right to know his own identity is a fundamental right, protected by the Equal Protection Clause.

Held, the statute is constitutional, and P has failed to establish good cause. The right to unseal records does not come within any recognized zone of privacy protected by the Constitution. Further, there is no fundamental right to examine adoption records. The law bears a rational relationship to a legitimate state interest. Confidentiality promotes the integrity of the adoption process and the rights of the natural and adopting parents. *In re Roger B,* 418 N.E.2d 751 (Ill. 1981).

Note: One court stated that the right of an adopted child to *inherit* from natural parents and other blood relatives may constitute a compelling reason to unseal adoption records. *Massey v. Parker,* 369 So.2d 1310 (La. 1979). However, most states do not provide for inheritance in such situations, so this rationale would not apply in those states.

3. **Registry:** Some states in recent years have addressed the desires of adoptees by establishing a *registry* of natural parents and adoptees. If the natural parent(s) and the adoptee both (acting independently of each other, of course) happen to register, then the state responds to this "match" by notifying each of the other's name and address. See Clark, p. 933, n. 57. California, Colorado, Connecticut, Florida and New York are some of the states having such registries.

B. **Open adoption:** Under the increasingly popular (but still rare) practice of *"open adoption,"* an adopted child may continue to have contact with her natural parents and/or natural siblings. An open adoption will almost never be ordered by the court over the objection of either the natural or adoptive parents, but may be enforced by the court if agreed to by both sets of parents.

1. **No general right of visitation:** The traditional approach to adoption, of course, is that at the moment of adoption, all contact between the adopted child and her natural family ceases. The utter confidentiality of adoption records described above is just one illustration of this more general cut-off of relations. The theory behind this approach is that a total cessation of relations is necessary in order for the child to bond completely to the adoptive family and not be torn between two families.

2. **Reason for changing views:** However, several factors have contributed to an increase in open adoptions.

   a. **Child's difficulty:** First, there is some scientific evidence that adopted children have great difficulty dealing with having been relinquished, and that these difficulties are exacerbated by the complete cut-off of contacts and even information about the natural family.

b. Birth mother's clout: Second, by some estimates there are more than 30 times as many prospective adoptive parents as there are white infants. C&G, p. 494. Consequently, birth mothers of white infants have a considerable degree of clout in deciding who should adopt their child. One manifestation of this clout is that the birth mother is often able to insist that the adoptive parents sign an agreement under which the birth mother is not only identified to the child, but has continuing *visitation* rights.

c. Older child: A final factor pushing towards open adoption is that where the child is *older* and/or has other natural siblings, the standard closed adoption is especially traumatic.

3. Judicial response: As noted, judges will virtually never order that members of the biological family have visitation rights, if the adoptive parents object. Open adoption issues thus arise only where the biological and adoptive parents *agree* that there should be such visitation. Because the child is not a chattel, and her best interests take priority, the court will never *automatically* enforce the agreement the way it would automatically enforce, say, a commercial contract. However, the trend seems to be to at least attach *some weight* to the agreement in deciding whether to allow visitation, rather than simply refusing to allow visitation on the grounds that open adoptions are against state public policy.

> **Example:** P is the natural mother of C, an infant. Just before the Ds adopt C (and to settle a dispute between P and the Ds about whether P has properly consented to the adoption), P and the Ds sign an agreement providing that P shall have the right to visit C twice a month for three hours until C turns 18. The agreement also provides that visitation shall generally be guided by the statutory rules applicable to the visitation rights of non-custodial parents in divorce cases. After the adoption, the Ds refuse to comply with the agreement, and P seeks specific enforcement of the visitation rights.
>
> *Held*, for P. Connecticut's visitation statute allows the court to grant the right of visitation "with respect to any minor child...to any person...[based upon] the best interests of the child...." The agreement here therefore does not violate the public policy of Connecticut. Case remanded to the trial court, for a hearing on whether visitation would indeed be in the child's best interests. *Michaud v. Wawruck*, 551 A.2d 738 (Ct. 1988).

V. CONSENT IN ADOPTION

A. Statutory requirements: Adoption statutes generally require the *consent of the natural parents* before a child can be placed for adoption.

1. **Formalities:** Many statutes contain detailed requirements regarding the form and procedure of the consent to adoption. Statutes frequently require written consent before witnesses, or provide that the consent cannot be given before a certain time, such as three days after birth. Formalities in state statutes must be ***observed strictly*** or the adoptive parents may find that the adoption is susceptible to attack later by the natural mother.

   > **Example:** W gives birth to an illegitimate child, C. While W is in the hospital, a hospital employee, A, persuades W to relinquish custody of C to A. W consents in a writing, witnessed by one person. Later a second consent is signed and witnessed by a second person. Neither consent contains the signatures of two witnesses as required by state law. A and her husband petition for adoption of C, and W seeks to regain custody.
   >
   > *Held*, W is awarded custody. W's consent is not valid because there was a failure to comply with the statute. Further, a mother is presumed to be a suitable person to raise her child with a right superior to others, and no evidence was offered that W was unfit. *In re Alsdurf,* 133 N.W.2d 479 (Minn. 1965).

2. **Who must consent:** State statutes usually specify ***who*** must consent. But even where there is no statute on point, the U.S. Constitution (by means of the Fourteenth Amendment's Due Process Clause) limits the right of a state to allow adoption over the objection of the parents. Thus even if a state child welfare agency, and/or the court, is absolutely convinced that the child would be better off with a particular adoptive family than with the natural family, the state is still not free to mandate the adoption over the objection of the natural parents — only if the natural parents are shown to be "unfit," justifying the termination of their parental rights, may their consent be dispensed with. Exactly who must consent varies from state to state, and depends both on statutory and constitutional principles.

   a. **Child born within wedlock:** Where the child is born ***within wedlock***, as a federal constitutional matter, consent of ***both parents*** is required for adoption. The exception is that if a natural parent's parental rights have already been involuntarily ***terminated*** for unfitness or abandonment (see *infra*, p. 183), then that parent's consent to the adoption is no longer needed.

   b. **Child born out of wedlock:** Where the child is born ***out of wedlock***, the situation is more complicated. The mother must of course consent (assuming that her parental rights have not been involuntarily terminated), just as in the in-wedlock situation. But the need for the ***father's*** consent is much less clear.

      i. **Father participates in caring:** Where the father has actively and consistently ***cared for*** and ***supported*** the child, the state may not constitutionally allow an adoption without the father's consent. See *Stanley v. Illinois*, 405 U.S. 645 (1972), discussed further *infra*, p. 180.

ii. Unknown father: At the other end of the spectrum, if the father never supports the child, and never even formally acknowledges paternity until after the adoption proceeding starts, then the state may constitutionally dispense with the father's consent (and may even dispense with *notice* to the father). *Quilloin v. Walcott*, 434 U.S. 246 (1978), discussed further *infra*, p. 181. At least, this rule applies where the father *knows* that he is the father.

iii. Father has no knowledge: Where the man who is in fact the natural father has *no knowledge* that he is the father (because the mother never tells him that she has become pregnant and they then drift apart, or because she falsely tells him that the father is someone else), there are no Supreme Court cases on point, and the law is muddled. Probably the states may constitutionally cut off the unknown father's adoption rights without notice to or consent by him, so that if the father later discovers that he is indeed the father, he will not be permitted to invalidate the adoption. The constitutional issues are discussed further *infra*, p. 182.

Note: Distinguish between what a state is *constitutionally entitled* to do, and what the state *does in fact* do. Although the states may probably (as noted above) constitutionally cut off the father's adoption rights without notice to him or consent by him, most state statutes do not in fact do this where it can be avoided.

Thus in the widely publicized case of *In Re B.G.C.*, 496 N.W.2d 239 (Iowa 1992), (the "Baby Jessica" case) the Iowa Supreme Court held that the Iowa adoption statute prohibited an adoption over the objection of the natural father, even though the natural mother had initially consented to the adoption, the mother had falsely stated that another man was the father, that man had consented, and physical custody had already been transferred to the would-be adoptive parents. The Iowa court was not saying that Iowa couldn't constitutionally cut off the natural father's rights in this situation, merely that the Iowa legislature hadn't chosen to do so.

Most states statutes follow the Iowa approach, which is that: (1) the natural father must be given notice where this is practicable, and (2) the father has a veto if he acts promptly, as soon as he learns he is the father, to block the adoption while the proceeding is still pending. (Once the adoption has become final, and the relatively short statute of limitations on attacking adoptions has run (see *infra*, p. 178), the father's rights are usually cut off even if he never received notice either that he was the father or that the adoption was being proposed.)

    iv. Right to establish procedures: The states may establish procedures by which the father of an out-of-wedlock child may *"register"* his assertion that he is the father. If the state sets up such a procedure, and the father does not register, then the child may constitutionally be given up for adoption without the father's consent, even if the court, the agency and the mother all know of the father's identity and whereabouts at the time of the adoption. *Lehr v. Robertson*, 463 U.S. 248 (1983) (discussed further *infra*, p. 182).

  c. Consent of non-parents: Where the child is not living with either natural parent, some states require the consent of the *adoption agency* or of the child's *guardian*. Thus if the child is entrusted to the custody of an agency, and the agency places the child in a foster care home, a state statute will frequently hold that no adoption (either by the foster parents or by a different prospective family) may occur without the agency's consent. However, most states hold that the court may oversee the agency approval process, and may order the adoption to go through without the agency's consent if the court finds that the agency's refusal to consent was unreasonable or arbitrary. The burden of proof, however, is on the would-be adoptive parents, not the agency, on the issue of unreasonableness.

3. Time for giving consent: Prospective adoptive parents who are in contact with the natural mother before the birth of the child frequently attempt to gain a *pre-birth* consent to the adoption. However, there is of course a serious risk that the natural mother will, after the birth, quickly change her mind, especially in light of the mother-child bonding that usually takes place during and shortly after the birth process. Therefore, many adoption statutes provide that *a consent given before birth is not valid*, and in fact that some minimum time (typically 72 hours) must elapse after birth before consent may be given. Clark, p. 879, n. 24. (But even under such a statute, if the mother gives too early a consent, then does not change her mind right away after the birth, her conduct may be found to have "ratified" the consent, so as to make it valid. See *id.*, n. 25.)

4. Age: The fact that a natural parent is not of *legal age* does *not* affect the validity of the consent. However, the extreme youth of the parent may, in conjunction with other factors, convince the court that the consent should be revocable on grounds of fraud or duress (discussed *infra*, p. 176).

C. Revocation of consent: Even where a consent is "valid" in the sense that all required formalities have been complied with (e.g., witnesses, time for giving consent, etc.), most states allow the consent to be **revoked** in at least some situations. Proceedings to revoke consent account for a large portion of all adoption-related litigation.

> **Note:** In this discussion of "revocation of consent," we are speaking about the rights of the natural parent(s) to undo the adoption *before it has become final*. Once the adoption has become final, it is of course much harder to undo, and courts and statutes usually do not speak in terms of revocation of consent. Attacks on adoptions that have become final are discussed *infra*, p. 178.

1. **Statutes:** Many states have enacted *statutes* to deal with whether, how and when consent to adoption may be revoked by the natural parent.

   a. **Time limit:** Many of the statutes provide what is in essence a very short *statute of limitations*. That is, after a short period of time (usually ranging from 48 hours to 10 days after the consent is given), it may no longer be revoked. Most of these time-limit provisions are made inapplicable where there is fraud or duress (see below). See Clark, p. 884, n. 65.

   b. **Fraud or duress:** Most revocation-of-consent statutes make it easier to revoke consent when there has been *fraud* or *duress* in procuring the consent. Often, this is done by imposing a longer time limit, or no time limit at all, on revocation for fraud or duress. The use of fraud or duress to revoke consent is discussed further *infra*, p. 176 (where this defense is analyzed both as to states having statutes on revocation and those deciding revocation issues solely by case law). Some statutes go further, and hold that fraud or duress is the *only* ground for revoking consent, at any time. See Clark, *id.* at n. 66.

   c. **Best interests of child:** Some statutes provide that as long as revocation occurs within the allotted time, it may be done "of right," that is, without any examination by the court into the reasons for the revocation. But other statutes hold that court approval is required, and that that approval shall be given only if the court finds that revocation would be in the *child's best interests*. See, e.g., Uniform Adoption Act §8(b).

   d. **No reason at all:** A few states have statutes allowing *automatic* revocation, at the *sole discretion of the birth mother* and without her having to show any reason at all. For instance, California has repealed its earlier statute requiring a showing the revocation would be in the best interests of the child, and now allows the birth mother to revoke *for any reason or no reason*, so long as the four month period between consent and the adoption's becoming final has not yet passed (and assuming that the mother has not waived the right of revocation, something that can only occur after the birth mother has been interviewed by the State Department of Social Services). See Cal. Civ. Code §§224.63, 224.64 (both effective 1/1/94). The new California procedure applies even where the child has been placed in the adoptive home, and requires the adoptive parents to immediately return the child to the birth mother upon revocation, without judicial intervention.

2. **Case law:** Where there is no statute dealing specifically with revocation of consent, the court is free to decide as a matter of judge-made law whether the facts justify allowing the adoptive parent(s) to revoke her consent. Decisions on grounds for revocation are all over the lot; some of the factors are as follows:

   a. **Not automatic:** Usually, the court does not treat the right to revoke as automatic; instead, the court scrutinizes the claim carefully, and will allow revocation only where there is *good reason*;

   b. **Fraud or duress:** *Fraud* or *duress* is usually considered a "good reason" justifying revocation (and, in some courts, it is the *only* reason);

   c. **Best interests of child:** The *best interests* of the *child* are generally considered. One consequence is that the *longer* the child has been living with the adoptive or foster parents, the less likely the court is to allow revocation. Clark, p. 887.

3. **Fraud or duress:** As noted, both statutes and case law recognize that the existence of *"fraud"* or *"duress"* are among the leading (and in some states the only) ground for revocation of consent to adoption. What, then, qualifies as "fraud" or "duress"?

   a. **Fraud:** For fraud, the natural parent(s) must generally show that she was induced to consent by means of a *material* misstatement of facts. For instance, if the natural mother could show that the adoptive parents induced her to consent by stating that she was consenting only to a *temporary* placement and could have her baby back whenever she wanted it, most courts would regard this as enough to establish fraud.

      i. **Intent:** Courts are split about whether the misstatement must be made "intentionally," i.e., with knowledge of its falsity and with an intent to induce the consent. Most courts would probably not insist that the misstater have knowledge of the falsity as long as the misstatement was sufficiently material.

      ii. **Constructive fraud:** The toughest question is whether *"constructive"* fraud should be sufficient for revocation. In particular, if the natural parent(s) is misled about the *identity* or nature of the adoptive parents, should this be deemed fraud? Examples might include: (1) the adoption agency says that it has picked out a loving family, whereas in fact (and unbeknownst to the agency) the adoptive father is a child abuser; or (2) the agency says that the adoptive parents are "a nice couple," which the birth mother interprets to mean a husband and wife, whereas in fact they are a pair of male homosexuals.

Courts are split about whether this sort of misrepresentation should be deemed as fraud justifying revocation. Clark, pp. 885-86. Revocation would be more likely to be allowed where either: (1) the misrepresenter was found to be in a fiduciary relationship with the birth parents (e.g., an adoption agency that treated the birth parents as its clients); (2) the misrepresentation went deeply to the heart of whether the adoptive parents would in fact be good parents; or (3) the misrepresentation is shown to have been intentional rather than merely reckless or negligent.

b. Duress: The clearest case for a finding of "duress" is that the natural mother was subjected to *wrongful* conduct to *strong-arm* her into consenting. For instance, if an adoption agency, without reasonable cause, told the birth mother that she was in the agency's opinion unfit to raise the child and that the agency would start proceedings to have the child taken from her involuntarily if she did not consent to adoption, this would almost certainly be considered the type of "duress" that constitutes grounds for revocation.

i. Duress of circumstances: The more difficult question is whether *"duress of circumstances"* should count. For instance, suppose the birth mother is a 16-year-old unmarried girl from a family of few financial resources, the father has no interest in marrying the mother or in participating in the child's upbringing, and the mother's parents advise her that the only sensible course is to give the child up for adoption and to return to school. The mother reluctantly consents, an adoptive placement is made, and three months after the consent the birth mother realizes that she has made a horrible mistake — she could raise the child herself by means of a full-time job and newly-available day care. In this situation, where the duress has come more from the circumstances than from any wrongful conduct by third persons, courts are generally *reluctant* to allow revocation of consent, especially where the child is already residing with the adoptive parents (even though the adoption is not yet final). See Clark, p. 886, arguing that "the effect on the child when such revocations occur is likely to be severe and this factor justifies denying the attempt at revocation." But occasionally courts have recognized this type of circumstantial duress as grounds for revocation. (Also, remember that in some states, such as California, statutes allow revocation for no reason at all, as long as the adoption has not yet become final; this would of course allow revocation in the "duress of circumstances" situation.)

4. **Finality of adoption:** All states provide a procedure by which at a certain moment an adoption becomes *final*. The significance of an adoption's finality is that this is the moment at which the natural parents' parental rights are *terminated*, and the adoptive parents are treated as being the parents in all legal respects (e.g., inheritance, or in entitlement not to have *their* parental rights terminated without a showing that they are unfit).

   a. **Length of time:** Because of a desire to make certain that the adoptive parents are fit, most states require passage of at least *several months* in between the time the child is placed with the adoptive parents and the moment of finality, to give social workers a chance to verify the fitness and suitability of the adoptive home. See, e.g., §12 of the Uniform Adoption Act, by which no adoption may become final until the child has lived in the adoptive home for at least six months after placement by an agency (or, in the case of an independent adoption, at least six months after state child welfare officials have been informed of the placement).

D. **Attack on final adoption:** Once the adoption has become "final," it is much harder, though not impossible, to set it aside.

1. **Time limit:** States generally set a very short *time limit* for attacking an adoption that has become final. Few states allow more than five years, and many allow much less. See, e.g., §15(b) of the Uniform Adoption Act (no decree may be questioned once one year has passed from the time it became final).

2. **Attack by natural parent:** Most attempts to set aside a final adoption decree are launched by one or both of the *natural parents*.

   a. **Fraud or duress by one who originally "consented":** Where the person attacking the decree is a natural parent who originally *consented* to the adoption, virtually the only grounds ever available to set aside the final decree are *fraud* and *duress*. Court typically take a narrower view of what constitutes fraud and duress here than in the case of pre-final attempts to revoke consent (see *supra*, p. 175). But if the natural parent can show, for instance, that the agency in making the placement knew that the adoptive parents would be unsuitable, and lied about this, the court may be willing to set aside even a final decree on grounds of fraud. See generally Clark, p. 936.

   b. **Parent who never received notice:** If the natural *father* never received notice of the adoption proceedings, he will have a good chance to set aside even a final decree, provided that he acts before the statute of limitations has run on attacking final decrees (see *supra*, p. 178). The father does not necessarily have a constitutional right to have the decree set aside in this situation, but state procedures may give him a statutory right to this relief. (But once the statute of limitations has run, even the natural father who can show that he never received any notice is out of luck.)

3. **Suit by adoptive parents:** With increasing frequency, the *adoptive parents* seek to undo the adoption. This is most likely to occur where, unbeknownst to the adoptive parents at the time of the placement, the child had a serious illness, a developmental disability, or a conduct disorder.

   a. **Statute:** Some states have now enacted statutes that allow for abrogation or relinquishment of the adoption in certain circumstances. For instance, in California, the adoptive parents may move to set aside the adoption if the child is shown to have had "a developmental disability or mental illness as a result of conditions existing before the adoption...of which conditions the adoptive parents...had no knowledge or notice before [the adoption]." The adoption may then be set aside by court order, provided that the suit to set is aside is filed within five years after the adoption became final. Cal. Fam. Code §9100.

   b. **Where no statute exists:** Most states do *not* have statutes allowing for abrogation or relinquishment of the adoption. In these states, it is far harder for the adoptive parents to undo the adoption. But occasionally, even in these states the adoptive parents have been able to undo the adoption where they can show that information about the child's disabilities was concealed from them. See, e.g., *In re Lisa Diane G.*, 537 A.2d 131 (R.I. 1988) (Rhode Island courts may set aside adoption if the adoption agency fraudulently concealed information about the child, such as the alleged concealment here of the child's behavioral problems).

VI. CONSTITUTIONAL ISSUES IN ADOPTION

A. **Constitutional issues generally:** An adoption affects the rights of the biological mother and father of the child. Since 1972, the Supreme Court has gradually held that biological parents have certain rights protected by the Due Process and Equal Protection Clauses, and that these rights must be taken into account in any adoption proceeding.

B. **Mother's rights:** The Court has always assumed, without explicitly deciding, that the natural *mother* has a substantive due process right not to have her child taken away from her and given up for adoption, unless she has been found to be an unfit parent (or to have abandoned the child), after notice and an opportunity to be heard.

C. Rights of father of child born in wedlock: Similarly, the Court has always assumed that the father of a child born *in wedlock* (or of a child whom the father has later *legitimated* through whatever proceedings the state supplies for this purpose) has a due process right not to have his parental rights terminated without a showing of unfitness.

> **Example:** Mother and Father, at a time when they are married to each other, have a child, C. When C is 4, Mother and Father are divorced, and the court gives custody to Mother. The next year, Mother marries Stepfather, and C lives with Mother and Stepfather. Stepfather petitions the court to be allowed to adopt C (a step which, under the law of every state, necessarily means that Father's parental rights would have to be terminated).
>
> Although the Supreme Court has never expressly so held, it seems clear that Father on these facts has a substantive due process right to veto the adoption unless there is a showing (after notice to him and an opportunity for him to be heard) that he is an unfit parent. Therefore, even if the court decides that it would be in C's best interests to be adopted by Stepfather, the court may not constitutionally take this step.

D. Father of child born out of wedlock: Virtually all litigation about the constitutional rights of natural parents to veto adoption proceedings has concerned the rights of *fathers* of children born *out of wedlock*. (We assume that the father has not, prior to the beginning of adoption proceedings, taken steps to legitimate the child; if he has taken such steps, then he is treated as if the child had been born in wedlock.) Here, although the Supreme Court has decided a number of cases, the rules remain very unclear, except at the outer ends of the spectrum.

1. **Father participates:** It is clear that the state may *not* simply deny to *all* fathers of out of wedlock children the right to veto an adoption. Where the father has offered to *support* the child financially, and has shown genuine and continuous interest in *participating* in the rearing of the child, then it is a violation of the father's substantive due process rights for the state to permit an adoption over the father's objection. *Stanley v. Illinois*, 405 U.S. 645 (1973).

   > **Example:** M and F live together for 18 years without being married. During that time, three children are born to them. M dies while the children are still minors. The state, acting under a statute that gives no parental rights to the father of an illegitimate child, takes the children as wards of the state. The state does not hold any hearing regarding F's suitability as guardian. F sues, claiming that he had a right under the Fourteenth Amendment's Due Process Clause to have a hearing on his fitness before the state can take away his children.

Held, for F. The statute violated both F's due process and equal protection rights, by presuming that an unwed father is an unfit parent without giving him notice or a hearing. Since the state takes over the custody of children of married parents, divorced parents or unmarried mothers only after a hearing and proof of neglect, it must do the same for unmarried fathers. *Stanley v. Illinois, supra.*

Note: Although *Stanley* involved merely the state's right to take custody of the child, not the right to put the child up for adoption, the case is understood to also mean that an unwed father who helps care for and support his children has a right not to have the children put up for adoption without notice and a hearing. Also, although the case only involved procedural issues (did F have the right to notice and a hearing?), later Supreme Court cases have assumed that *Stanley* stands for the proposition that an unwed father who participates in the raising of his children has a **substantive** right to veto an adoption, not just a procedural right to have a notice and a hearing.

2. **Father does not participate or support:** At the other end of the spectrum, consider an unwed father who does **not** participate in the children's upbringing, or help support them financially. At least where the father has had an opportunity to do so (e.g., he knows that the child is his, and knows where the mother is living with the child), after the passage of some period of time the father no longer has a constitutional right to veto a proposed adoption. This is quite clear where the adoption would be by a step-parent, and is probably the case where the adoption would be by a stranger.

   Example: M and F have a child, C, out of wedlock. M and F never marry each other or live together. When C is three, M marries X. When C is 12, X seeks to adopt C. F is given notice of the adoption proceedings, and objects. The court nonetheless allows the adoption (and consequent termination of F's parental rights). F has never attempted to legitimate C, and has never had actual custody or daily responsibility for C. F now argues that the adoption violates his equal protection and due process rights.

   Held, the adoption was proper. Where an unwed father has never had custody or daily responsibility for his child and has never attempted to legitimate the child, and where the proposed adoption would merely "give full recognition to a family unit already in existence," the state may constitutionally allow the adoption based merely on a finding that it is in the child's best interests. *Quilloin v. Walcott*, 434 U.S. 246 (1978).

   Note: Observe that the court in *Quilloin* relied in part on the fact that the adoption there was by a step-father, not by a stranger. The Supreme Court has never decided whether different rules should apply in the adoption-by-strangers situation, which is discussed below.

3. **Father fails to register as "putative father":** Where the state gives men a chance to *register* the fact that they are the biological father of a child, and a father fails to take advantage of this opportunity, then not only does the father not have a substantive right to block the adoption, but he does not even have the right to receive *notice* of the proposed adoption, or an opportunity to be heard. This is true even though the court and/or the natural mother are on notice of the father's identity and whereabouts. *Lehr v. Robertson*, 463 U.S. 248 (1983). (Apparently this rationale applies only where the father has not just failed to use the registry but has also failed to participate financially or emotionally in the upbringing of the child; presumably a father who does participate in upbringing will not lose his right to notice or an opportunity to be heard merely because he has failed to comply with a state paternity registration provision.)

4. **Adoption at birth by strangers:** Now, assume that while the child is still a *newborn*, and before the father has had any opportunity to participate in the child's upbringing, the mother consents to an adoption (typically, to complete strangers). The Supreme Court has never directly addressed this issue. Clearly, the father has a stronger claim to be allowed to veto the adoption here, since he has not yet "failed" to participate in the child's upbringing — he has simply not yet had the opportunity. Furthermore, if the adoption is by strangers, then the rationale present in the step-parent adoption cases — that the adoption is merely validating the pre-existing natural relationship — would not apply. However, it seems probable that the Supreme Court would allow an adoption over the father's objections in this situation, if the father has failed to take advantage of a state paternity registry such as the one in *Lehr*; the few lower court cases on the subject have so held. See Clark, p. 861.

VII. TERMINATION OF PARENTAL RIGHTS AND DUTIES

A. **Introduction:** Adoption involves a two-step process:

1. **Termination of rights:** The rights and responsibilities of a child and his natural parents to each other are *terminated*; and

2. **Creation of rights:** The rights and responsibilities of parent and child are created between the child and his adoptive parents.

   Here, we focus on the first of these two steps.

B. **Termination of rights:** The termination of the rights and responsibilities between natural parent and child can be *voluntary* or *involuntary*.

1. **Voluntary termination:** The natural parents may ***consent*** to the termination of their parental rights. This is a "voluntary" termination. Generally, such a voluntary termination is carried out in conjunction with the parents' consent to adoption of the child.

   a. **Deal between parents:** Suppose as part of the breakup of a relationship, the non-custodial parent wishes to be relieved of child support, and the custodial parent is willing to accept this provided that the non-custodial parent (typically, the father) agrees to have his parental rights terminated. Should such a "deal" be allowed by the courts? Where the child is born out of wedlock, most courts would probably answer "yes," since there is ample precedent for holding that the father of an out-of-wedlock child has no real parental rights unless he participates actively in raising and supporting the child. But where the child is born to a married couple, the principal case on the issue has held that such a deal should ***not*** be permitted unless there is clear evidence that the deal would be in the best interests of the ***child***, not just the parents. *Ex parte Brooks*, 513 So.2d 614 (Ala. 1987).

   Example: H and W are divorced while W is three months pregnant with a son, David. During the first four years of David's life, he has lived with W, and H has never seen him or supported him. W (who has a reasonable income of her own) is not interested in obtaining child support from H. W fears that H will meddle in how W raises David if H remains the father. Therefore, H and W agree that in return for W's absolving H of any duty to pay child support, H will consent to the termination of his parental rights. There is no evidence that H has harmed David or interfered with W's custody of him.

   Held, H's parental rights are ***not*** terminated. The termination here "appears to be overwhelmingly for the convenience of the parents," and would not benefit David at all. The statutory provision allowing for termination of parental rights "was not intended as a means for allowing a parent to abandon his child thereby to avoid his obligation to support the child. ..." In the absence of clear and convincing evidence that termination is in David's best interests, the court denies the petition. *Ex parte Brooks, supra*.

2. **Involuntary termination:** The natural parents of a child may be judged ***unable*** or ***unfit*** to care for their child. If such a ruling is rendered, consent of the natural parents to the termination of parental rights (and to the adoption or foster placement of the child) is not necessary. Here, the termination of parental rights is, of course, ***involuntary***.

   Example: W has a child, C, who is not the child of H, her husband. Paternity is never established. W is diagnosed as having multiple sclerosis when C is born. Because W is unable to care for C, he is placed in a foster home. The foster parents petition for adoption, but W refuses to consent even though she is a paraplegic.

Held, the petition for adoption is granted. A parent has no property right in a child, and the right of custody is not absolute. Where it is shown by *"clear and convincing evidence"* that parental consent to adoption of a child is being withheld contrary to the "best interests of the child," parental rights may be terminated. Since W depends on others for most of her physical needs, she cannot care for C, and never developed a parent-child relationship with C. *Matter of Adoption of J.S.R.*, 374 A.2d 860 (D.C.App. 1977).

a. **Grounds for termination:** To terminate the rights of parents, a mere finding that the termination is in the child's *best interests* is *not sufficient*. It must be shown that continued custody by the parents will be *detrimental to the child.* Typical situations include:

   i. **Injury:** The parents have caused serious *physical* or *psychological harm* to the child;

   ii. **Nonsupport:** The parents have failed to *support* the child for a specified period (one year, in many states); or

   iii. **Other grounds:** The parents have taken other acts or omissions which, depending on their seriousness, may justify termination of their rights. These include *gross neglect* of the child, drug or alcohol *dependency,* and *unfitness* of the parent which is seriously detrimental to the child's welfare.

3. **Effect of divorce:** A *divorce* granting sole custody of a child to one parent does *not* terminate the non-custodial parent's rights and responsibilities with respect to the child. Consequently, *both parents* must normally *consent* to any adoption of the child.

   Example: W marries H2, her second husband, who petitions to adopt M's two children by W's first husband, H1. H1 objects, but the adoption is granted. *Held* (on appeal), the adoption decree is overturned. In the case of divorce, one parent is granted custody based on the welfare of the children. That standard does not terminate the necessity of consent by the parent not having custody. Where there is no consent to the adoption, there must be some conduct by the nonconsenting parent which demonstrates an intent to abandon the children or forfeit the natural rights of parenthood. No such evidence was presented here. *In the Matter of Adoption of Smith*, 366 P.2d 875 (Or. 1961).

4. **Child's standing to sue for termination:** Normally, a proceeding to terminate parental rights is brought by either state officials (e.g., the Department of Child Welfare) or by an adult seeking to adopt the child.

But may the ***child himself*** sue to, in effect, ***"divorce his parents"***? If by this question we mean, may a child who feels abandoned or mistreated, acting on his own, petition the court to have his parents' rights terminated, few such cases have ever arisen. However, in one celebrated case, an 11-year-old boy was successful in having his natural mother's rights cut off on the grounds that she had abandoned him by placing him in foster care; an adoption was then allowed as the boy wished. That case, involving "Gregory K.," is *Kingsley v. Kingsley,* 623 So.2d 780 (Fla.App. 1993). But the appellate court in *Kingsley* held that as a minor, Gregory should ***not*** have been permitted to sue on his own, but only by means of a court-appointed "next friend" or guardian ad litem. (However, the appellate court did not overturn the termination and adoption.)

   i. **Must show unfitness:** Also, keep in mind that in the case of any suit to terminate parental rights — whether the suit is instigated by the child, by the prospective adoptive parents, or the state — a mere showing that the child would be happier or better off in some adoptive or foster setting will ***not*** be sufficient to terminate the natural parent(s)' rights. Only where the natural parent is shown to be ***unfit*** (in the sense of affirmatively damaging the child), or to have abandoned the child, will the petition for involuntary termination be granted. Thus in *Kingsley, supra,* the basis for the parent-child "divorce" was that Gregory's natural mother had in effect "abandoned" him by placing him in foster care.

C. **Defenses:** The Constitution guarantees certain rights to persons. These rights may provide a defense to involuntary termination of parental rights.

1. **"Void for vagueness":** A statute which allows a child to be taken from his natural parents must be sufficiently explicit so that it informs people ***fairly and reasonably*** of the conduct which is forbidden. If the statute fails to do this it is ***"void for vagueness,"*** in violation of the Due Process Clause.

   Example: An Iowa statute provides that the rights of parents may be terminated where they "have continuously or repeatedly refused to give the child necessary parental care and protection," or "are unfit by reason of ... conduct found by the court likely to be detrimental to the physical or mental health or morals of the child." This statute was held void for vagueness. *Alsager v. District Court of Polk County,* 406 F.Supp. 10 (Iowa 1978).

   Example: Statutes in a number of other jurisdictions, which are similar to the Iowa statute in the previous example, have been upheld. Thus, in *Matter of Doe,* 666 P.2d 771 (N.M. 1983), the court held that a statute which authorized the termination of the parent—child relationship where it "has disintegrated" was not unconstitutionally vague.

2. **Notice:** Due process requires reasonable ***notice*** and an ***opportunity to be heard***. Thus, the natural mother and father must normally be given notice before the rights of either are terminated.

> **Example:** A state law permits adoption of a child by a stepfather without the consent of the natural father if he has failed to contribute to the child's support to the extent of his ability for two years. The statute was held unconstitutional as violative of the Due Process Clause. *Armstrong v. Manzo*, 380 U.S. 545 (1965).

> **Note:** The notice requirement applies to unwed fathers. *State ex rel Lewis v. Lutheran Social Services of Wisconsin*, 207 N.W.2d 826 (Wis. 1973).

3. **Right to counsel:** Indigent parents do ***not*** have an absolute right to ***counsel*** before their rights are terminated. In *Lassiter v. Dept. of Social Services of Durham County*, 452 U.S. 18, *rehearing denied* 453 U.S. 927 (1981), the Court held that an indigent mother, whose parental rights the state was trying to terminate, was not automatically entitled to appointed counsel. The need for appointed counsel should be determined by the trial court on a ***case by case*** basis. In *Lassiter* the mother's claim to counsel failed because, in essence, the Court decided that her case was so weak that counsel could not have helped her.

   a. **Criteria used:** The trial court should consider the following factors in deciding whether to appoint counsel:

      i. **Private interests at stake:** Parents have a strong interest in a continuation of the family unit and raising their own children. The child needs a stable, loving homelife for his physical, emotional and spiritual well-being.

      ii. **Government interest:** The state has an urgent interest in the welfare of the child.

      iii. **Risk of erroneous decision:** If the court makes an incorrect decision regarding the termination of a parent — child relationship, the child may be returned to an abusive home or placed in the often unstable world of foster care.

4. **Standard of proof:** Before the rights of parents in their natural child may be terminated, the Due Process Clause requires that the state support its allegations by at least ***clear and convincing evidence***. This is a higher standard than preponderance of the evidence used in the ordinary civil case. *Santosky v. Kramer*, 445 U.S. 745 (1982).

   a. **Temporary custody order:** But where the state seeks ***temporary custody*** of endangered children, it must show the risk of harm only by a ***fair preponderance of the evidence.*** This best protects the interests of the child because the child's safety is involved, and the deprivation of parents' rights is not final. *In re Juvenile Appeal,* 445 A.2d 1313 (Conn. 1983).

VIII. FOSTER CARE

A. **Foster care generally:** Where a child's own family cannot care for him, and adoption is either not desirable at the moment, or not possible, the appropriate remedy is generally ***foster care.*** Common situations calling for foster care are:

1. **Hard to place:** The child is ***hard to place*** for adoption, perhaps because of developmental disabilities, emotional problems, physical handicaps, or because the child is older.

2. **Possible return to natural parent:** The natural parent(s) is ***currently*** not able to care for the child, but there is a reasonable chance that he or she may be able to do so at some time in the future. Therefore, adoption, because of its finality, would be inappropriate. For instance, if the natural mother is currently dependent on ***drugs,*** but has entered a treatment facility, temporary foster care would probably be the appropriate solution.

B. **Adoption contrasted:** Foster care is care for a child in a ***family.*** It is ***non-institutional*** substitute care for a ***planned period,*** either temporary or extended. By contrast, adoptive placement is the ***permanent substitution*** of one home for another.

C. **Status of foster parents:** The typical foster placement occurs when a state or local child welfare agency determines that the natural parents are unable, at least at the present, to care for the child properly. Typically the agency then signs a "boarding home" agreement with the foster parents. The agreement usually provides that:

1. **Return:** The placement is only ***temporary,*** and the foster parents must ***return*** the child immediately upon the demand of the agency;

2. **No adoption:** The foster parents will ***not*** attempt to ***adopt*** the child; and

3. **Financial support:** The state will ***pay*** the foster parents some or all of the estimated costs of caring for the child.

D. **Custody and adoption disputes involving foster parents:** In the typical case where the foster parents sign the type of "return child on demand" agreement described above, it would seem unlikely that the foster parents would ever end up asserting either a continued right to custody or the right to adopt the child. Nonetheless, such disputes do sometimes arise.

1. **Dispute between foster and natural parents:** Where the nature of the dispute is that the natural parent(s) wishes to have the child returned, the foster parents almost always *lose*. Recall (see *supra*, p. 184) that the natural parents' parental rights can only be terminated upon a finding of permanent unfitness. Therefore, unless the court has made such a finding of unfitness, the natural parent has an *absolute right* to have the child returned, even if the judge believes that the child would be "better off" remaining in the foster family. In the extreme case, this result will be reached even though the child has been with a particular foster family for long enough that the child now views the foster family as his "psychological family." Clark, p. 835.

2. **Dispute between foster parents and agency:** Now, assume that the dispute does not involve the natural parents (either because their parental rights have been formally terminated, or because they show no interest in regaining custody). Instead, the dispute is between the foster parents (who wish to keep custody or even adopt) and the *agency* that made the placement (which now wishes to remove the child for either another foster placement or an adoption placement). Here, the foster parents have a substantially greater chance of prevailing.

    a. **Probably no due process right:** Foster parents, even those that have lived with the child long enough to develop a deep emotional tie, probably do *not* have a constitutional *due process* interest in continuing to have custody. The Supreme Court so indicated, without expressly deciding, in *Smith v. Organization of Foster Families for Equality and Reform*, 431 U.S. 816 (1977). Lower courts interpreting *Smith* have concluded that foster parents have no liberty interest in maintaining custody of children placed with them by the state. Clark, p. 834.

    b. **Cases split on outcome:** Nonetheless, courts sometimes do side with the foster parents against the agency, and permit the foster parents to maintain custody or adopt, where this would clearly be in the child's best interest.

        i. **Child's best interests:** On the face of it, courts that look merely to the child's best interests, and permit the foster parents to maintain custody or adopt when this will be in the child's interests, seem correct — why should the foster placement ever be terminated where maintaining it would be in the child's interests, in view of the emotional bond between the foster family and the child?

        ii. **Integrity of system:** The difficulty is that there is a strong countervailing interest, the interest in the *integrity* of the *foster placement system.* If the "return the child on demand" clause is not stringently enforced, people are likely to volunteer to be foster parents as a shortcut to adopting, and the whole temporary-placement system may break down. See Clark, pp. 835-36.

    iii. Possibility of adoption by others: In deciding a custody/ adoption dispute between the foster parents and the agency, the court should and frequently does consider the likelihood that the child will be adopted by some third party in the near future. If such a suitable adoption seems likely, then the case for removing the child from the foster home is relatively strong. If, on the other hand, the likely effect of removing the child is merely a succession of other temporary foster placements, then probably the child should be left with the otherwise-suitable foster family with whom he is presently living, especially where an emotional bond has developed. Clark, p. 836.

IX. JURISDICTIONAL ASPECTS OF ADOPTION

A. Basis of jurisdiction: Jurisdiction refers to the authority of the court to grant the adoption. A valid adoption may be created in the state of the *child's domicile,* in the state where the *adoptive parents are domiciled* when the child is before the court, or in a state where the adoptive parents and either the adoptive child or the person having legal custody of the child are subject to its *personal jurisdiction.*

    Note: Most cases in which jurisdictional issues are raised are concerned with the requirements of the local statute which sets forth the court's jurisdiction.

1. Raising issue: Jurisdictional issues of an adoption proceeding, if any, are generally raised either at the *inception of the adoption proceedings* to determine whether the court has jurisdiction to grant the adoption, or *after entry of the decree* of adoption to determine whether it should be given recognition.

    Example: H and W, residents of State A, give custody of their child, C, to P because they are unable to provide adequately for C. W also gives C's birth certificate to P with a letter granting permission to take C out of the state. P moves to State B and later petitions to adopt C. H and W oppose the adoption and contend that B's court lacks jurisdiction.

    Held, State B may hear the adoption proceeding. P has legal custody of C and is domiciled there. Personal jurisdiction over P is sufficient, even though the domicile of C is that of her natural parents. *A. v. M.,* 180 A.2d 541 (N.J. 1962).

2. **Interstate recognition:** The Full Faith and Credit Clause, Article IV, Section 1, requires the recognition of the adoption decree of one state by other states.

> **Example:** H and W are domiciled in State A, when a child, C, is abandoned on their doorstep. H and W, in compliance with A's laws, adopt C through a proceeding in which all three appear in court. H, W, and C move to State B, where they establish a new domicile. H and W die intestate in B, and C claims to be their heir. A sister of H claims to be their heir, asserting that the adoption proceedings in A are invalid under B's laws.
>
> *Held*, C will inherit. Since C was validly adopted under the laws of A, the law of domicile at the time of the adoption will be given full faith and credit in B. Thus B must recognize the adoption as valid. *Woodward's Appeal,* 70 A. 453 (Conn. 1908).

3. **Indian Child Welfare Act (ICWA):** The *Indian Child Welfare Act* was passed because of Congress' concern that many Native American children were being placed through adoption or foster care placement into non-Native American families. The Act was passed to protect both the rights of the Indian child as an Indian, and the rights of Indian tribes in retaining their children in their society. It gives exclusive jurisdiction over children domiciled on Indian reservations to *tribal courts*. Consequently, a child born on an Indian reservation normally *cannot be placed for adoption by state officials*, even with the *consent of the natural mother*.

> **Example:** M resides on an Indian reservation. She leaves the reservation, gives birth to twins, and places them for adoption. A state court approves the adoption by a non-Indian couple. The Tribe moves to vacate the adoption because the tribal court has exclusive jurisdiction under the ICWA. The motion is denied because M intentionally left the reservation to give birth and arrange for adoption, and the children were never physically on the reservation.
>
> *Held*, the adoption is vacated. "Domicile" is established by physical presence in a place with intent to remain there. Since minors are legally incapable of forming the requisite intent to establish domicile, their domicile is determined by that of their parents. In the case of an illegitimate child, as the present case, the domicile of the mother is traditionally used. M and the father are domiciled on the Indian reservation. At birth the twins were also domiciled on the reservation even though they had never been there. Tribal jurisdiction cannot be defeated by actions of individual members of the tribe; that would be inconsistent with what Congress intended in the Act. Thus the state court lacked jurisdiction to enter a decree of adoption. *Mississippi Bank of Choctaw Indians v. Holyfield,* 490 U.S. 30 (1989).

X. ADOPTION OF ADULTS

A. **Statutory provisions:** Almost all states have some type of law permitting adoption of adults. The provisions of these statutes vary from jurisdiction to jurisdiction.

   1. **Permitted:** Some statutes expressly provide for the adoption of adults;

   2. **Not permitted:** Some statutes expressly limit adoption to minors;

   3. **Limited to "children":** Some statutes merely provide for the adoption of children. In these jurisdictions some courts have interpreted the statute to mean "minors," while other courts have found it to mean a relationship, thereby including adults.

B. **Purpose:** Adult adoptions, in most instances, are used to provide an *inheritance* device. Other considerations include insurance and tax impact.

> **Example:** In a state where adult adoptions are allowed, H, a 56-year-old man, attempts to adopt W, his 45-year-old wife. The purpose of the adoption is to allow W to inherit under a testamentary trust established by H's mother — the trust provides that its principal is to be distributed at H's death to his "heir at law." Under state law, an adopted child is regarded as an heir unless specifically disinherited.
>
> *Held*, the adoption is valid. The adoption is within the authority of the statute, and it does not create an incestuous relationship. *Bedinger v. Graybill's Executor*, 302 S.W.2d 594 (Ky. 1957).

> **Note:** Most states would probably not agree with the result in *Bedinger*. However, some states have passed "designation of heir" statutes, in order to achieve the result of *Bedinger* without the need for an adoption.

   3. **Adoption between homosexuals:** In recent years, one member of a *homosexual couple* has sometimes attempted to adopt the other. As with other types of adult adoption, the purpose is usually to facilitate inheritance, transfer of health or life insurance benefits, or achievement of some other property-related objective. Several of the few cases that have considered homosexual adoption have been hostile to it, on the grounds that it furthers immorality or would thwart the intention of the legislature in enacting the adoption statute.

> **Example:** H, age 57, petitions to adopt S, age 50. H and S are homosexuals who have lived together for 25 years. They desire an adoption for various reasons, including, broadly, that "we are a family and seek to formalize such." The relevant statute allows for adult adoptions, and is silent on the express issue of whether one member of a gay couple may adopt another. However, the statute provides that adoption is "the legal proceeding whereby a person

takes another person into the relation of **child** and thereby incurs the responsibilities of **parent**."

Held, the adoption here is not permitted under the statute. While adult adoptions are generally allowed by the statute, they may occur only in those situations where there are some incidents of a parent-child relationship. If the adoption laws are to be changed so as to permit sexual lovers — whether homosexual or heterosexual — to adopt one another, it is for the legislature, not the court, to do so. *In re Robert Paul P.*, 471 N.E.2d 424 (N.Y. 1984).

Note: Observe that the rationale of the court in *Robert Paul P.* would have been equally applicable to prevent the husband-wife adoption in *Bedinger, supra*.

4. **Duty of support:** When an adult is adopted, there is no duty to support the adoptee as there is when a child is adopted.

C. **Procedure:** The adoption of an adult is not as complicated as that for adoption of a minor. The adopting adult is not investigated, and there is usually no need for a court determination that the adoption is in the best interest of the adoptee. Usually, only the **consent** of the adult to be adopted is required.

XI. INHERITANCE RIGHTS OF ADOPTED CHILDREN

A. **General rule:** The modern trend, and the rule in almost all states, is to treat the adopted child **solely** as a member of the **adoptive** family for inheritance purposes, and to **terminate all rights of inheritance** between the child and his **entire natural family**. (In most states, there is a partial exception for adoptions by a step-parent, which have the effect of making the child the heir of the adoptive parent, continuing the child as the heir of the natural parent married to the adoptive parent, and terminating the child as an heir of the other natural parent.)

Example 1: C is the child of H1 and W, who are divorced. W marries H2, who adopts C. C's inheritance rights from W are not cut off (because the adoption did not terminate W's parental rights), but such rights from H1 are cut off. Uniform Probate Code §2-109.

Note: Adoption statutes can dictate the intestate inheritance rights of a child and his parents, both natural and adoptive. However, they cannot dictate to whom a person may leave property. Thus in the example above, despite the fact that C does not have intestate inheritance rights to H1's property, H1 may nevertheless make C an heir under his will.

Example 2: Same facts as Example 1 above. Now, assume that after the adoption, H1 dies. Then, H1's father, F, dies, leaving his estate "to H1, but if H1 shall predecease me, then in equal shares to any child of H1 living at my death." C will not receive anything from F's estate, because C's adoption by H2 not only cut off C's right to adopt *from* H1, but also his right to adopt *through* H1.

1. **Rights of child:** An adopted child inherits *from* adoptive parents through intestate succession. An adopted child also inherits *through* adoptive parents in most states.

   a. **Construction of will:** Most states, either by statute or case law, provide that in construing wills and trusts, a document using the word "child" or "issue" shall be deemed to include adoptive as well as natural children.

      Example: G, the father of S, drafts a will in 1980. The will provides that in the event G's only child, S, predeceases G, G's estate is to go to S's "issue." At the time, S has only one child, C1, who is his natural child. In 1985, S adopts C2. In 1990, G dies. Most states, by statute or case law, provide that the reference to "issue" should be deemed to include adoptive as well as natural children. Therefore, G's estate would be split between C1 and C2.

      i. **Construction recognizing blood relationship:** States are split as to whether the rule of construction described in the above paragraph should also apply where its effect would be to *prevent* an adopted child from taking by will or trust from or through the natural parent. Here, whatever the statute says about the effect of adoption and the construction to be given to words like "child" and "issue," the court is likely to choose an interpretation that will best match the wishes of the testator or settlor. Thus most but not all courts would agree with the decision in the case set forth in the following example.

         Example: N is the nephew of T. T's will provides that if N predeceases T, N's share will go "to the children of [N's] body." At the time this will is drawn, N is married to W, and they have two natural children, C1 and C2. N and W then divorce, and W marries X, who adopts C1 and C2. Next, N dies, followed by T. May C1 and C2 inherit under T's will?

         Held, yes. It is true that the adoption statute provides that all rights and duties between the child and the natural parent cease with adoption. However, the statute does not prevent T or any other person from voluntarily transferring property to the children by will. T knew of C1 and C2's existence when she made her will, and must have intended them to inherit. Therefore, the court will honor this intention. (If T had died *intestate*, the statute would have prevented the children from inheriting, because their adoption would have cut off their right to inherit through as well as from N.) *In re Estate of Zastrow*, 166 N.W.2d 251 (Wis. 1969).

2. **Inheritance from adopted child:** Where it is the adopted *child* who dies, virtually all states provide that the *adoptive* parents and relatives, not the natural parents and family, inherit from the adopted child.

B. **Equitable adoption:** The doctrine of *"equitable adoption"* is sometimes used when a child is given to foster parents who agree to adopt the child. Where the foster parents care for the child but never legally adopt him, a court may hold that there has been an equitable adoption. This usually must be shown by *clear and convincing evidence*. It is generally used to allow the child to *inherit* from the foster parents.

> **Example:** C is in the custody of her aunt and uncle. H and W promise the aunt and uncle that they will adopt C if C's father consents. C is delivered to H and W, who change C's name, raise her and hold C out as their daughter. H and W never formally adopt C. H dies intestate and C seeks a share of the estate as H's adopted daughter. *Held*, for C. There was an oral contract to adopt, and it was performed in all respects except the formal adoption. The court will use its *equitable powers* to declare C an heir so that she may inherit by intestate succession. *Long v. Willey*, 391 S.W.2d 301 (Mo.1965).

ASSISTED REPRODUCTION

Introductory note: This chapter deals with a number of special techniques for bringing about reproduction, most of which make use of modern medical technology. The techniques we examine here are: artificial insemination; surrogate motherhood (including "gestational surrogacy"); egg donation; and test-tube embryos.

I. ARTIFICIAL INSEMINATION

A. Definition: *Artificial insemination* is the impregnation of a woman with semen of a donor through means other than sexual intercourse. The donor may be the woman's husband or a third party.

   1. AIH: If the donor is the *husband*, the insemination is referred to as *"AIH"* ("Artificial Insemination by Husband").

   2. AID: If the donor is a man other than the woman's husband — the most common situation — the insemination is referred to as *"AID"* ("Artificial Insemination by Donor").

   3. CAI: If the sperm of the husband is *mixed* with that of a third party, the insemination is referred to as *"CAI"* ("Confused Artificial Insemination"). This method is used principally for psychological reasons, where the husband's sperm are medically unlikely to be able to impregnate the woman, but it is desirable for the husband to think that there is some chance that the child is genetically related to him.

   > **Note:** Normally, artificial insemination is used where the woman who is impregnated expects to raise the child as her own. It is this use of AI that we are talking about in the present section. AI is also used in conjunction with surrogate motherhood — in which a woman carries and gives birth to a child but the parties anticipate that she will not raise the child as her own — but this kind of arrangement is discussed in the next section ("Surrogate Motherhood"), not here.

B. Status of children: When AI is used, a number of legal questions can arise regarding the status of the child and the rights/duties of the various adult males involved.

   1. AID issues: Some of the issues that can arise when AID is used are:

   a. Visitation and custody by donor: To what extent may the *donor* have the right to be treated as the parent of the child, for purposes of *visitation* and *custody*?

b. **Child support by donor:** To what extent may the mother (or a state welfare agency making payments to the mother for the child's support) sue the donor for ***child support***?

c. **Child support by husband:** To what extent may the mother's ***husband*** be forced to pay ***child support*** for a child that is, of course, genetically not his?

d. **Inheritance from either donor or husband:** To what extent is the child deemed the "legal child" of the donor and/or the mother's husband?

e. **Legitimacy:** Where the woman is married at the time of birth, assuming that the husband rather than the donor is deemed the legal father, is the child ***legitimate***? (This matters for both inheritance and parental rights — if a child is illegitimate, then unless there is a later legitimation, the child cannot inherit from or through the father. Similarly, unless the father actively participates in raising and supporting the child, his parental rights can be terminated even without a showing that he is unfit to be a parent, so that he would lose any rights to custody and/or visitation.)

Note: Normally, all of these issues will be resolved by the resolution of a single, more basic, issue: legal "paternity." If the child is deemed to be the "legal child" of the donor, then the donor would have visitation rights (and conceivably even custody if shown to be a more fit parent than the mother), and would probably have an obligation to pay child support.

If the mother is married at the time of birth, and her husband was found to be the child's legal father, then the donor would have no visitation or custody rights and no obligation to pay child support, and the husband would be the parent for all legal purposes, including child support, custody/visitation (if there were a later divorce), and inheritance from or through the husband or by the husband from the child.

If the mother was unmarried at the time of the child's birth, and the donor was found not to be the legal father, then the child would simply have no legal father (and this would not change if the mother were to marry later, unless her new husband adopted the child).

In general, as is discussed in more detail below, if the mother is married at the time of birth, the law treats the husband, not the donor, as the legal father, and if the mother is not married, states are split as to whether and under what circumstances the donor is the legal father.

2. **AIH:** In the relatively unusual situation where AIH is used, none of these issues generally arises — the mother's husband is the child's

legal father for all purposes, just as if the child had been conceived by sexual intercourse.

3. **Married couple using AID:** Where a *married couple* uses *AID*, some states have statutes dealing specifically with the issue of parentage, and some states do not.

   a. **No statute on point:** Where no statute deals specifically with parentage in the AID situation (and most states still do *not* have such a statute), the courts must decide the issue of parentage by construing a general parenthood statute that was enacted without consideration of the AID problem. Frequently, the general statute does not even give a clue as to how the legislature would have decided the issue of parentage in an AID setting. Most courts have concluded that the strong state policy in favor of supporting families, and the presumption of legitimacy, dictate a conclusion that the woman's *husband* at the time of birth should be *treated as the legal father* for all purposes, and that the child should be deemed *legitimate*.

      i. **Child support by husband:** Thus in the leading case of *People v. Sorensen*, 437 P.2d 495 (Cal. 1968), the court concluded that the husband was the father, and was thus required to pay *child support*.

      ii. **Husband's right to veto adoption of child:** Similarly, a New York lower court has held that the man married to the mother at the time of the birth is the legal father, and that after the two were divorced, that man could veto the child's adoption by the mother's new husband. "New York has a strong policy in favor of legitimacy," which justifies the conclusion that "a child born of consensual AID during a valid marriage is a legitimate child entitled to the rights and privileges of a naturally conceived child of the same marriage. The father of such child is therefore the 'parent'...whose consent is required to the adoption of such child by another." *In re Adoption of Anonymous*, 345 N.Y.S.2d 430 (Surr.Ct. 1973).

      iii. **Consent of husband:** The case for regarding the mother's husband as the legal father is obviously much stronger where the husband *consented* to the AID. Thus both the *Sorenson* and *Anonymous* decisions relied heavily on this fact. There are few if any cases deciding whether an artificial insemination done over the husband's objection, or without his knowledge, should produce a different result. Probably, however, the strong state interest in legitimacy would mean that even in this situation, a man who was married to the woman at the time of the birth would be deemed the legal father where there was no statute on point.

iv. **Equitable adoption:** At least where the husband has consented to the insemination, one legal doctrine that courts can use to justify a finding that the husband is the legal father is the doctrine of *"equitable adoption."* Clark, p. 153. Under this doctrine (discussed *supra*, p. 194), when one raises a child under an express or implied promise to adopt that child, the court will use its equitable powers to treat the adoption as having taken place for at least some purposes (e.g., inheritance). Here, where the husband has consented to the insemination, he could be regarded as having implicitly promised to adopt, justifying the conclusion that he is the legal father even without formal adoption proceedings.

b. **Statute:** About 20 states have statutes specifically dealing with the issue of who is the parent when a married woman gives birth via AID. See Clark, p. 153, n. 141. These statutes all give a procedure by which the woman's *husband*, not the donor, will be deemed the legal father. A few of these statutes provide for the husband to be deemed the legal father regardless of the circumstances behind the insemination. The vast majority of them, however, insist on the first, and sometimes second, of the following two conditions before the husband will be deemed to be the father:

i. **Physician:** That the insemination be performed by or under the direction of a *physician* (see, e.g., §5(a) of the Uniform Parentage Act, in force in six states); and

ii. **Husband's consent:** That the insemination be performed with the *consent* of the husband (sometimes required to be in *writing*). *Id.*

Note 1: Frequently these statutes provide that the *donor* is *not* the legal father. Since a child can only have one legal father, even where the statute is silent on the donor's status, he is obviously not the legal father where the statute provides that the mother's husband *is* the legal father. But these statutes sometimes (e.g., Uniform Parentage Act §5(b)) provide that the donor is not the legal father even when the provisions making the husband the father are not complied with. Thus UPA §5(b) seems to provide that the donor is not the legal father where the insemination is done through a physician, even if the woman's husband does not give the consent required for *him* to be deemed the father. The UPA would therefore lead to a situation where, if the mother's husband did not consent, *neither* the donor nor the husband would be the child's legal father (and the child would in fact have no legal father).

Note 2: Suppose that in a state having a statute like the ones just described, the procedural requirements are not complied with (e.g., the parties dispense with a physician, or the husband either does not consent at all or does not consent in writing.) The statute clearly cannot be relied on to make the husband be the father. It is not clear whether the child should be viewed as having no legal father, or whether the husband can be found to be the legal father under common law rather than statutory principles. Clark, p. 154, advocates the latter solution, which he says has the virtue of achieving the statutes' basic objective. *Id.*

4. **Unmarried woman using AID:** Where the woman is *unmarried* both at the time of insemination and at the time of birth, the only two possibilities are of course that the donor is the legal father or that there is no legal father. Again, some states have statutes on point and others do not.

   a. **No statute on point:** Where there is no statute on point, probably a slight majority of the few cases on point have held that the donor *is* the legal father. At least, this is likely to be a court's conclusion where: (i) the donor is known to the woman; and (ii) no physician intercedes.

      i. **Leading case:** The leading case is *Jhordan C. v. Mary K.*, 224 Cal.Rptr. 530 (Super.Ct.Cal. 1986), in which the court granted the donor's request to be treated as the legal father of the child. California had a statute that provided a mechanism whereby the donor would not be treated as the legal father. However, as is generally the case with such statutes, the statute specifically required that the insemination be done by a licensed physician. Because the parties did not comply, the mother lost the protection of the statute, and the court decided — apparently as a common law matter — that the donor was the legal father. (The court also emphasized that the donor had occasionally participated in the child's life, but it is not clear that this was necessary to the result.)

   b. **Statute on point:** Some of the statutes that make the husband be the natural father when a married woman has AID, further provide that the donor is not the natural father where the insemination is of an unmarried woman. These statute thus protect both the woman and the donor in the typical situation, since each presumably desires that the donor have neither rights nor responsibilities of fatherhood. But observe that such statutes typically set out strict procedural requirements — such as participation of a physician — and that where the requirements are not complied with, the donor may end up being the legal father anyway (as happened in *Jhordan C., supra.*) Additionally, many statutes apply only to married women, leaving the status of a donor to an unmarried woman in limbo.

II. SURROGATE MOTHERHOOD

A. **Conventional surrogacy:** In what might be called "conventional surrogate motherhood," a married couple who cannot have children naturally agree with another woman — the surrogate — to have the surrogate artificially inseminated with the husband's sperm. The parties all understand — and usually attempt to contract — that the surrogate will waive all parental rights to the child. If all goes well, the husband's wife will then immediately adopt the baby. (No action by the husband should be necessary, since by hypothesis he is the natural father.) As with conventional artificial insemination, some states have statutes dealing specifically with conventional surrogacy and some do not.

1. **Where no statute is on point:** Most states do not have a statute dealing with surrogacy. In these states, courts are generally *hostile* to the concept. There are only a few decisions on point, because most surrogacy arrangements go as planned and do not lead to litigation. The leading case on conventional surrogacy, *In re Baby M.* (discussed *infra*, p. 201) held that surrogacy contracts are void as against public policy, leading to the result that the two "genetic" parents were the legal parents.

   Most litigation involving conventional surrogacy arises where the surrogate *changes her mind* either before or shortly after giving birth, and refuses to surrender her parental rights even though she has agreed (usually in writing) to do so. If the court follows the usual judicial approach of invalidating the contract as being against public policy, here are the usual messy results:

   a. **No specific performance:** The court disregards the surrogacy agreement completely. This means, of course, that the court does not grant specific performance of it, and typically resolves the case as if there had been no agreement at all.

   b. **Surrogate is legal mother:** The state may have a statute dealing with artificial insemination. However, that statute, although it probably provides that the sperm donor is not the father (see *supra*, p. 198), certainly will not say that the surrogate is not the legal mother. Consequently, under common-law principles (and probably under the state's general parentage act), *the surrogate is the legal mother.* (Remember, we are talking only about "conventional" surrogacy, in which the surrogate has contributed the egg as well as gestated the baby, not "gestational surrogacy," discussed below, p. 205, in which the surrogate supplies only gestation, not the egg.)

   c. **Adoption:** Since the surrogate is the legal mother, the case then is typically viewed an *adoption* case — the issue is, should the surrogate's parental rights be involuntarily terminated, either on the theory that the surrogate has already consented to adoption and should not be allowed to revoke, or on the theory that the surrogate is an unfit parent? Given that (by hypothesis) the court has already found the surrogacy contract to be against public policy, the court is likely to hold that any consent embodied in it is not valid, and that therefore the surrogate's parental rights should *not* be terminated, and *the adoption should not go forward.* Thus we are left with the situation where the man is the legal father, the surrogate is the legal mother, and the man's wife — even though she was intended originally by all parties to be the mother — *has no parental rights whatsoever.*

   d. Custody: The case then typically turns into a custody battle — should custody be in the man, the surrogate, or shared jointly? The current physical care arrangements for the child are likely to be very important in the determination, so that if the surrogate refuses to ever relinquish the child and is still in physical possession at the time of trial, there is a good chance she will get custody; if the surrogate relinquishes the child (as in the *Baby M.* case, below), there is a good chance that custody will go to the father.

   e. Visitation: The court must then decide whether to give *visitation* rights to the parent who lost the custody battle. At least some of the time (most notably, in the *Baby M.* case, below), the court has granted such visitation rights to the surrogate where the surrogate has lost the custody battle.

2. *Baby M* case: The principal appellate case dealing with conventional surrogacy is ***In re Baby M.***, 537 A.2d 1227 (N.J. 1988), in which the New Jersey Supreme Court: (i) held that surrogacy contracts are invalid as against public policy, (ii) declined to terminate the surrogate's parental rights, (iii) awarded custody to the father, but (iv) granted visitation rights to the surrogate.

   a. Facts: In *Baby M.*, William and Elizabeth Stern, a married couple, were afraid to have children naturally because Mrs. Stern had multiple sclerosis, and there was some medical risk to her from a pregnancy. In an arrangement "brokered" by the Infertility Center of New York, Mr. Stern agreed with Mary Beth Whitehead and her husband that Mrs. Whitehead would be artificially inseminated with Mr. Stern's sperm, that Mrs. Whitehead would carry the baby, deliver it to the Sterns and terminate her own maternal rights in it, and that upon doing so Mrs. Whitehead would receive $10,000 from Mr. Stern. The contract assumed that Mrs. Stern (although she was not a party to it) would adopt the child.

      i. Change of heart: Baby M. was born. At or soon after the child's birth, Mrs. Whitehead realized that she did not want to give her up. She did so, however, three days after birth. The next day, she begged to have the baby back for just one week, after which she would (she promised) return her. The Sterns acquiesced. Mrs. Whitehead did not return the child as promised, so the Sterns started an action to enforce the contract. The Sterns obtained an order that Mrs. Whitehead turn over the child; she fled to Florida with the child, and police in Florida forcibly removed the child and returned her to the Sterns.

   ii. **Trial court decision:** The trial court upheld the surrogacy contract, ordered that Mrs. Whitehead's parental rights be terminated, and allowed the baby to be adopted by Mrs. Stern.

b. **Trial court reversed:** The New Jersey Supreme Court reversed.

   i. **Contract invalid:** First, the court held that the *surrogacy contract* was *invalid*, because it conflicted with both the statutes and public policy of New Jersey. On the statutory side, the agreement violated New Jersey's *"baby selling"* law, which prohibits the payment of money in connection with an adoption placement; since Mrs. Whitehead was to receive $10,000 only if she surrendered her parental rights, the essence of the financial arrangement was payment for adoption, not payment for gestational services. The contract's provisions for terminating Mrs. Whitehead's rights also violated other New Jersey procedural statutes governing the termination of parental rights (e.g., the requirement that the child be surrendered to an approved state or private adoption agency). The contract also violated various public policies of New Jersey: "it guarantees the separation of a child from its mother; it looks to adoption regardless of suitability; it totally ignores the child; it takes the child from the mother regardless of her wishes and her maternal fitness; and it does all of this … through the use of money."

   ii. **Constitutional claims rejected:** The court rejected the Sterns' argument that a refusal to enforce the contract would violate the Sterns' constitutional right of procreation. The court construed this right very narrowly as "simply*(D3the right to have natural children, with or through sexual intercourse or artificial insemination. It is no more than that." Mr. Stern had not been deprived of this right, and the right did not extend, as he claimed, to a right to have custody. The court also rejected Mrs. Stern's claim that it was a violation of her equal protection rights for the state to treat a sperm donor as not being the legal parent but to make the surrogate the legal mother — the court believed that there were large practical differences between sperm donation and surrogacy, justifying the distinction.

c. **Custody:** The court then decided that Mr. Stern, not Mrs. Whitehead, should have *custody* over the baby. The court handled this as a garden-variety custody determination, based upon the child's best interests. Here, the Whiteheads' precarious financial trouble, Mr. Whitehead's alcoholism, Mrs. Whitehead's difficulties in handling her older child, all compared unfavorably with the Sterns' stability and their most recent 1-1/2 year track record of raising the baby.

d Visitation: The court granted *visitation rights* to Mrs. Whitehead (though it left it to the trial court on remand to decide the extent of these rights). (Mrs. Whitehead continues, as of 1992, to have weekend and summer visitation rights with the baby. Areen, p. 1053, n. 1.)

e. No adoption: Observe that one important consequence of the court's refusal to enforce the surrogacy contract is that **Mrs.** Stern did **not** get to **adopt** the baby, and will never get to do so unless Mrs. Whitehead either consents to this, is shown to have abandoned the child, or is found to be unfit to continue as the non-custodial parent.

3. Statutes: Since the *Baby M.* case, at least 11 states have passed **statutes** attempting to deal with conventional surrogacy. None of these statutes makes it easy to arrange and enforce a surrogacy contract, and some make it impossible.

a. Unenforceable: Some states — Arizona, Indiana and North Dakota, for instance — have made **any** sort of surrogacy contract **unenforceable**. Michigan, in fact, has made surrogacy a **crime** (which the others have not). Another group of states has not rendered all surrogacy contracts unenforceable, but has made any contract calling for the payment of any **compensation** to the surrogate unenforceable; since few if any women are willing to engage in the burdens of surrogacy without any form of compensation, this type of "no compensation" statute — enacted in Kentucky, Louisiana, Nebraska, Utah and Washington — makes surrogacy arrangements de facto but not de jure unenforceable. See generally 68 Ind.L.J. 205, 217 (1992).

i. Consequences of non-enforcement: Where the statute does not criminalize surrogacy, but renders the contract unenforceable, probably the court will decide any dispute based on common-law principles, as the court did in *Baby M.*, *supra*. If so, the husband and the surrogate would be the two legal parents, and custody and visitation issues would be resolved as they would be in a divorce between those two individuals.

b. Regulation: As of 1993, only two states — Virginia and New Hampshire — purported to *regulate* surrogacy contracts. Only one of these, Virginia, has created a scheme under which a surrogacy contract might be enforced against the will of the surrogate.

i. **Virginia approach:** Under the Virginia approach, if the contract is *pre-authorized* by a *judge* before insemination, and all parties jump through various other procedural hoops (e.g., all parties receive counselling; the intended mother is either infertile or unable to bear children without risk; the surrogate is married and has had at least one successful pregnancy; etc.), the surrogate may terminate the contract until she is starting her seventh month of pregnancy, but then *loses this right to terminate*. So in the case of a properly pre-authorized contract, a surrogate in Virginia would not have the right to change her mind late in the pregnancy or after the child's birth, and the contract would be enforced to the extent of making the "intended" husband and wife be the legal parents, with no visitation or other parental rights in the surrogate. Even in Virginia, the contract in order to be valid may not allow compensation except for any expenses associated with the pregnancy, again making the proposition relatively unattractive to the surrogate. See generally Va. Code §20-160(a) et seq.

ii. **Uniform Act:** The Uniform Status of Children of Assisted Conception Act (1988) makes surrogacy more palatable and enforceable than any state has so far. Under Alternative A to this Act, judicially pre-authorized surrogacy contracts are enforced, so that the intended parents become the legal parents, and the surrogate has no parental rights. As with the Virginia statute discussed above (which in fact is to some extent based on Alternative A of the Uniform Act), the surrogate may unilaterally terminate the contract until the end of her sixth month of pregnancy. A key feature, §9(a), allows for the payment of consideration, without limiting it to direct expenses of pregnancy. So in a state enacting Alternative A of the Uniform Act, surrogacy would be a practical and enforceable method. However, as of 1993 only Virginia has enacted anything resembling Alternative A, and it has — by limiting payment to direct pregnancy-related expenses — made it unattractive.

c. **Advice:** Most surrogacy arrangements — even though they are legally unenforceable — nonetheless work out as all parties expect. It is only in the relatively rare case where the surrogate changes her mind that there are major legal difficulties. Therefore, it may be rational for the intended parents to enter into an agreement even though they know is unenforceable. They should probably hold some of the payment in escrow pending delivery of the baby and termination of the surrogate's maternal rights. However, observe that if the surrogate changes her mind, things could easily work out far worse for the intended parents than they did in the *Baby M.* case — in the worst of all worlds (from the intended parents' viewpoint), the father/sperm donor could be found to be the legal father, be denied custody and even visitation rights (perhaps on the grounds of willful violation of the public policy of not enforcing surrogacy contracts), and yet be required to pay *child support* for a child he may never get to see.

B. Gestational surrogacy: The second type of surrogacy is usually called "gestational surrogacy." Gestational surrogacy is made possible by the development of *in vitro fertilization*, i.e., conception in a "test tube."

1. **How it works:** Gestational surrogacy is typically used where a married couple wishes to have children, and the wife is capable of supplying eggs but not capable of carrying a child through gestation (e.g., because she has had a partial hysterectomy). An egg is removed from the woman in a surgical procedure, then fertilized with the man's sperm in a laboratory petri dish. The resulting zygote or embryo is then implanted into the gestational surrogate, who carries it to term and gives birth to it. Obviously this arrangement has the peculiarity that the woman who gives birth to the child *is not its genetic mother*.

2. **Conflict between two types of "mother":** If the gestational surrogate refuses to give up the child, we now have a conflict between the "genetic" mother and the "birth" mother. Thus whereas in the conventional surrogacy case, the surrogate would probably be automatically found to be the legal mother if the surrogacy contract is not enforced, in the gestational case, it is not at all clear who the legal mother should be deemed to be if the contract is disregarded.

3. **Few statutes on point:** Because gestational surrogacy is both rare and new, few states have statutes on point.

    a. **Uniform Act:** However, the Uniform Status of Children of Assisted Conception Act, drafted in 1988, does purport to deal with gestational surrogacy. It basically treats gestational surrogacy like conventional surrogacy. Thus if the surrogacy contract is not judicially pre-authorized, then the woman who gives birth to the child becomes the legal mother (even though she is not genetically related to the child). If the contract is judicially pre-authorized, then the surrogate may *not* terminate the contract once she becomes pregnant. Section 7 of the Act. This is in striking contrast to the Act's treatment of conventional surrogacy, which allows the conventional surrogate, because she has supplied the egg, to recant up until the start of her seventh month of pregnancy.

    b. **Virginia:** So far, Virginia is the only state to adopt, even in part, the Uniform Act's treatment of gestational surrogacy. Virginia basically follows the Act's approach, so that a judicially pre-authorized surrogacy contract in Virginia is enforceable, and the surrogate may not terminate when she becomes pregnant. Va. Code §20-161(B).

4. **No statute on point:** In the vast majority of states having no statute dealing with gestational surrogacy, how should the court decide a conflict between the woman who donates the egg and the woman who gives birth to the child? So far, only one highest state court, that of California, has addressed this issue; California held that the parties' *intentions* (as manifested by the surrogacy agreement) should govern in this situation, and therefore found in favor of the ***mother who supplied the egg***, not the birth mother. *Johnson v. Calvert*, 851 P.2d 776 (Cal. 1993).

   a. **Facts:** In *Johnson*, a married couple, Mark and Crispina, wished to have a child. Crispina could not have children naturally because she had had a hysterectomy; however, she could produce eggs. Anna signed a contract with Mark and Crispina whereby an embryo created from the sperm of Mark and the egg of Crispina would be implanted in Anna, and Anna would after giving birth relinquish all parental rights to the child in favor of Mark and Crispina. Mark and Crispina agreed to pay Anna $10,000 in a series of installments. All went according to plan medically, but due to an escalating series of disagreements, Anna refused to turn over the child.

   b. **Statute unclear:** The decision in *Johnson* stemmed from the particular provisions of California statutes, so it may not have too much value for other jurisdictions. Under one California provision, the woman who gives birth to a child is deemed to be the mother. Under another provision, a person can be eliminated as a possible *father* on the basis of blood tests, and still another provision makes the rules for determining fatherhood applicable to motherhood as well. Therefore, one statutory provision made Crispina, the intended mother/egg donor, the legal mother, and another provision made Anna, the gestational surrogate/birth mother, the legal mother.

   c. **Intent as the tie-breaker:** Since the relevant statutory provisions conflicted with each other, the court decided to look to the ***intent*** of the parties as in effect the tie-breaker. The court reasoned that "Anna would not have been given the opportunity to gestate or deliver the child had she, prior to implantation of the zygote, manifested her own intent to be the child's mother. No reason appears why Anna's later change of heart should vitiate the determination that Crispina is the child's natural mother. ... [A]lthough the Act recognizes both genetic consanguinity and giving birth as means of establishing a mother and child relationship, when the two means do not coincide in one woman, she who ***intended to procreate*** the child — that is, she who intended to *bring about the birth* of the child that she intended to raise as her own — is the natural mother under California law."

    d. Dissent: A dissent in *Johnson* argued that since the statutory provisions were in conflict, the issue of motherhood should be decided by reference to the *best interests of the child*, on a case-by-case basis.

    e. Compare with *Baby M. case:* Observe that in contrast to the *Baby M.* case (*supra*, p. 201), here, the surrogacy contract was in effect enforced. Thus the result in both cases can be summarized by saying that *genetics* was the predominant factor — the court enforced the parties' intent in only one of the two cases, and the court gave victory to the birth mother in only one of the two cases, but *the genetic mother won each time*.

III. OTHER ISSUES

A. Egg donation: Now, consider the situation in which a woman *donates her eggs* to be implanted in the womb of another woman (whom we'll refer to as the "intended mother"). This donated egg might be fertilized in a test tube with the sperm of the intended father, or it might be implanted before fertilization, to be fertilized by the intended father's sperm by ordinary sexual reproduction. In either event, the egg donor is in a position analogous to a sperm donor — her only contribution has been to supply genetic material, not to give birth.

    1. Result: In this situation, it seems clear that courts should apply the rules governing artificial insemination. This would mean that *the egg donor is never the mother*, and has *no rights* to the resulting child. This is the result explicitly reached by the Uniform Status of Children of Assisted Conception Act, §1(2) and §4(a).

B. "Ownership" of embryo: When in vitro fertilization is used to create a "test tube" embryo, which parent, if either, "owns" the embryo? More particularly, can the woman have it implanted in herself over the man's objection? If the woman does not want to have it implanted in herself, may either party, over the other's objection, donate the embryo to a third party for gestational surrogacy? The one case to have considered the issue so far has concluded that both parents should *share control* over the embryo, with each having a *veto power* over the other's disposition of it. *Davis v. Davis*, 59 U.S.L.W. 2205 (Tenn.Ct.App. 1990).

    1. Facts and holding: In *Davis*, while Mary Sue and Junior were married, they used in vitro fertilization to produce seven embryos. The parties divorced and each remarried, while the embryos remained frozen. Mary Sue sought "custody" over the embryos, so that she could donate them for the use of childless couples. Junior objected to this, arguing that he did not want to become a "father" under these circumstances. The court held in favor of Junior, concluding that granting Mary Sue control over the embryos would constitute "impermissible state action in violation of Junior's constitutionally protected right ***not to beget a child*** where no pregnancy has taken place."

LEGITIMACY AND ILLEGITIMACY

I. INTRODUCTION

A. Generally: A child is said to be "illegitimate" if he or she was born *out of wedlock* or unlawfully begotten.

> **Note on terms:** The term "illegitimate" is gradually falling out of favor as being unfairly judgmental, and "out of wedlock" is coming to be used in its stead. However, since the relevant Supreme Court cases continue to use "illegitimate," we use that term here.

1. Traditional view: Historically, the law governing illegitimate children was based on the premise that their father was irresponsible and unconcerned about the welfare of his children. Laws enacted on that premise gave unwed fathers no rights with respect to their children in the areas of custody, adoption, or visitation.

2. Modern view: With the discernible shift in attitudes towards marriage among some groups, and the conscious decision of some couples to live together outside the marriage relationship, the traditional view is no longer valid. Courts now uphold the rights of the concerned, unwed father with respect to his children.

B. Constitutional analysis: The classification of individuals according to whether or not they are legitimate is *not* a *suspect classification* subjecting it to *strict scrutiny* by a court. But in determining whether the statutory classification is valid, the Court generally applies a level of *heightened scrutiny* to discrimination against illegitimate persons. This requires the state to show that the law is *substantially related* to a legitimate state interest. *Clark v. Jeter, infra,* p. 214

1. Case law is confused: In a series of cases the Supreme Court has found that various statutes which discriminate against illegitimate children violate the Equal Protection Clause of the Fourteenth Amendment. Notwithstanding those decisions, the Court has upheld some statutes which impose some disability on illegitimate persons. It is difficult, if not impossible, to reconcile all of those decisions.

a. Workers' compensation: A state may *not* exclude illegitimate children from sharing equally with other children in the recovery of *workers compensation* benefits. *Webber v. Aetna Casualty and Surety Co.,* 406 U.S. 164 (1972).

b. Wrongful death: A state may *not* create a right of action in favor of children for the *wrongful death* of a parent and exclude illegitimate children from the benefits of that right. *Levy v. Louisiana,* 391 U.S. 68 (1968).

c. **Public assistance:** State welfare legislation *may* discriminate against illegitimate children by limiting benefits to households of married adults and their children. *New Jersey Welfare Rights Organization v. Cahill,* 411 U.S. 619 (1974).

d. **Inheritance:** State intestate *inheritance* schemes which deprive *acknowledged* illegitimate children of inheritance rights granted to legitimate heirs are likely to constitute unconstitutional discrimination against them. *Trimble v. Gordon, infra,* p. 216.

e. **Other rights:** Once a state grants a judicially enforceable right to children who need *support* from their natural father, there is no constitutionally sufficient reason to deny that right to acknowledged illegitimate children. *Gomez v. Perez, infra* p. 212.

II. COMMON LAW BACKGROUND

A. **Generally:** At common law a child was considered illegitimate if his parents *never married,* or his parents married *after* his birth.

> **Note:** A child was considered legitimate, even if conception took place before the marriage, so long as the marriage took place *before* his birth. Clark, p. 151.

1. **Presumption of legitimacy:** At common law a child of a married woman was *presumed* to be *legitimate*. However, this presumption could be rebutted if it was proved that the husband was impotent or "beyond the four seas" (out of the country).

a. **Modern status:** The presumption of legitimacy of children born to a married couple continues to be applied today. In fact, the presumption, and the policy behind it, are so strong that the relation between a *natural* father and his child born during the mother's marriage to another man will apparently receive *no constitutional protection*.

> **Example:** At a time when H and W are married and living together, W has an adulterous affair with a neighbor, P. W conceives and gives birth to a child, Victoria. The birth certificate lists H as Victoria's father, and he always holds her out to the world as his daughter. Genetic tests, however, show a 98% probability that Victoria's father is P, not H. For various brief periods, W and Victoria reside with P, and P holds Victoria out as his daughter. H and W eventually reconcile, and oppose P's efforts to obtain visitation rights. A state statute provides that "the issue of a wife cohabiting with her husband, who is not impotent or sterile, is *conclusively*

presumed to be a child of the marriage." P asserts that he has a constitutionally protected liberty interest in being allowed to visit Victoria. H and W argue that protection of the marital unit which they form with Victoria outweighs any liberty interest that P might have in visitation.

Held (in a case with no majority opinion), for H and W. According to the plurality, P can have a liberty interest in his relationship with Victoria only if that relationship is one which has been historically protected by our society. The relation between a natural father and his child born during the mother's marriage to another man has never been specially protected or recognized by our society. The fact that many states may permit one in P's position to prove paternity is irrelevant, because the test is whether states give parental *prerogatives* to one in P's position, and the answer is that they do not. Similarly, any liberty interest that Victoria may have in being permitted to maintain her relationship with P is a weak one that is outweighed by the need to protect the family unit formed within the confines of a marriage. (Four dissenters contend that P should be found to have a liberty interest strong enough to entitle him to continue his relationship with Victoria.) *Michael H. v. Gerald D.*, 491 U.S. 110 (1989).

2. **Effect of annulment:** At common law a child of an *annulled* marriage, whether void or voidable, was considered illegitimate since the annulment decree was retroactive to the date of the marriage. This rule is generally not followed today.

B. **Rights of illegitimate child:** At early common law an illegitimate child was considered a child of no one, and he had no right to inherit from or through his parents. In addition, the parents had no duty to support him.

1. **Elizabethan Law:** In 1576, the Elizabethan Poor Law provided for a quasi-criminal procedure against the natural father of an illegitimate child for the support of his child.

2. **Reason for change:** The Poor Law was designed to relieve the general public of the burden of supporting illegitimate children. It was quasi-criminal in nature because the failure to provide support was an offense against society as well as a wrong to the child.

   Note: The quasi-criminal aspect of the procedure under the English Poor Law can be found in some jurisdictions of the United States even at the present time.

III. MODERN APPROACH TO ILLEGITIMACY

A. **Common law changed:** Most of the harsher aspects of the common law treatment of illegitimate children, such as limitations on rights to support and to inherit, have been changed. The Equal Protection Clause of the Fourteenth Amendment has been the vehicle utilized in most of the decisions.

> **Example:** The law in State A provides for a judicially enforceable right of support for a legitimate child from a natural father. No such right is afforded to an illegitimate child. C, an illegitimate child, brings suit against her natural father for support.
>
> *Held*, C is entitled to support. Once a state recognizes a judicially enforceable right of children to support from their natural fathers, there is no constitutionally sufficient justification for denying that right to a child merely because her natural father has not married her mother. For a state to do so is invidious discrimination, violative of the Equal Protection Clause. *Gomez v. Perez,* 409 U.S. 535 (1973).

1. **Establishing paternity:** In a suit to establish paternity, the standard of proof of a *preponderance of the evidence* is sufficient to comply with the Due Process Clause of the Fourteenth Amendment.

> **Example:** P, an unmarried woman, gives birth to a child. P sues D for child support alleging that D is the child's father. The jury is instructed that P must prove her case by a preponderance of the evidence, and D is found to be the father. D moves for a new trial contending that the standard of proof should be clear and convincing evidence.
>
> *Held*, in paternity cases the proper standard is preponderance of the evidence. Most states use that standard to determine paternity in a civil action for support. There is no constitutional requirement for a higher standard of proof because the decision "will not trammel any pre-existing rights." D's only interest is to avoid a financial obligation. *Rivera v. Minnich,* 483 U.S. 574 (1987).

> **Note:** The Court distinguished *Santosky v. Kramer, supra,* p. 186, which held that clear and convincing evidence was required to terminate a parent child relationship. In *Santosky* the state sought to destroy all legal recognition of the parental relationship and deprive the parents of the companionship, care and custody of their child. In that situation it is appropriate that the state have a greater burden of proof. By contrast, in paternity cases the father's only interest is avoiding financial obligations. The parties are relatively equal and each should share the roughly equal risk at trial where a final judgment will be entered.

2. **No tort action:** Courts have generally *not* allowed an illegitimate child to maintain an action against his *parents* for *damages* for being born illegitimate.

Example: P, who is illegitimate, brings suit against D, his father. P alleges that D seduced P's mother by promising to marry her, but that D could not keep his promise because he was already married. P seeks damages for deprivation of the right to be born legitimate, to have a legal father, to inherit from P's paternal ancestors, and for being stigmatized as a bastard.

Held, P's suit is dismissed. Although D committed a willful tort and P suffered an injury, to recognize P's claim would create a new tort: a cause of action for wrongful life. The legal and social implications of such a tort would be enormous. It is more appropriate for the legislature to study and declare its policy on such suits than for courts to do so. *Zepeda v. Zepeda,* 190 N.E.2d 849 (Ill. 1963).

B. **Legitimation statutes:** Children born out of wedlock may be *legitimized*. Legitimization is the legal procedure set by statutes under which illegitimate persons may be declared to be legitimate in certain situations.

   1. **Types of statutes:** All fifty states have passed some type of statute providing for the legitimization of children born out of wedlock. These statutes are quite divergent and can be classified roughly as follows:

      a. **All legitimate:** Statutes recognizing *all* children as the legitimate children of their natural parents.

      b. **Subsequent marriage:** Statutes recognizing the *subsequent marriage* of an illegitimate child's natural parents as a method of legitimization.

      c. **Subsequent marriage and acknowledgment:** Statutes recognizing the *subsequent marriage* of an illegitimate child's natural parents along with some form of *acknowledgment of paternity* by the natural father as a method of legitimization.

      d. **Acknowledgment:** Statutes recognizing a child born out of wedlock as being legitimate if the child is *acknowledged* by his natural father. (Some statutes add the requirement that the child be taken into the father's family.)

      e. **Court procedure:** Statutes recognizing a child born out of wedlock as being legitimate if the child is *declared legitimate* in a prescribed *court proceeding*.

      Note: A state might have more than one of the above statutory provisions dealing with legitimation. For instance, a state might allow both subsequent marriage of the natural parents and court paternity proceedings, as methods of legitimation.

   2. **Acknowledgment:** *"Acknowledgment"* is the *admission* by a natural father that an illegitimate child is his child. Acknowledgment can take many forms, and its validity depends on statutory requirements.

Example: Where an acknowledgment must be in writing, any written document containing an admission of paternity will generally suffice. It is not necessary that the document be written for the purpose of providing acknowledgment of the child involved. Where acknowledgment is not required to be written, an oral admission of paternity is sufficient.

3. **Applicable law:** The law of the ***domicile of the parent*** of an illegitimate child normally determines whether or not an act of the parent has legitimized the child. The law of the child's domicile does not govern.

C. **Child support:** The obligation of child support extends to illegitimate children. Where the child is illegitimate, the court must determine paternity. This is usually through a civil suit by the mother or, where public assistance is involved, by a state agency.

1. **Cost of blood tests:** If the defendant in a paternity action lacks financial resources to pay for blood tests, failure of the state to pay for such tests may, in some instances, deny the defendant due process.

    Example: The defendant in *Little v. Streater,* 452 U.S. 1 (1981), was an indigent against whom a ***paternity action*** had been brought. The Court held D had a due process right to ***state-subsidized blood grouping tests*** to determine whether he could have been the child's father.

2. **Child's right to support:** An illegitimate child has an ***equal protection*** right not to be denied ***child support*** from his natural father based on arbitrary state rules. The Supreme Court now applies mid-intermediate-level scrutiny to classifications based on legitimacy; one important consequence is that the state may not place an unduly brief ***time limit*** on the bringing of a paternity/child-support claim. While we do not know what the shortest time limit would be that would not be unconstitutional, we know that a cut-off when the child is ***six years old*** is ***too brief***. *Clark v. Jeter*, set forth in the following example.

    Example: Tiffany is born out of wedlock to Cherlyn and Gene. (Blood tests show a 99% probability that Gene is Tiffany's father.) When Tiffany is 10, Cherlyn brings a suit on her behalf seeking a determination that Gene is Tiffany's father, and seeking child support. A Pennsylvania statute says that any paternity action must be brought within six years of the child's birth. Cherlyn asserts that this short cut-off for paternity actions violates Tiffany's equal protection rights.

    Held, the statute violates Tiffany's equal protection rights. The court will apply intermediate scrutiny to classifications based on legitimacy; under this standard, the classification must be "substantially related to an important governmental objective." The state may have a substantial governmental interest in avoiding the litigation of stale or fraudulent claims, but a statute of limitations as brief as six years is not needed to carry out this objective (especially since newer genetically based testing techniques are reliable long past this age). *Clark v. Jeter*, 486 U.S. 456 (1988).

   a. Federal statute: Any state that does not wish to lose federal Aid to Families with Dependent Children funds must allow paternity suits to be brought until the child is *18 years old*. See the federal Child Support Enforcement Act Amendments of 1984, 42 U.S.C. §666(a)(5). Because of the great importance of these funds to the states, it is likely that all states will keep an 18-year limit on their books.

IV. INHERITANCE RIGHTS OF ILLEGITIMATES

A. Background: The recognition of rights of illegitimate persons to inherit by intestate succession developed slowly.

   1. Common law: An illegitimate child was deemed a child of no one, and had no right to inherit. No one other than his or her own issue could inherit from an illegitimate person.

   2. United States: An illegitimate child was the child of the mother and could inherit from her and her relatives, and they from him. Under the old view, an illegitimate child was *not* treated as a child of the father unless legitimated or acknowledged by the father.

   3. Modern view: The rights of illegitimate children to inherit from their natural fathers have been greatly expanded. Present law on the inheritance rights of illegitimate children is discussed immediately below.

B. Constitutional issues: Just as the Supreme Court has found that constitutional provisions, especially the Equal Protection Clause, limit certain types of government discrimination against illegitimates (see *supra*, p. 209), so the Court has held that the Constitution limits the ways in which a state may restrict the *inheritance* rights of illegitimates. The respects in which the states may treat out-of-wedlock children less favorably than in-wedlock ones for inheritance remain unclear. However, it is now clear that any such discrimination will be subjected to *intermediate-level* scrutiny, and will thus be sustained only if the classification scheme is shown to be *substantially related* to an *important* governmental objective. Many of the old-fashioned statutes (such as those completely cutting off the inheritance rights of illegitimate children) are clearly invalid under this test.

   1. Can't totally foreclose: It is clear that the state may *not totally foreclose* all illegitimates from taking under the state intestacy statute. In particular, the state may not impose a blanket rule that even *acknowledged* children cannot inherit from their father. *Trimble v. Gordon*, 430 U.S. 762 (1977). (Although *Trimble* is no longer recent law, its core holding — that the state must provide at least *some* method by which out-of-wedlock children can be acknowledged and thus permitted to inherit — is almost certainly still good law.)

2. **State can foreclose unacknowledged children:** Conversely, the state probably *may* prevent inheritance by an out-of-wedlock child who remains *unacknowledged* at the time of his parents' death. In *Lalli v. Lalli*, 439 U.S. 259 (1978), the Court upheld a New York Statute which prevented illegitimate children from inheriting by intestate succession from their fathers, unless a court made a *finding of paternity* during the father's *lifetime*. Thus whereas *Trimble* seems to show that the state may not completely foreclose all out-of-wedlock children from inheriting, *Lalli* seems to mean that the states may insist on a judicial finding of paternity, made while the parent is still alive, as a condition to inheritance for out-of-wedlock children.

3. **No early cut-off:** Finally, if the state wants to insist on a judicial finding of paternity as a condition of the right to inherit (as the state did in *Lalli, supra*), the state may not impose too early a *cut-off* of that right. For instance, the state may not say that no paternity action may be brought after the child turns seven; see *Clark v. Jeter, supra*, p. 215. As a practical matter, in light of federal legislation, if the state wants to foreclose a child's inheritance rights due to lack of a judicial finding of paternity, the state must give the child until the age of 18 to bring the suit. (If the child is under 18 when the father dies, and no paternity suit has yet been started, it is not clear whether the state may deny the child the right to inherit. *Lalli, supra*, suggests that the state may treat the parent's death as cutting off the chance to bring a paternity suit in this situation, no matter how young the child is, but this is not at all certain.)

ESSAY EXAM
QUESTIONS AND ANSWERS

Here are some suggestions about how to answer an essay exam question:

1. Remember that you are taking an essay examination. The complete essay examination answer must contain not only the "answer" to the question, but of greater importance, must also contain your **analysis,** the applicable **black letter law,** and an **explanation** of how you have applied the black letter law to the facts and reasoned to the "answer."

2. Begin by **reading the question** thoroughly.

3. Next, **reread the question;** read it as it is written, not as you think it is written.

4. As you read, spot **key concepts, ideas, issues** and applicable **legal terms,** principles and concepts.

5. **Organize your thoughts** into an orderly, logical sequence.

6. **Analyze** the fact pattern and the key issues, terms, principles and concepts which you have spotted.

7. **Work out a game plan** for your answer, including the sequence of those things which you are going to write about, the priority for writing, the space to be allocated to each and an allocation of your time for writing.

8. Make a brief **word-phrase outline** of your proposed answer.

9. Use at least 25% of the time allotted for answering the question to do all of the things outlined above **before you begin to write** the answer. An organized answer can be written quickly. If you are not organized when you begin your answer, time will be wasted adding issues, crossing out part of your answer which is not relevant, and writing too much about minor issues.

10. Begin writing with a short, clear, **decisive answer** to the question precisely as it is asked. For example, if the question reads: "Rule on plaintiff's motion," your answer should begin: "Motion granted," or "Motion overruled." The balance of your answer explains how you reasoned to that conclusion.

11. Write your answer in **clear, professional, lawyer-like English prose** using full and complete **legal terminology.** Remember: This is an essay examination in the English language, at the graduate level, in a learned profession.

12. Be certain to include **full sentences of black letter law** on each of the key issues. Failure to do this is the most frequent mistake made by students.

13. **Do not merely rehash the facts.** A complete answer requires analysis, black letter law and application of that black letter law to the facts.

Rehashing of the facts is not enough.

14. **Use short, complete, simple sentences.** Avoid long, wandering, convoluted sentences which deal with several issues and subjects.

15. **Reason to a lawyer-like conclusion.** If you have time and space, add a wrap-up concluding sentence to your answer.

16. **Reread your answer** to make certain that you have made no unintended errors or omissions, and to ensure clarity and completeness of your answer.

17. **Use the full time allotted** for the question—no more and no less.

> **Note:** The following questions have been selected from various examinations of Professor Paul McLane Conway of Georgetown Law Center, Washington, D.C., and are reprinted here with his permission. Their inclusion is designed to acquaint the student with the kinds of questions which may be found on law school examinations. A sample answer, which has been prepared by the author, follows each question.

QUESTIONS

QUESTION 1: Tarzan and Jane have been dating for many years. When Jane becomes pregnant, she suggests they marry. Tarzan resists the idea of marriage, fearful that settling down with one woman would tarnish his image as a "swinger." Jane becomes furious with Tarzan's irresponsibility and issues an ultimatum: Either Tarzan settles down or she takes off. "But dear," protests Tarzan, "marriage is such a hassle. And you know how messy it can get if the marriage goes sour — the resentment, the pain, the endless litigation.... And the husband always gets shafted in the end!" Jane, a determined woman, comes up with a solution to calm Tarzan's fears. She suggests they sign a contract limiting the amount to which she would be entitled should their marriage falter. Jane hastens to assure Tarzan that she has no thoughts of ever leaving him, and that the separation agreement is merely a device "to take those silly worries out of your head." Tarzan is impressed by Jane's quick thinking and agrees to marry her.

The two marry and subsequently sign an agreement providing for a lump-sum of $20,000 payable to Jane, along with a weekly payment of $100 for the support of their daughter, Girl, "in the improbable event that we, the undersigned, decide to split." The years pass. By chance Tarzan is spotted by a visiting Mutual of Omaha film crew and receives a lucrative screen contract. His income quadruples and he, Jane and Girl live a life of unaccustomed luxury. The pressures of stardom take their toll on the family. Tarzan is away from home much of the time. To fill up her lonely hours Jane acquires a job as a tour guide in a local escort service. One night Tarzan returns home unexpectedly to find Jane giving a "tour" of the bedroom to Marlin Perkins, Jr., alias Buster Crabbe. "I'll teach you to 'cheeta' on me," grunts Tarzan. He promptly sues Jane for divorce on the ground of adultery.

(a) In the divorce proceeding Tarzan argues that the separation agreement governs his obligations to Jane. Respond.

(b) Assume that the separation agreement is approved by the court and merged in the divorce decree:

If Tarzan fails to make the lump-sum and child support payments, may he be held in contempt? Would your answer be different if the agreement had been incorporated by reference, but not merged, in the divorce decree?

(c) For fifteen years Tarzan faithfully makes the child support payments. At the end of that period he petitions the court to reduce the amount he must pay for child support, claiming that he quit his acting job and can no longer afford to pay $100 per week. What result?

QUESTION 2: Husband seeks an injunction restraining his wife from interfering with the attendance of their seven year old child in a private school. The wife wishes to have the child attend a public school. This is part of a family dispute. There is no question concerning the custody of the child since the parents and child are living together as a family group. In the absence of a statute does a court of equity have "inherent jurisdiction" to resolve the dispute as to which school the child should attend?

QUESTION 3: June Green and Mulhamid Mulhamid met in Cairo, Egypt where June was on vacation. She is an American. He is a citizen of Egypt and wished to emigrate to the U.S. but was unable to obtain a visa. He offered to pay her $20,000 if she would marry him for the purpose of getting him into the U.S. on a permanent basis. The immigration laws permit the entry of spouses of American citizens outside the usual quotas. June agreed on the condition that they would never live together as husband and wife. Mulhamid paid her the money, the marriage was performed and they both came to the United States. Upon their arrival in New York they part. Two years later June hears that Mulhamid has become a very successful oriental rug dealer and is earning large sums of money. As a result she brings an action for maintenance and support. What result?

QUESTION 4: Discuss briefly the key elements of proof in an action for adultery based on circumstantial evidence.

QUESTION 5: Would the following events entitle either spouse to a modification of alimony?

(a) The wife married a second husband, who was much less wealthy than her first. Her first husband moved to terminate alimony payments, arguing that this should follow automatically from his wife's remarriage.

(b) The wife met and fell in love with another man, but her attorney advised her that if she married him, she would risk losing her alimony, so she and her new boyfriend moved into an apartment together without bothering to marry, although they represented themselves as being married. The husband moved to terminate alimony.

(c) At the time of the divorce the husband's income was $18,000 per year, and the court awarded alimony in the amount of $500 per month. Two years later the husband invented a valuable electronic device and his income from patent royalties, together with his salary, became $60,000 per year. The wife moved for an increase in alimony, giving evidence also that inflation had produced an increase in her living expenses.

(d) The alimony order read that the wife was to receive $500 per month "until further order of this court." The husband died some years later leaving a substantial estate. His executor refused to make any further payments of alimony. Six months after the husband died, the executor moved to terminate the alimony. Does the divorce court have the authority to order periodic alimony which is to continue beyond the husband's death, particularly since, if they had remained married, the wife would have had no right to be supported beyond his death?

(e) The alimony order gave the wife $500 per month. Two years later the parties made an agreement by which she agreed to accept $300 per month in full satisfaction of her claims for the future. The husband then moved for a modification of the original award to $300 per month. Must the court grant his motion? Alternatively, assume that the husband made no such motion, but thenceforth paid at the rate of $300 per month. Three years later the wife brings a proceeding for enforcement of the original order of $500 per month. Can she prevail in this proceeding?

QUESTION 6: On what basis may a court distribute property following an annulment?

QUESTION 7:

(a) In a Reciprocal Enforcement of Support action the initiating court must find two things. Name them.

(b) In Reciprocal Support actions what role does the Full Faith and Credit Clause of the U.S. Constitution play?

QUESTION 8: Having opened your office in the general practice of law and in particular specializing in family law or domestic relations, you are consulted by Mrs. D, who says that she has information to the effect that Mr. D is about to flee the marital abode and the jurisdiction. What action would you consider on her behalf to prevent Mr. D's fleeing?

QUESTION 9: Briefly define the following terms:

(a) divorce *a mensa et thoro*

(b) affinity

Please answer Questions 10-13 true or false, and give a short statement defending your position:

QUESTION 10: Jack and Jill agree to an amicable divorce. The decree does not mention alimony which Jill neither needs nor wants. Eight months later Jill becomes seriously ill and she petitions to revise and modify the decree to provide for alimony. Jill invokes the continuing jurisdiction of the court and states that unless she is granted relief she will become a public charge. Jack will prevail.

QUESTION 11: H & W lived together as a married couple in State X, which has a no-fault divorce law and in which adultery is not a ground for divorce. Because of H's adultery W leaves and moves to State Y where adultery is a ground for divorce. W sues for divorce in Y on the ground of adultery and H defends. H will prevail because X was the center of gravity, because he had done no act or omission within State Y and because H & W were residents of State X during the time of the alleged breach of the marital duty.

QUESTION 12: An unconsummated ceremonial marriage is no more than an engagement to marry.

QUESTION 13: "Clear and convincing" proof of cohabitation and reputation will sustain a common law marriage.

SAMPLE ANSWERS

SAMPLE ANSWER 1:

(a) The settlement agreement does not govern Tarzan's obligations, because of the present inadequacy of the amount.

The agreement was signed when the parties were living together and not preparing to separate. Under older decisions the agreement would not be enforceable on that ground alone. Modern statutes and court decisions would not follow that old rule, reasoning that it does not encourage divorce, and the parties should be allowed to settle their own affairs.

It should be noted that a separation agreement is a contract and it must be supported by consideration. If Tarzan and Jane made mutual promises of some kind in the agreement, that requirement would be satisfied. For example, Jane might have promised to care for Girl which would be sufficient consideration for Tarzan's promise to pay.

Strictly speaking, the agreement cannot be considered a separation agreement because the parties were not separated, nor about to separate, when it was signed. However, a court may treat it like a prenuptial agreement because it was agreed to orally before the marriage. The Statute of Frauds requires a prenuptial agreement to be in writing. But an oral prenuptial contract is enforceable where a writing is signed after the marriage (Clark, p.2). This rule applies in the example given because the parties agreed to sign it before the marriage.

The modern rule requires that a prenuptial agreement make adequate provision for the spouses considering the circumstances at the date of execution *and* the date of enforcement. This is considered the better view (Clark, p. 9), but it has not been adopted by all courts. In the present case, Tarzan's income increased substantially since the agreement was made; a modern court should consider that fact and reject the agreement as inadequate.

(b) Tarzan may be held in contempt.

Where the separation agreement has been merged into the divorce decree, alimony and support are enforceable by contempt. In some states property settlement orders such as a lump-sum payment are not enforceable by contempt because they regard it as imprisonment for a debt which is prohibited by the Constitution. However, probably most courts would also enforce the lump sum payment by contempt. Frequently there is a practical difficulty in distinguishing between alimony and property divisions.

An effect of the merger of the settlement agreement in the divorce decree is to extinguish the private contract rights of the agreement which become part of the court order (judgment). The duty of Tarzan to make support payments may be enforced by contempt proceedings because they violate a court judgment. Courts regard alimony and child support payments as a statement of the husband's obligation to support his family and not as the payment of a debt. Thus, the constitutional prohibition against imprisonment for a debt does not apply to alimony and child support. Tarzan may be held in contempt for failure to make the $100 per week child support payments.

Yes, the answer would be different if the agreement had been incorporated by reference but not merged into the decree. For the remedy of contempt to be available the agreement must be merged into the divorce decree. If the agreement is not merged, then ordinary contract remedies must be used.

(c) The court will deny Tarzan's petition.

Tarzan may not evade his child support obligations by voluntarily quitting his job and refusing to find employment elsewhere. It would deny Tarzan's petition, and he could be held in contempt if payments were not made. If the loss of income is only temporary, lasting until Tarzan finds other employment, the court would still deny Tarzan's petition. A temporary loss of income is not a valid basis upon which to reduce child support payments. See Clark, p. 729. See also *Herndon v. Herndon*, 305 N.W.2d 917 (S.D. 1981).

Courts will modify child support provisions when it is in the best interests of the child regardless of whether the agreement has been merged into the divorce decree. Therefore, even if there were a valid reason to modify the amount of child support, the answer given in the preceding paragraph would not be changed. Tarzan's petition should be denied because the refusal to work, or the temporary loss of income, is not a sufficient reason to modify child support payments.

SAMPLE ANSWER 2: A court of equity would have jurisdiction to hear and decide the dispute, but it would not exercise its jurisdiction.

The general rule is that courts will not resolve family disputes while the spouses are living together and have no grounds for separation or divorce. One reason for the rule is that there is no assurance that a judge would be able to resolve the dispute better that the spouses. Therefore, a court should not inject itself into a family problem while they continue to live together. See *McGuire v. McGuire*, 59 N.W.2d 336 (Neb. 1953), p. 62.

SAMPLE ANSWER 3: June would lose her suit. Many courts have held that a marriage contracted for the sole purpose of immigration is invalid. Where parties consent to marriage in a ceremony, but do not have the intent to assume the status of a married couple, a court should find the marriage invalid. The reasons for the rule include the failure to consummate the marriage and the lack of intent to establish a life together and assume the responsibilities which married status entails. Some courts, however, have upheld such limited purpose marriages. They reason that the marriage is valid after a lawful ceremony regardless of the motives of the parties. See Clark, pp. 122-24.

SAMPLE ANSWER 4: Adultery may be established by circumstantial evidence. When this is done two elements must be shown: (a) The spouse charged has a ***disposition*** to commit adultery; and (b) There was an ***opportunity*** to commit it. One court concluded that there was sufficient evidence to establish adultery where the parties were seen together in a tavern and later on the same night in an automobile. That occurred on three different occasions late in the evening and in the early morning hours. They were seen embracing, petting and kissing on those occasions. When the couple was in the car no one else was around, and there was sufficient time and opportunity for them to have had sexual relations. These facts show the two elements: disposition and opportunity. See *Ermis v. Ermis*, 39 N.W.2d 485 (Wis. 1949).

Other evidence may be available to show adultery. A wife may be shown to have committed adultery through blood tests which establish that her husband is not the father of her child, or by establishing non-access of the husband when the child was conceived. A *prima facie* case of adultery may be made against a husband if he contracts a venereal disease during the marriage.

SAMPLE ANSWER 5:

(a) Remarriage is recognized as a change of circumstances which warrants termination of alimony.

Some states have statutes which automatically terminate the obligation to pay alimony upon remarriage. In other states the decree must be modified by the court to end the obligation. The reasons are that upon remarriage, new support obligations arise between the parties, and public policy requires a termination of support from the earlier marriage. Other courts reason that the claim for alimony is "abandoned" by the subsequent marriage.

(b) Modern decisions allow termination of alimony in this situation.

Under traditional rules the fact that the spouse receiving alimony was cohabiting with a person of the opposite sex was not a sufficient reason to terminate alimony. That rule has been questioned in recent decisions. The termination of alimony is not automatic under the modern rule: It is a circumstance which should be considered by the court. Where the alimony is for support only and completely independent (severable) from any property settlement, issues arise as to whether there is a need to continue the alimony and whether part of the alimony is being used to support the lover of the ex-spouse. In the example the ex-wife and her boyfriend held themselves out to be married. If that occurred in a state which recognized common law marriages, alimony would be terminated as of the time of the common law marriage. A court might also be inclined to terminate alimony because the ex-wife is attempting to enjoy the benefits of actual marriage in order to avoid loss of alimony. Thus, the mere holding out as being married may be sufficient to terminate alimony in some state. See p. 124, *supra*.

(c) A general increase in the cost of living is a sufficient reason to increase the amount of alimony due the wife, so long as the husband is financially able to pay the increased amount. In this example it is clear that he can pay such an increase, so alimony would be increased to compensate her for increased cost of living expenses. However, alimony may not be raised merely because the husband later earns substantially more money. The reason is that the purpose of alimony is to provide for the needs of one spouse, and assuming that the original alimony award provided adequate support, the mere ability to pay more does not justify modification of the initial award. If the original award was less than the spouse reasonably needed, but was set low because the husband could not afford to pay more, then a court may increase the amount if the husband subsequently earns more. See p. 123 *supra*. See also *Arnold v. Arnold*, 76 N.E.2d 335 (Ill. App. 1947).

(d) The court should not order the alimony continued because there was no clear language to show that alimony should survive the husband's death.

Most courts have found authority to order periodic alimony payments after the death of the husband from their interpretation of the applicable alimony statute; courts do not have inherent power to order alimony. However, when the spouse paying alimony dies, courts are reluctant to order the continuation of alimony unless it conforms with the intent of the parties. This is so because requiring the estate to be held open for a long period to make alimony payments may cause hardship on others and frustrate the distribution of the estate in accordance with the will. The fact that the husband's obligation to support his wife would have ended with his death had they remained married does not control because in that event the wife would have been entitled to a share of her husband's estate. See Clark, pp. 668-71.

(e) When the parties mutually agree to modify alimony payments, it must be submitted to the court for approval in order for it to be binding on them. Although the court is not obligated to accept the modification, it will normally do so unless there is evidence of fraud or overreaching by one party. If court approval of the alimony modification is not obtained, then the agreement to modify it is not binding. If the husband in the example did not move the court to change the amount of alimony payable, the wife could later enforce the original order. She would be entitled to the additional $200 per month.

SAMPLE ANSWER 6: A court should distribute property equitably following an annulment. This may mean an equal distribution, but not necessarily. For example, if most of the marital property was given to the couple by the wife's father, then most of the property should be awarded to the wife. In a state where no alimony may be awarded after an annulment, the property division may be very favorable to the spouse who would otherwise receive alimony. A court will consider all relevant facts, including the length of the marriage, the needs of the parties, their contribution towards acquiring it, and services as a homemaker. In this way a court may use property division as a substitute for alimony. See Clark, pp. 139-40.

SAMPLE ANSWER 7:

(a) In an action under the Uniform Reciprocal Enforcement of Support Act, a complaint is filed by the person seeking to enforce the support obligation. The court in the initiating state must find that: (1) The complaint sets forth sufficient facts from which the duty of support may be imposed: and (2) A court in another state (the responding state) may obtain jurisdiction over the defendant. If the court in the initiating state finds those two essentials, it certifies its decision and transmits copies of the complaint, its certification and the Act to the court in the responding state which has jurisdiction over the defendant. Action by the court in the initiating state does not constitute a finding that support is due, but only that further proceedings are warranted. See Chart IV, p. 150, *supra.*

(b) The defendant may raise any defense he may have before the court in the responding state, but no counter-claims may be raised. The court then determines the merits of the claims of the parties and may either dismiss the complaint or enter an order of support. Support orders may be registered as provided by the Act and enforced by contempt or other means. Insofar as such support order (decree) is final it must be given full faith and credit by other states. Usually accrued, installments, even though not paid, are considered final, and the support order may be modified only as to future support. If the plaintiff brought a second action under the Act to increase the amount of support, the Full Faith and Credit Clause could be used as a defense to modification of the initial support order for accrued support payments in jurisdictions where they are considered a final judgment. See Clark, p. 281.

SAMPLE ANSWER 8: A writ of *ne exeat* should be considered to prevent Mr. D from leaving the jurisdiction. The object of such a writ is to keep a defendant within the court's jurisdiction so that he may be compelled to perform court orders and decrees where it is necessary for the preservation and enforcement of the plaintiff's rights. The writ may also be used to prevent the defendant from taking property out of the jurisdiction. The granting of the writ is discretionary, and evidence must be presented to the court to show that the defendant intends to leave the jurisdiction or take property out of the jurisdiction, and that granting the writ is necessary to protect the plaintiff's rights. If the writ is issued, the defendant may be required to post a bond. See *Kirby v. Kirby*, 206 S.W.2d 404 (Tenn. 1947).

SAMPLE ANSWER 9:

(a) A divorce *a mensa et thoro* is a divorce from bed and board, or a legal separation. Ecclesiastical courts granted this limited divorce for adultery or cruelty without a right to remarry. A divorce *a mensa et thoro* should be distinguished from a divorce *a vinculo matrimonii* which is a divorce from the banns of matrimony or absolute divorce.

(b) A marriage is permitted between unrelated persons. A prohibited relation may result from consanguinity (blood) or from affinity. A relationship by affinity occurs where one of the partners is related by marriage to a blood relative of the other. For example, under the common law a man could not marry the sister of his deceased wife because he was related to her by his earlier marriage. Some states prohibit such marriages, but the trend is to eliminate affinity as a ground to prohibit a marriage. Most courts terminate all affinity relationships produced by the marriage when the marriage ends by death, divorce or annulment.

SAMPLE ANSWER 10: True, assuming that the court had personal jurisdiction over the parties to award alimony when the divorce was granted.

The reason is that the matter is *res judicata.* If Jill could have asserted her claim for alimony in the divorce action, she may not later put her former husband to the expense of a second suit on the same claim absent fraud or mistake. In *Weidman v. Weidman,* 48 N.E. 506 (Ohio 1897), the court held that the wife waived alimony by failing to claim it. If Jill argues that her illness is a change of circumstance justifying modification, the court will reject it. "The usual rationale for this rule is that when there is no alimony in the original decree, there is nothing to modify, or that after the original decree (which ordered no alimony) the parties were no longer husband and wife and there was therefore no further obligation on one to support the other." Clark, p. 634.

There are statutes in a few states which permit a claim for alimony to be raised at any time. In those states Jill may prevail. It should be noted that if jurisdiction to modify the decree is **expressly reserved,** then alimony may be awarded subsequently. The facts do not show that such a provision was contained in the decree. See Clark, pp. 633-36.

SAMPLE ANSWER 11: False. So long as W has met the residency requirements of State Y she may sue for divorce in that state. H's defenses are not valid. The fact that H and W had lived in State X, and that H's adultery occurred in State X, does not limit divorce actions to that state. See Clark, pp. 413-14.

SAMPLE ANSWER 12: False. Consummation of a marriage means the parties have had sexual intercourse. So long as there is a ceremonial marriage, the couple is validly married regardless or whether the marriage is consummated. If a common law marriage is involved the answer would be different. Since common law marriage requires cohabitation as husband and wife, such a marriage must be consummated to be valid. See Clark, p.39.

SAMPLE ANSWER 13: True, assuming that common law marriages are recognized in the jurisdiction. This is the test used by many courts. A lesser standard of proof is sufficient in some jurisdictions. At common law evidence of consent or agreement of the parties was also necessary, but courts which

adhere to that requirement infer the consent or agreement from the fact of cohabitation, see p. 20, *supra*.

TABLE OF CASES

SUBJECT MATTER INDEX

Products for 1998-99 Academic Year

emanuel ®

Emanuel Law Outlines

Steve Emanuel's Outlines have been the most popular in the country for years. Over twenty years of graduates swear by them. In the 1997–98 school year, law students bought an average of 3.0 Emanuels each – that's 130,000 Emanuels.

Civil Procedure ◆	$18.95
Constitutional Law	23.95
Contracts ◆	17.95
Corporations	18.95
Criminal Law ◆	14.95
Criminal Procedure	15.95
Evidence	17.95
Property ◆	17.95
Secured Transactions	14.95
Torts (General Ed.) ◆	17.95
Torts (Prosser Casebook Ed.)	17.95

Keyed to '94 Ed. Prosser, Wade & Schwartz

Special Offer... First Year Set

All outlines marked ◆ *plus* Steve Emanuel's 1st Year
Q & A's *plus* Strategies & Tactics for the First Year
Law Student. Everything you need to make it through
your first year.   **$97.50**

Lazar Emanuel's *Latin for Lawyers*

A complete glossary and dictionary to help you wade through the complex terminology of the law.

New title   *$15.95*

Siegel's First Year Set - Civil Procedure, Contracts, Criminal Law, Property, and Torts, at a discounted price (see below).

$79.95 if purchased separately   *$59.95*

The Professor Series

All titles in these series are written by leading law professors. Each follows the Emanuel style and format. Each has big, easy-to-read type; extensive citations and notes; and clear, crisp writing. Most have capsule summaries and sample exam Q & A's.

Agency & Partnership	$15.95
Bankruptcy	15.95
Environmental Law	15.95
Family Law	15.95
Federal Income Taxation	15.95
Intellectual Property	17.95
International Law	16.95
Labor Law	15.95
Negotiable Instruments & Payment Systems	14.95
Products Liability	13.95
Professional Responsibility (*new title*)	17.95
Property (*new title*)	17.95
Torts	13.95
Wills & Trusts	15.95

Question & Answer Collections

Siegel's Essay & Multiple–Choice Q & A's

Each book contains 20 to 25 essay questions with model answers, plus 90 to 110 Multistate-style multiple-choice Q & A's. The objective is to acquaint the student with the techniques needed to handle law school exams successfully. Titles are:

Civil Procedure	Evidence
Constitutional Law	Professional Responsibility
Contracts	Real Property
Corporations	Torts
Criminal Law	Wills & Trusts
Criminal Procedure	

Each title   *$15.95*

The Finz Multistate Method

967 MBE (Multistate Bar Exam)–style multiple choice questions and answers for all six Multistate subjects, each with detailed answers – *plus* a complete 200 question practice exam modeled on the MBE. Perfect for law school and ***bar exam*** review.

$33.95

Steve Emanuel's First Year Q&A's

1,144 objective–style short-answer questions with detailed answers, in first year subjects. A single volume covers Civil Procedure, Contracts, Criminal Law, Criminal Procedure, Property, and Torts.

$18.95

Law In A Flash Flashcards

Flashcards

Civil Procedure 1 ◆	$16.95
Civil Procedure 2 ◆	16.95
Constitutional Law ▲	16.95
Contracts ◆▲	16.95
Corporations	16.95
Criminal Law ◆▲	16.95
Criminal Procedure ▲	16.95
Evidence ▲	16.95
Future Interests ▲	16.95
Professional Responsibility (953 cards)	32.95
Real Property ◆▲	16.95
Sales (UCC Article 2) ▲	16.95
Torts ◆▲	16.95
Wills & Trusts	16.95

Flashcard Sets

First Year Law Set	95.00
(includes all sets marked ◆ *plus* the book Strategies & Tactics for First Year Law.)	
Multistate Bar Review Set	165.00
(includes all sets marked ▲ *plus* the book Strategies & Tactics for MBE)	

Law In A Flash Software

(for Windows® 3.1 and Windows® 95 only)

- Contains the complete text of the corresponding *Law In A Flash* printed flashcards
- Side-by-side comparison of your own answer to the card's preformulated answer
- Fully customizable, savable sessions – pick which topics to review and in what order
- Mark cards for further review or printing

Every *Law In A Flash* title and set is available as software.

Requirements: 386, 486, or Pentium-based computer running Windows® 3.1 or Windows® 95; 16 megabytes RAM; 3.5" high-density floppy drive; 3MB free space per title

Individual titles	$19.95
Professional Responsibility (covers 953 cards)	34.95
First Year Law Set*	115.00
Multistate Bar Review Set*	195.00

* These software sets contain the same titles as printed card sets *plus* the corresponding *Strategies & Tactics* books (see below).

Law In A Flash Combo Packs

Flashcards + software, together at a substantial saving.

Individual titles in combo packs	$29.95
Professional Responsibility combo pack	46.95

(Sorry, LIAF Combo packs are not available in sets.)

Strategies & Tactics Series

Strategies & Tactics for the MBE

Packed with the most valuable advice you can find on how to successfully attack the MBE. Each MBE subject is covered, including Criminal Procedure (part of Criminal Law), Future Interests (part of Real Property), and Sales (part of Contracts). The book contains 350 actual past MBE questions broken down by subject, plus a full-length 200-question practice MBE. Each question has a ***fully-detailed answer*** which describes in detail not only why the correct answer is correct, but why each of the wrong answer choices is wrong.

☞ Covers all the new MBE specifications tested on and after July, 1997.

$34.95

Strategies & Tactics for the First Year Law Student

A complete guide to your first year of law school, from the first day of class to studying for exams. Packed with the inside information that will help you survive what most consider the worst year of law school and come out on top.

☞ Completely revised for 1997.

$12.95

Strategies & Tactics for the MPRE

Packed with exam tactics that help lead you to the right answers and expert advice on spotting and avoiding the traps set by the Bar Examiners. Contains actual questions from past MPRE's, with detailed answers.

$19.95

simplicity

LEXIS-NEXIS

Is Now

www.lexis-nexis.com/lawschool

- No software to load!
- Access from anywhere – at any time!
- An easier-to-use graphical interface!

Bookmark us today.

We'd like to know . . . .
Professor Series on Family Law (4th Ed.)

We value your opinions on our study aids. After all, we design them for *your* use, and if you think we could do something better, we want to know about it. Please take a moment to fill out this survey and feedback form and return it to us.

We'll enter you in our monthly drawing where 5 people will win the study aid of their choice! If you don't want to identify yourself, that's OK, but you'll be ineligible for the drawing.

Name: _____ Address: _____

City: _____ State: _____ Zip: _____ E-mail: _____

Law school attended: _____ Graduation year: _____

Please rate this product on a scale of 1 to 5:

General readability (style, format, etc.)................................. *Poor* ① ② ③ ④ ⑤ *Excellent*

Length of outline (number of pages) .... *Too short* ① ② ③ ④ ⑤ *Too long*

Table of Contents .... *Too detailed* ① ② ③ ④ ⑤ *Not enough detail*

End-of-book questions and answers....................................... *Not useful* ① ② ③ ④ ⑤ *Useful*

End-of-book tables & subject-matter index........................... *Not useful* ① ② ③ ④ ⑤ *Useful*

Outline's coverage of material presented in class .... *Incomplete* ① ② ③ ④ ⑤ *Complete*

OVERALL RATING.. *Poor* ① ② ③ ④ ⑤ ***Excellent***

Suggestions for improvement: _____

_____

_____

_____

☛ **What other study aids did you use in this course?** _____

_____

☛ **If you liked any features of these other study aids, describe them:** _____

_____

_____

☛ **What casebook(s) did you use in this course?** _____

☛ **For other subjects, what study aids other than Emanuel do you use, and what features do you like about them?** ____

_____

_____

☛ **Please list the items you would like us to add to our product line:**

Outline subjects: _____

Flashcard subjects: _____

Other products (e.g., software, multimedia, etc.): _____

☛ **If you win our drawing, what one study aid would you like?** _____

Send to: *Emanuel Law* **Survey**   OR   Fax to: *(914) 834-5186*
           1865 Palmer Avenue, Suite 202
           Larchmont, NY 10538

**Please
complete & return
the Survey Form
on the other side**